X-FORCE BY BENJAMIN PERCY VOL. 2. Contains material originally published in magazine form as X-FORCE (2019) #7-12. First printing 2020. ISBN 978-1-302-91989-4. Published by MARVEL WORLDWIDE, INC., a subsidiary of MARVEL ENTERTAINMENT, LLC. OFFICE OF PUBLICATION: 1290 Avenue of the Americas, New York, NY 10104. © 2020 MARVEL No similarity between any of the names, characters, persons, and/or institutions in this magazine with those of any living or dead person or institution is intended, and any such similarity which may exist is purely coincidental. **Printed in Canada.** KEVIN FEIGE, Chief Creative Officer; DAN BUCKLEY, President, Marvel Entertainment; JOHN NEE, Publisher; JOE QUESADA, EVP & Creative Director; TOM BREVOORT, SVP of Publishing; DAVID BOGART, Associate Publisher & SVP of Talent Affairs; Publishing & Partnership; DAVID GABRIEL, VP of Print & Digital Publishing; JEFF YOUNGQUIST, VP of Production & Special Projects; DAN CARR, Executive Director of Publishing Technology; ALEX MORALES, Director of Publishing Operations; DAN EDINGTON, Managing Editor; RICKEY PURDIN, Director of Talent Relations; SUSAN CRESPI, Production Manager; STAN LEE, Chairman Emeritus. For information regarding advertising in Marvel Comics or on Marvel.com, please contact Vit DeBellis, Custom Solutions & Integrated Advertising Manager, at vdebellis@marvel.com. For Marvel subscription inquiries, please call 888-511-5480. **Manufactured between 10/16/2020 and 11/17/2020 by SOLISCO PRINTERS, SCOTT, QC, CANADA.**

10 9 8 7 6 5 4 3 2 1

Writer: **Benjamin Percy**
Artists: **Jan Bazaldua** (#7-8, #11-12)
                              & Joshua Cassara (#9-10)
Color Artists: **Guru-eFX** (#7-8, #10-12) **&**
                              Dean White (#9)
Letterer: **VC's Joe Caramagna**

Cover Art: **Dustin Weaver &**
                              Edgar Delgado

Head of X: **Jonathan Hickman**
Design: **Tom Muller**
Assistant Editors: **Chris Robinson &**
                              Lauren Amaro
Editors: **Jordan D. White &**
                              Mark Basso

Collection Editor: **Jennifer Grünwald**
Assistant Managing Editor: **Maia Loy**
Assistant Managing Editor: **Lisa Montalbano**
Editor, Special Projects: **Mark D. Beazley**
VP Production & Special Projects: **Jeff Youngquist**
SVP Print, Sales & Marketing: **David Gabriel**
Editor in Chief: **C.B. Cebulski**

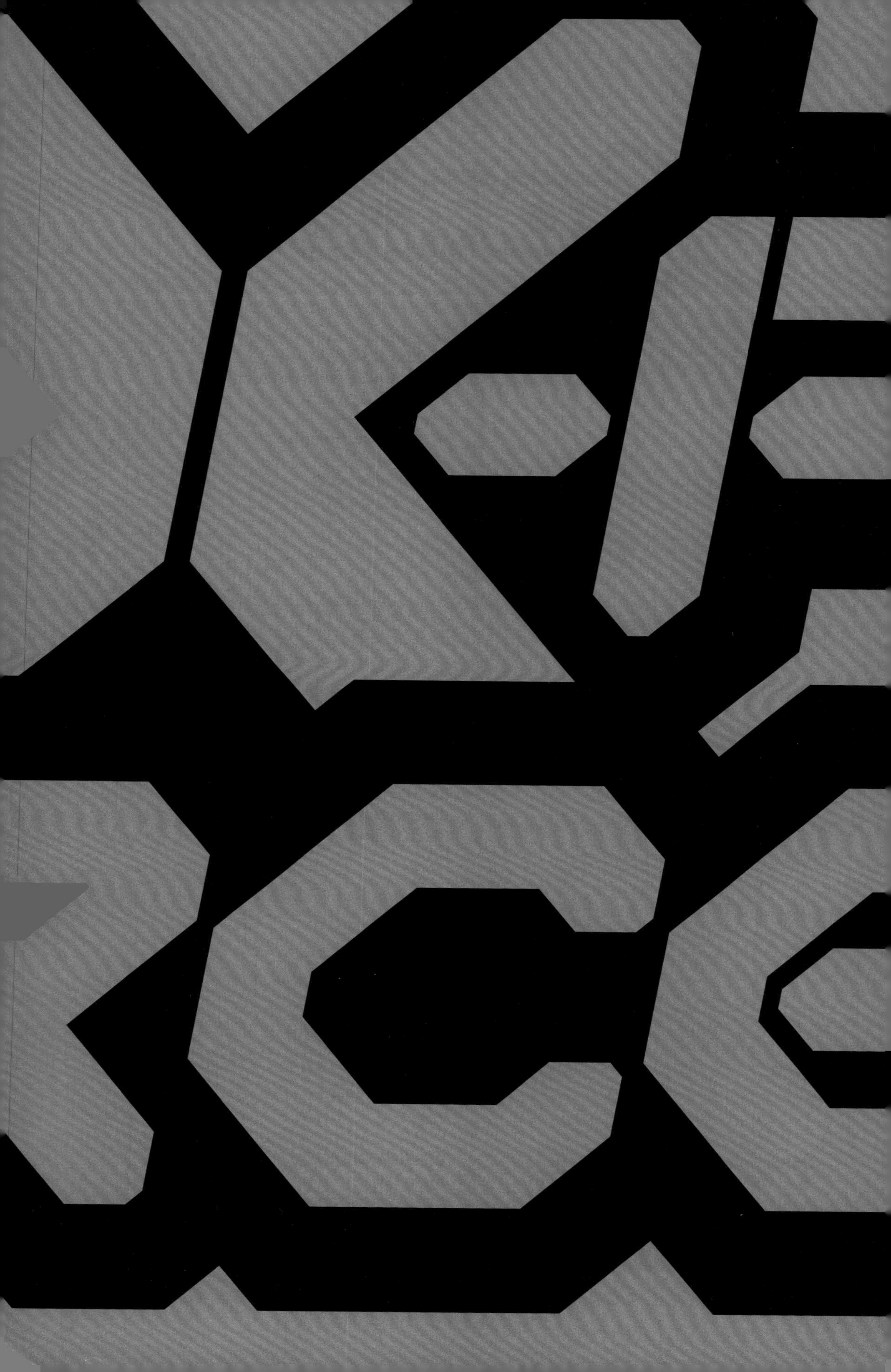

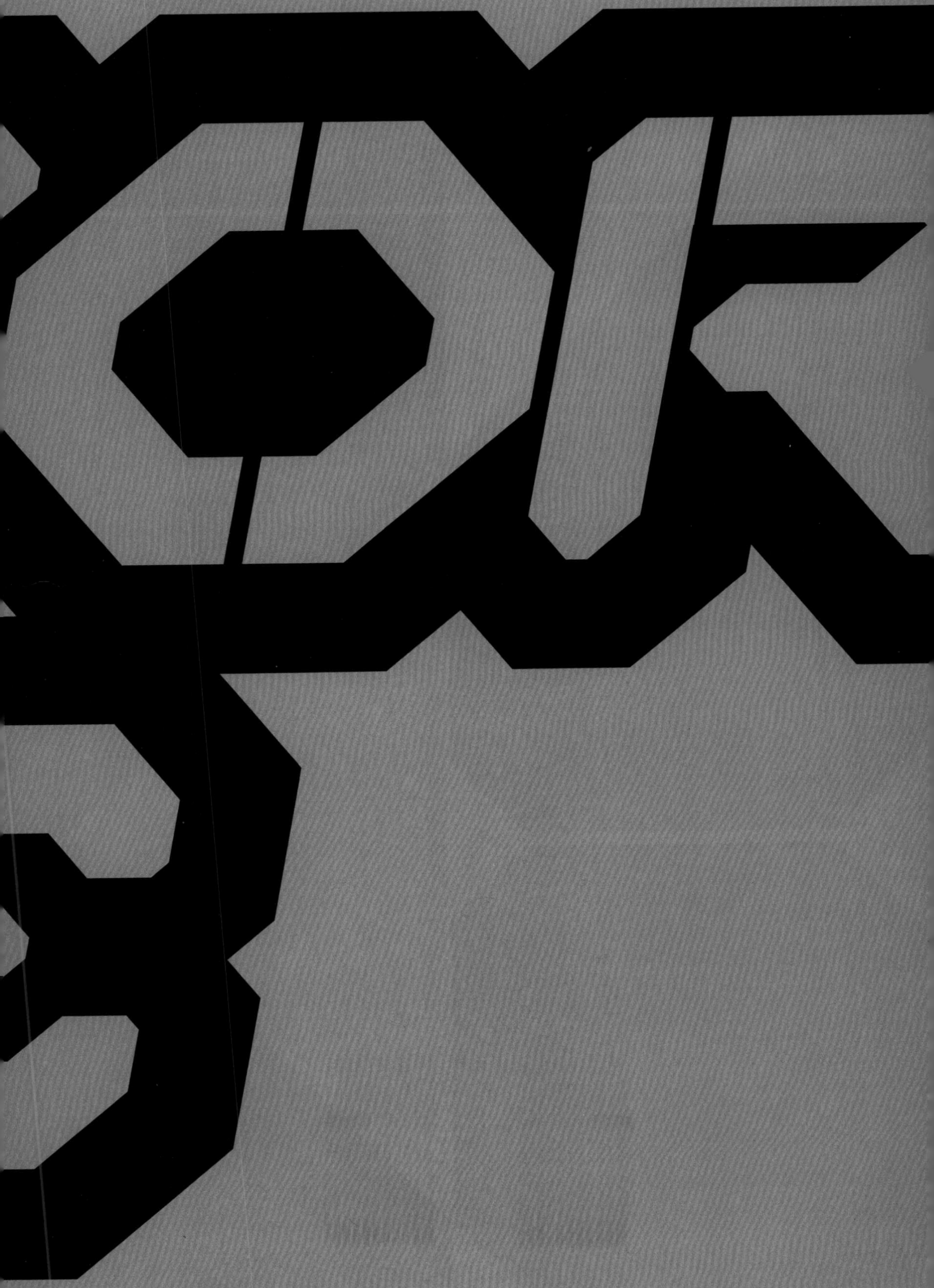

[dawn_of_x]

[kra_]
[koa_]

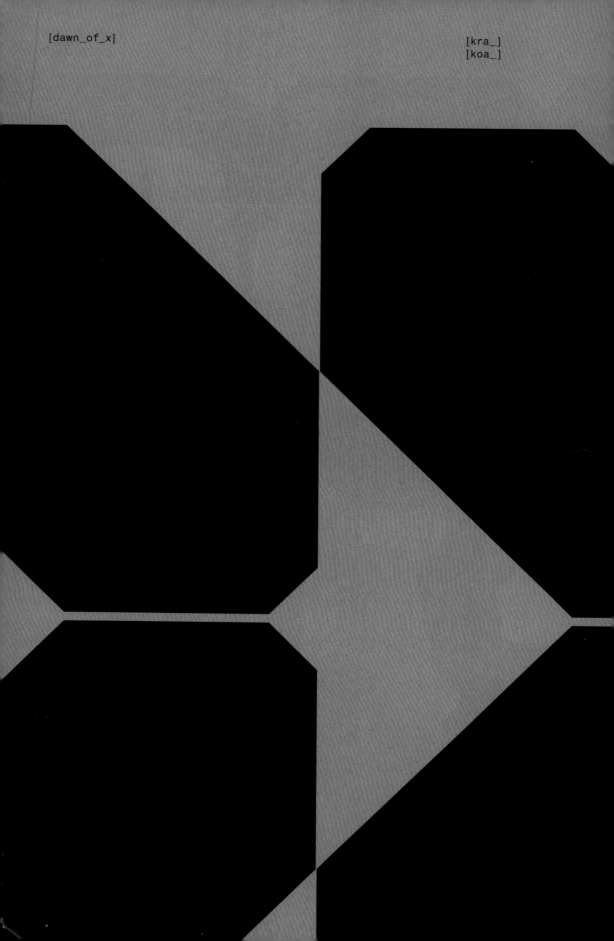

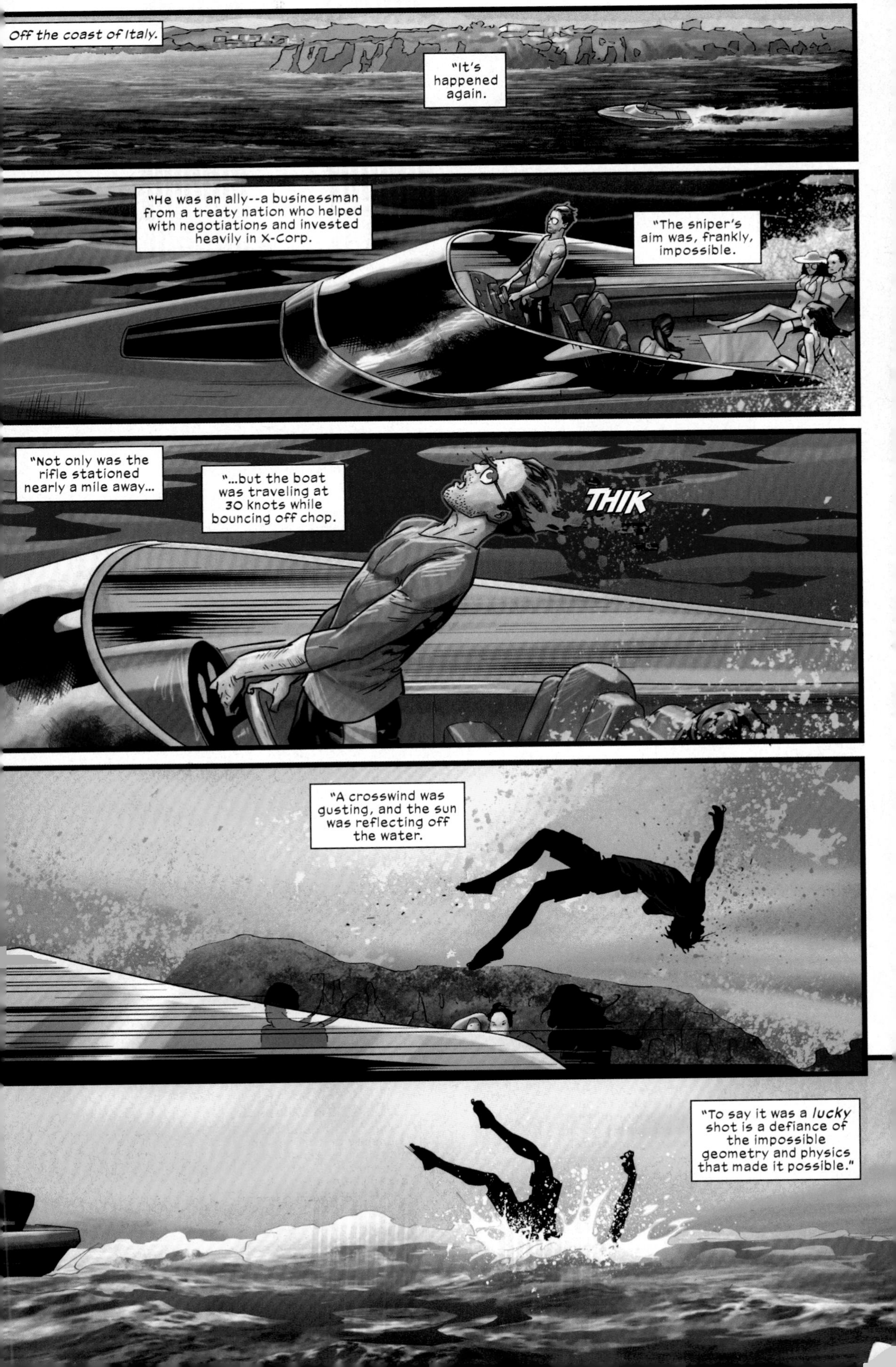
Off the coast of Italy.
"It's happened again.
"He was an ally--a businessman from a treaty nation who helped with negotiations and invested heavily in X-Corp.
"The sniper's aim was, frankly, impossible.
"Not only was the rifle stationed nearly a mile away...
"...but the boat was traveling at 30 knots while bouncing off chop.
THIK
"A crosswind was gusting, and the sun was reflecting off the water.
"To say it was a *lucky* shot is a defiance of the impossible geometry and physics that made it possible."

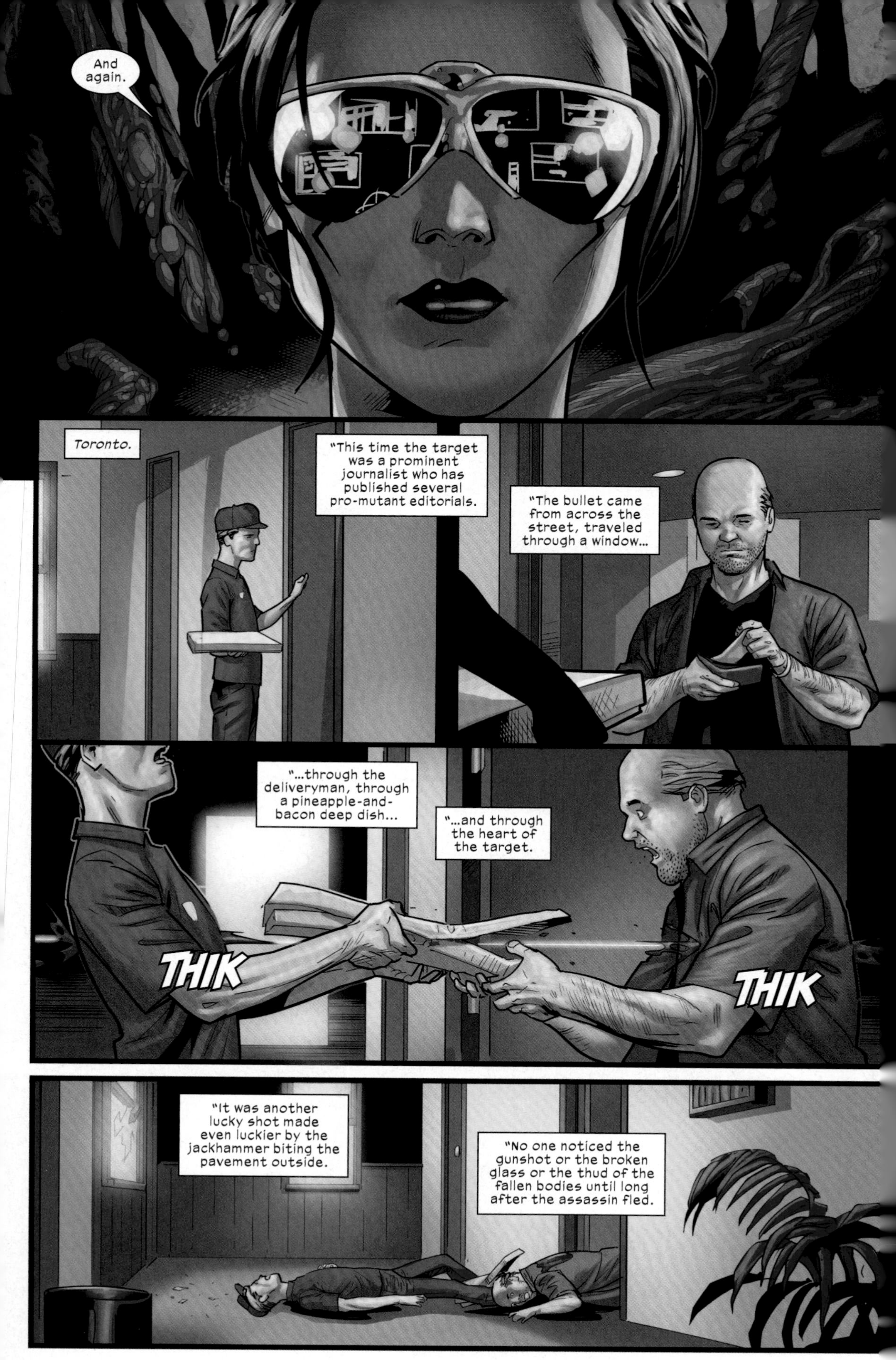
And again.
Toronto.
"This time the target was a prominent journalist who has published several pro-mutant editorials.
"The bullet came from across the street, traveled through a window...
"...through the deliveryman, through a pineapple-and-bacon deep dish...
"...and through the heart of the target.
THIK
THIK
"It was another lucky shot made even luckier by the jackhammer biting the pavement outside.
"No one noticed the gunshot or the broken glass or the thud of the fallen bodies until long after the assassin fled.

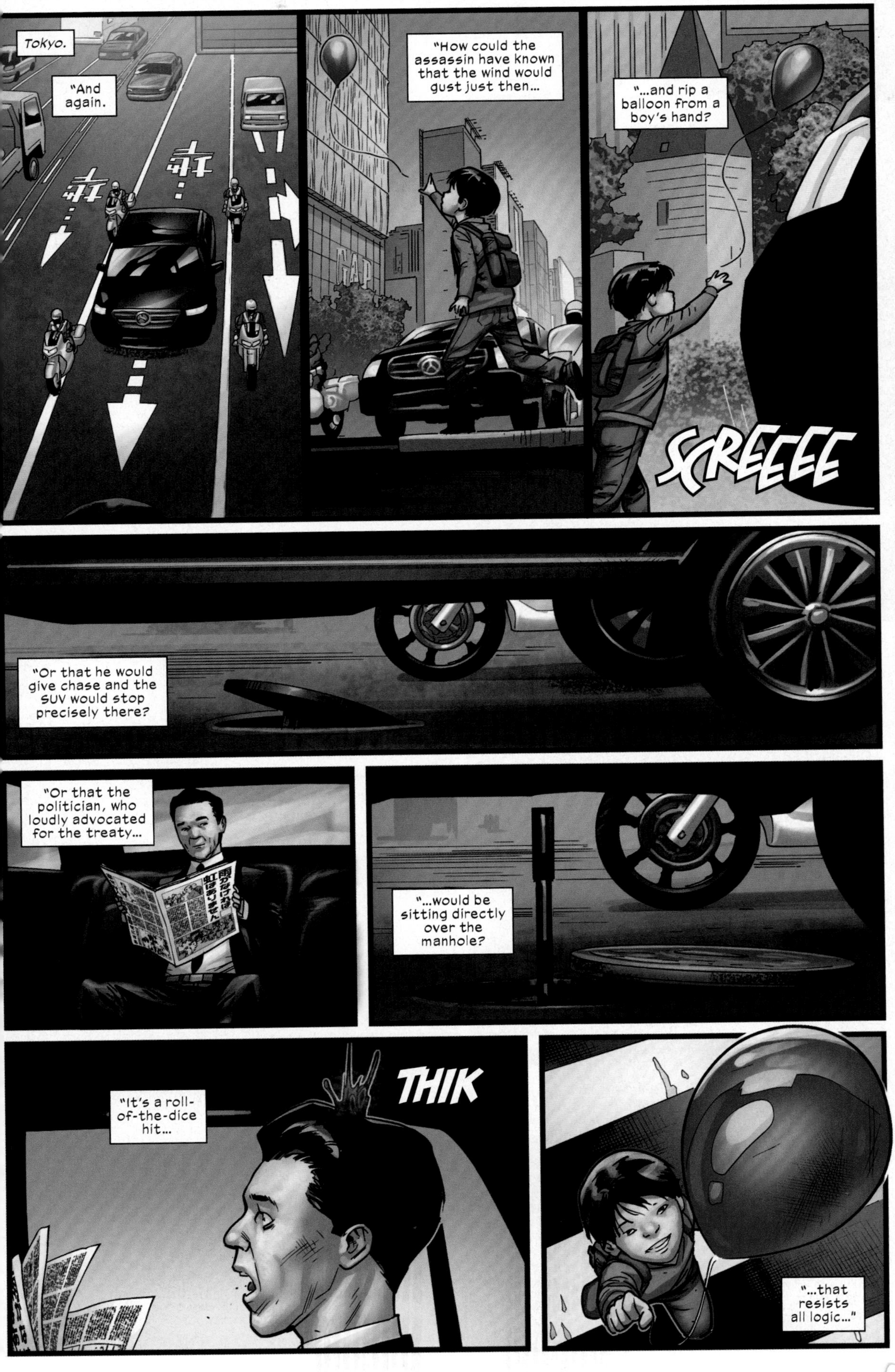
Tokyo.
"And again.
"How could the assassin have known that the wind would gust just then...
"...and rip a balloon from a boy's hand?
SCREEEE
"Or that he would give chase and the SUV would stop precisely there?
"Or that the politician, who loudly advocated for the treaty...
"...would be sitting directly over the manhole?
"It's a roll-of-the-dice hit...
THIK
"...that resists all logic..."

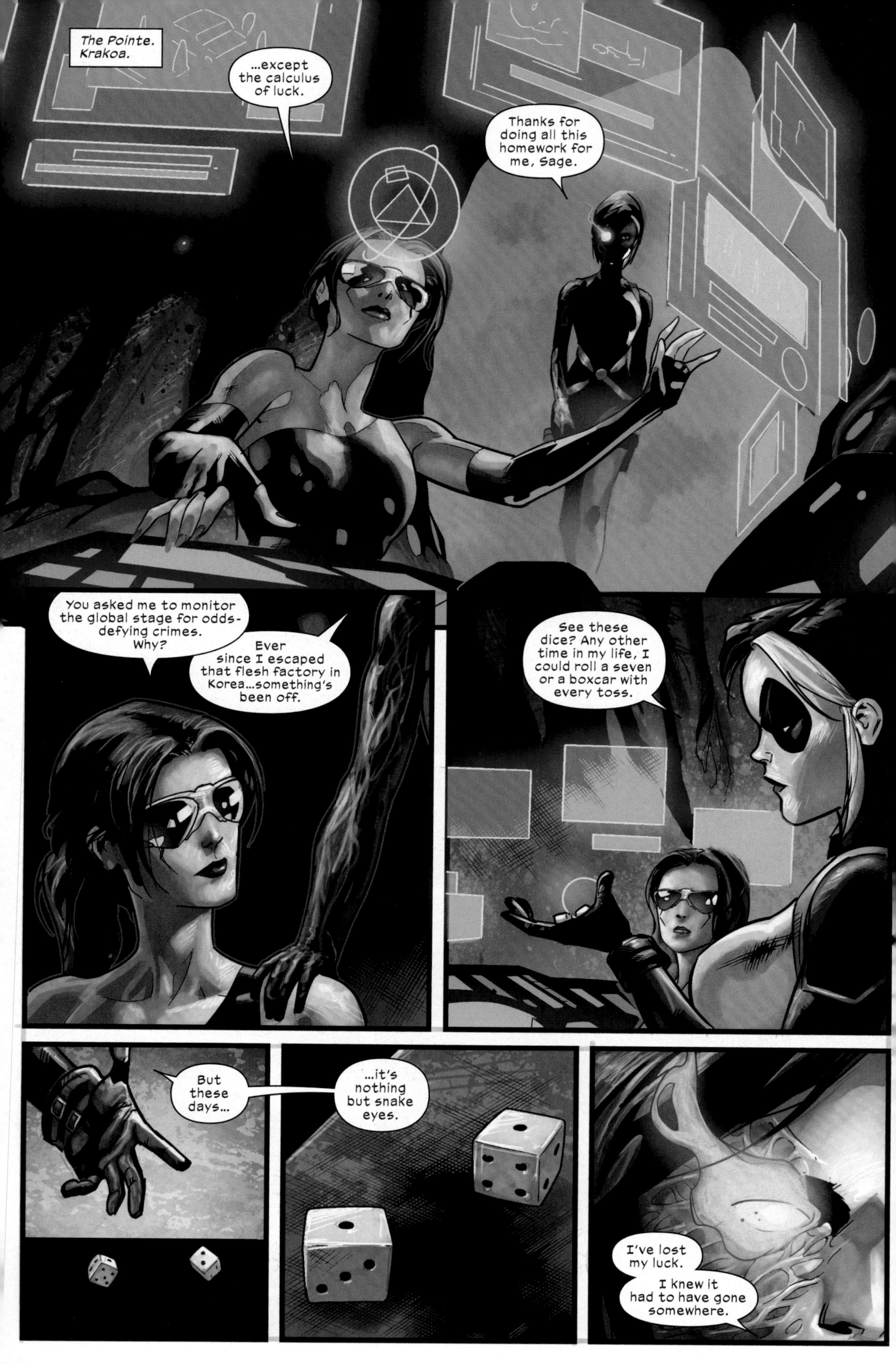
The Pointe. Krakoa.
...except the calculus of luck.
Thanks for doing all this homework for me, Sage.
You asked me to monitor the global stage for odds-defying crimes. Why?
Ever since I escaped that flesh factory in Korea...something's been off.
See these dice? Any other time in my life, I could roll a seven or a boxcar with every toss.
But these days...
...it's nothing but snake eyes.
I've lost my luck.
I knew it had to have gone somewhere.

[kra_[0.7]
[koa_[0.7]

[kra_[0.X]
[koa_[0.X]

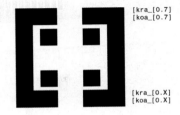

LADY LUCK

Before X-FORCE was formed, Professor X sent Colossus and Domino on separate missions for the benefit of Krakoa and mutantkind. While Colossus was killed in Russia, Domino was sent to investigate a mysterious organization that calls itself XENO. She was captured and skinned alive. Since then, Domino was rescued and her injuries treated with vegetative skin grafts. Colossus was resurrected but remains disturbed...

Sage

Domino

Colossus

[kra_[0.7]...]
[koa_[0.7]...]

[A._Spy_Agency]

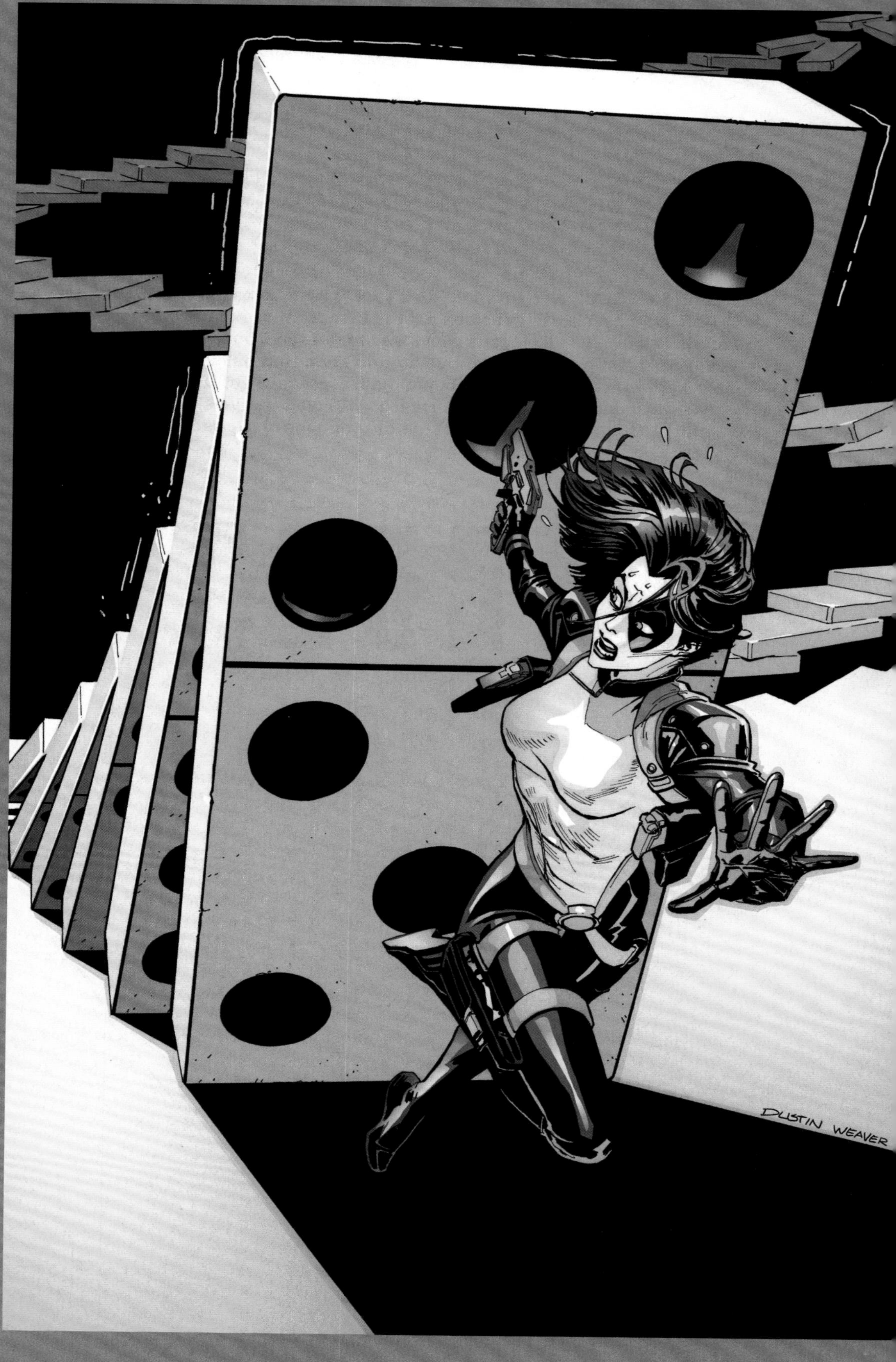
DUSTIN WEAVER

Domino Has Fallen

BEAST'S LOGBOOK: SPYWARE

I paid Forge a visit in the Armory -- and I must say that he can be, like Logan, rather impossible. There is a certain locker room bravado about him I find perplexing, like a language I only half understand. For instance, he refused to shake my hand but instead dragged me into what he called a "bro hug." Then he challenged me to a "feat of strength," asking if I would test out this sappy "muck bomb" he had developed that -- or so I gather -- glues one in place. He wondered if a "big boy" like me might be able to thrash free of the binding. I refused him and said I very much would prefer to get down to business. He then referred to me as a "bookish peckerwood ████████" but did so with a friendly laugh and clapped me on the shoulder hard enough to make me stagger. I'm not sure how to process this, honestly. Is he being friendly or cruel? Is it possible to be both?

But the man can build. I will give him that. And I wanted him to build me something.

I asked him if he had ever heard of ringing rocks -- sonorous stones that chime like a bell when struck. These are a form of diabase and felsenmeer. I wondered if the opposite could be true. If they could be made absorbent as well so that they might sing back to me.

"And what would you want them to sing about?" he asked, and I said, "Whatever they might hear." As a counter in a kitchen. As a vase in an office. As the tilework in a bathroom. "I would like very much to know what people are saying about us, if you catch my meaning."

"Oh, I do," he said, and his mustache bristled with his smile. "Let's make the world sing, then."

He was going to work on the development of a singing stone. And he thought he might experiment as well with some mosses whose porousness could prove effective at absorbing sound.

So a first step has been taken.

And the second step shall be working our spyware unnoticed into the White House, RoXXon, Stark Unlimited and Avengers Mountain, among others.

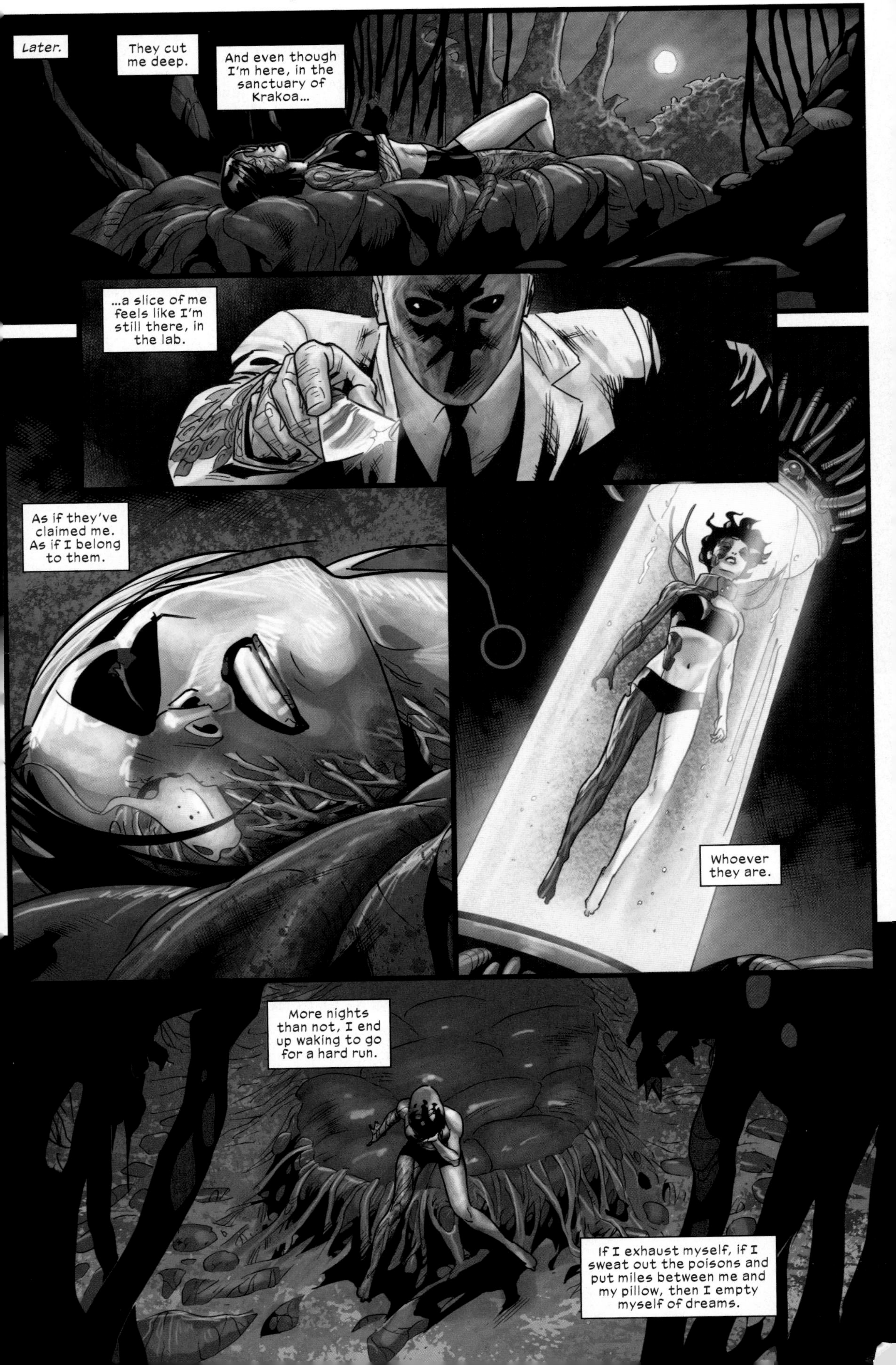
Later.
They cut me deep.
And even though I'm here, in the sanctuary of Krakoa...
...a slice of me feels like I'm still there, in the lab.
As if they've claimed me. As if I belong to them.
Whoever they are.
More nights than not, I end up waking to go for a hard run.
If I exhaust myself, if I sweat out the poisons and put miles between me and my pillow, then I empty myself of dreams.

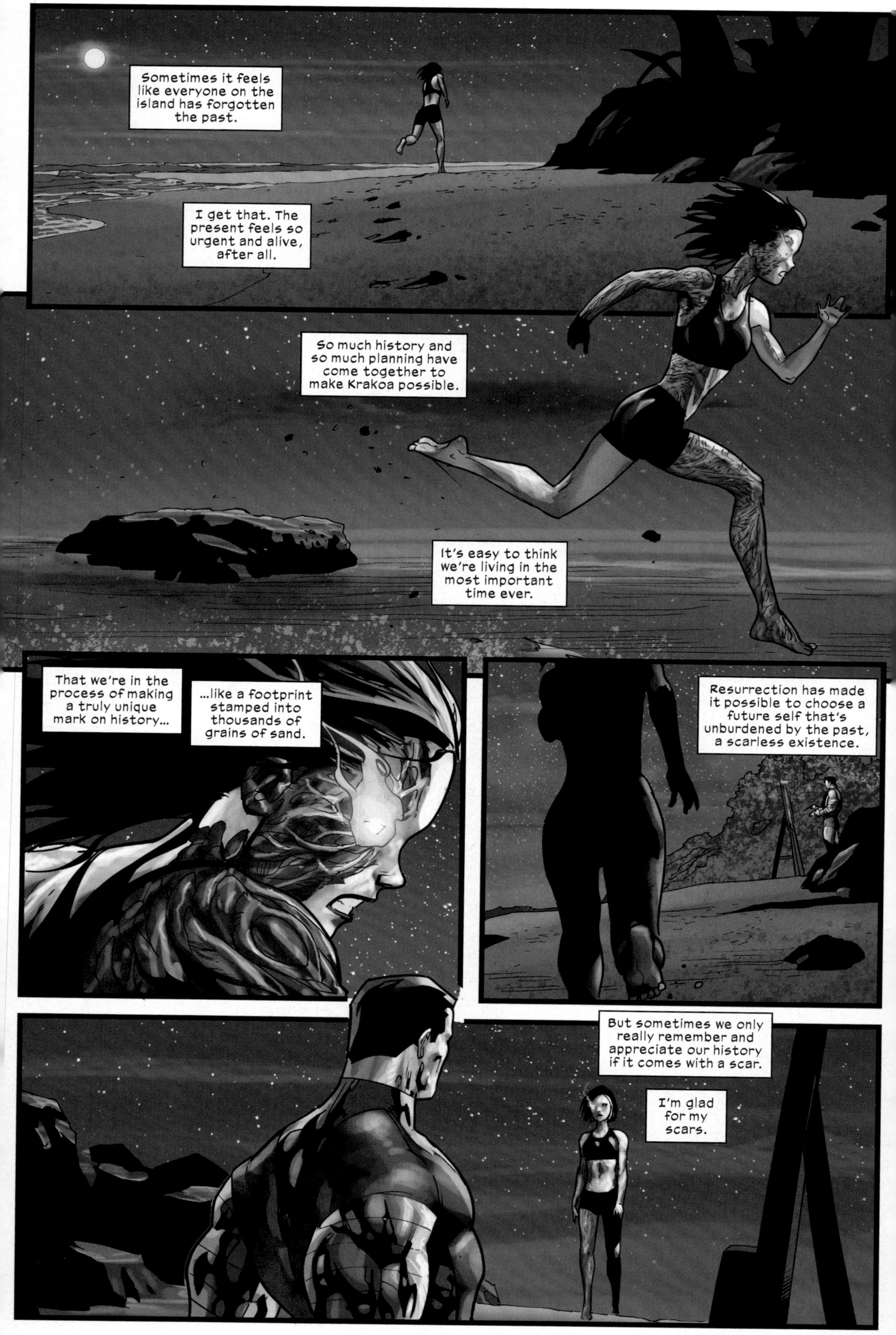
Sometimes it feels like everyone on the island has forgotten the past.
I get that. The present feels so urgent and alive, after all.
So much history and so much planning have come together to make Krakoa possible.
It's easy to think we're living in the most important time ever.
That we're in the process of making a truly unique mark on history...
...like a footprint stamped into thousands of grains of sand.
Resurrection has made it possible to choose a future self that's unburdened by the past, a scarless existence.
But sometimes we only really remember and appreciate our history if it comes with a scar.
I'm glad for my scars.

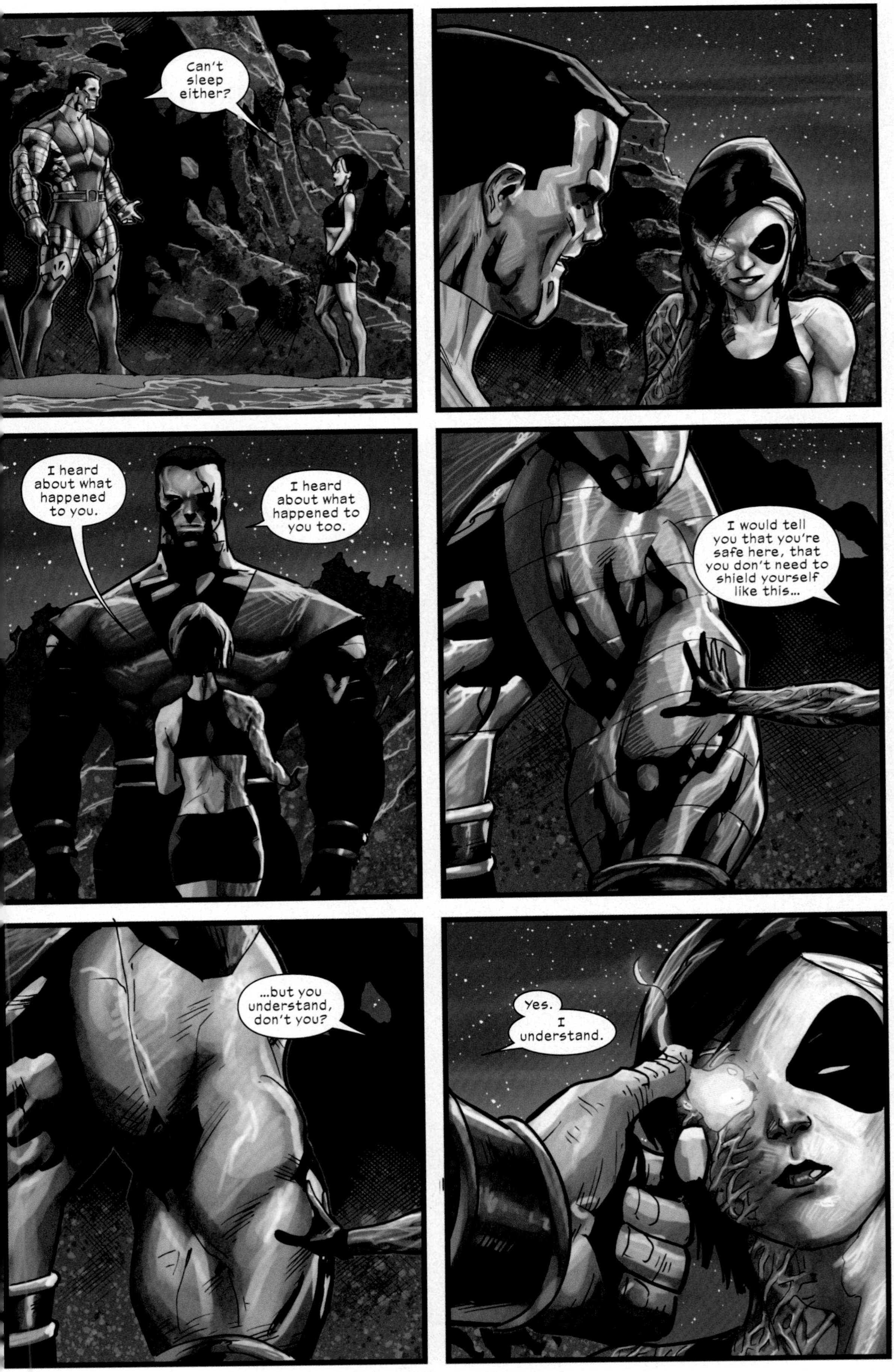

Can't sleep either?
I heard about what happened to you.
I heard about what happened to you too.
I would tell you that you're safe here, that you don't need to shield yourself like this...
...but you understand, don't you?
Yes. I understand.

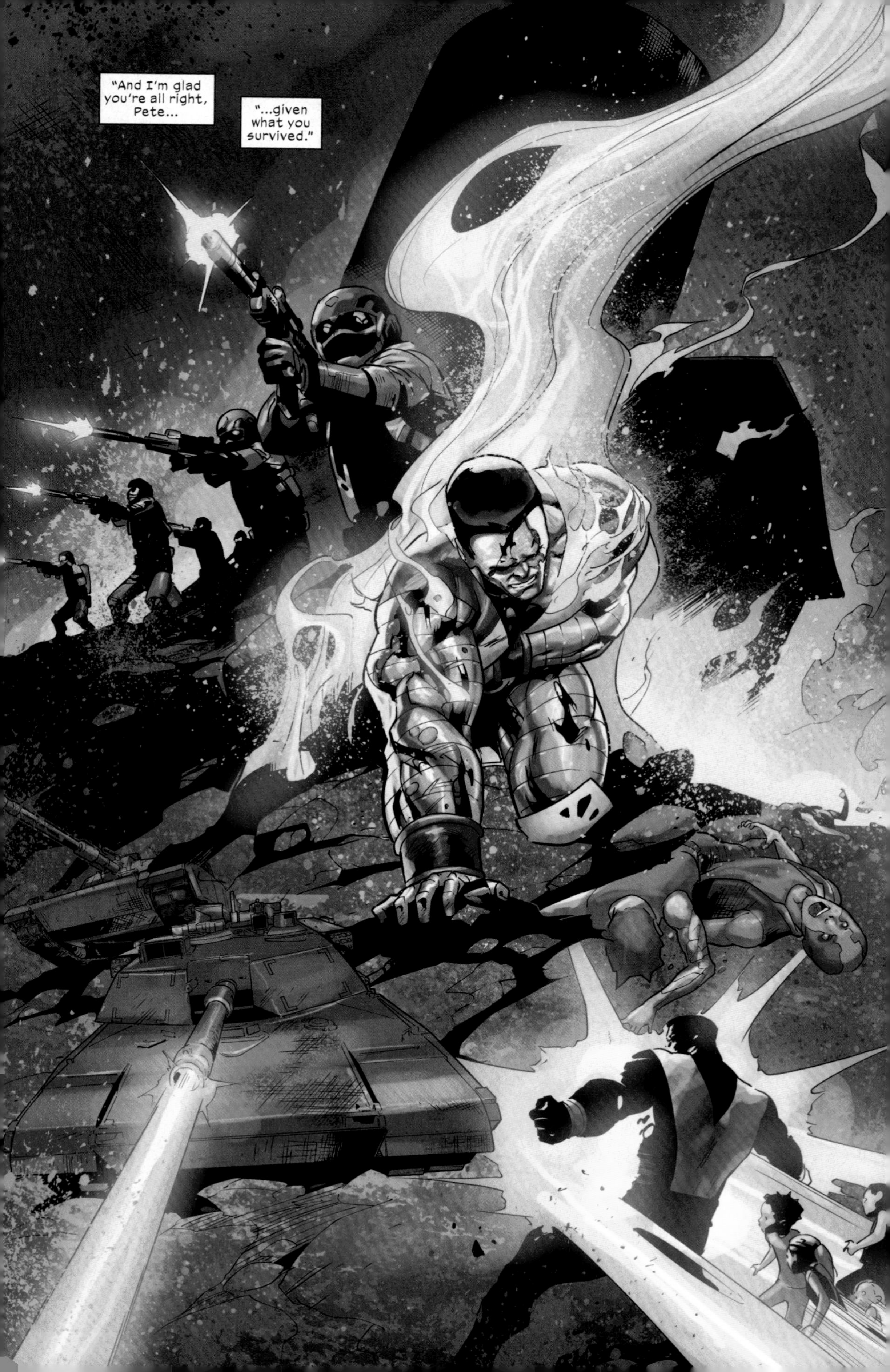
"And I'm glad you're all right, Pete...
"...given what you survived."

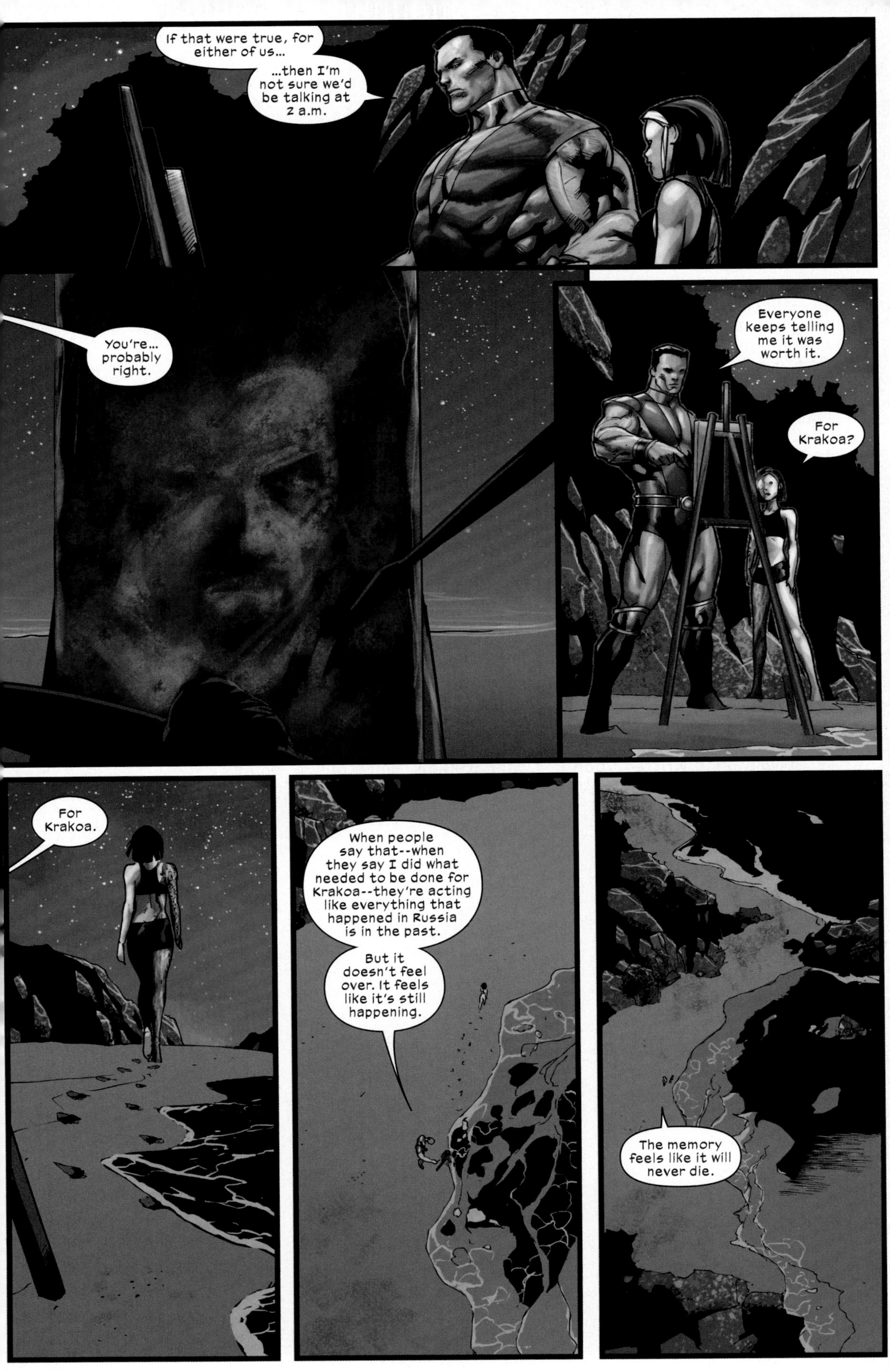
If that were true, for either of us...
...then I'm not sure we'd be talking at 2 a.m.
You're... probably right.
Everyone keeps telling me it was worth it.
For Krakoa?
For Krakoa.
When people say that--when they say I did what needed to be done for Krakoa--they're acting like everything that happened in Russia is in the past.
But it doesn't feel over. It feels like it's still happening.
The memory feels like it will never die.

BEAST'S LOGBOOK: THE SCRAP OF PAPER

I like to take a good ramble now and then to clear my thoughts and to study the island further. I might have been gone an hour -- during which time I collected many fascinating samples of Krakoan insects and fungi and mosses and flowers -- and upon my return to the Pointe, I discovered something curious waiting for me.

Perhaps it is a reach to say that it was waiting for me, but the way it was lying on the floor near my desk...just so...I couldn't help but feel that someone wanted me to find it and yet couldn't bring themselves to offer it directly.

A scrap of paper. Scorched at the edges.

I myself prefer the tactile. I would choose a handwritten letter over a comm request any day. And I keep an extensive library at my home pod. But paper is something of a curiosity here on Krakoa -- and certainly here at the Pointe -- since so much of our work is done digitally or through organic interface.

I asked Sage about it, and she said she did not know. I asked if anyone had been by, and she said not to her knowledge.

Now, this was not merely paper but the highest quality ivory cardstock. A thick quality weave that is almost the texture of cloth. Deckle-edged where it had not been burned. A writer's stationery.

What was once written upon it, I cannot know, since only a single word remained...

летописец

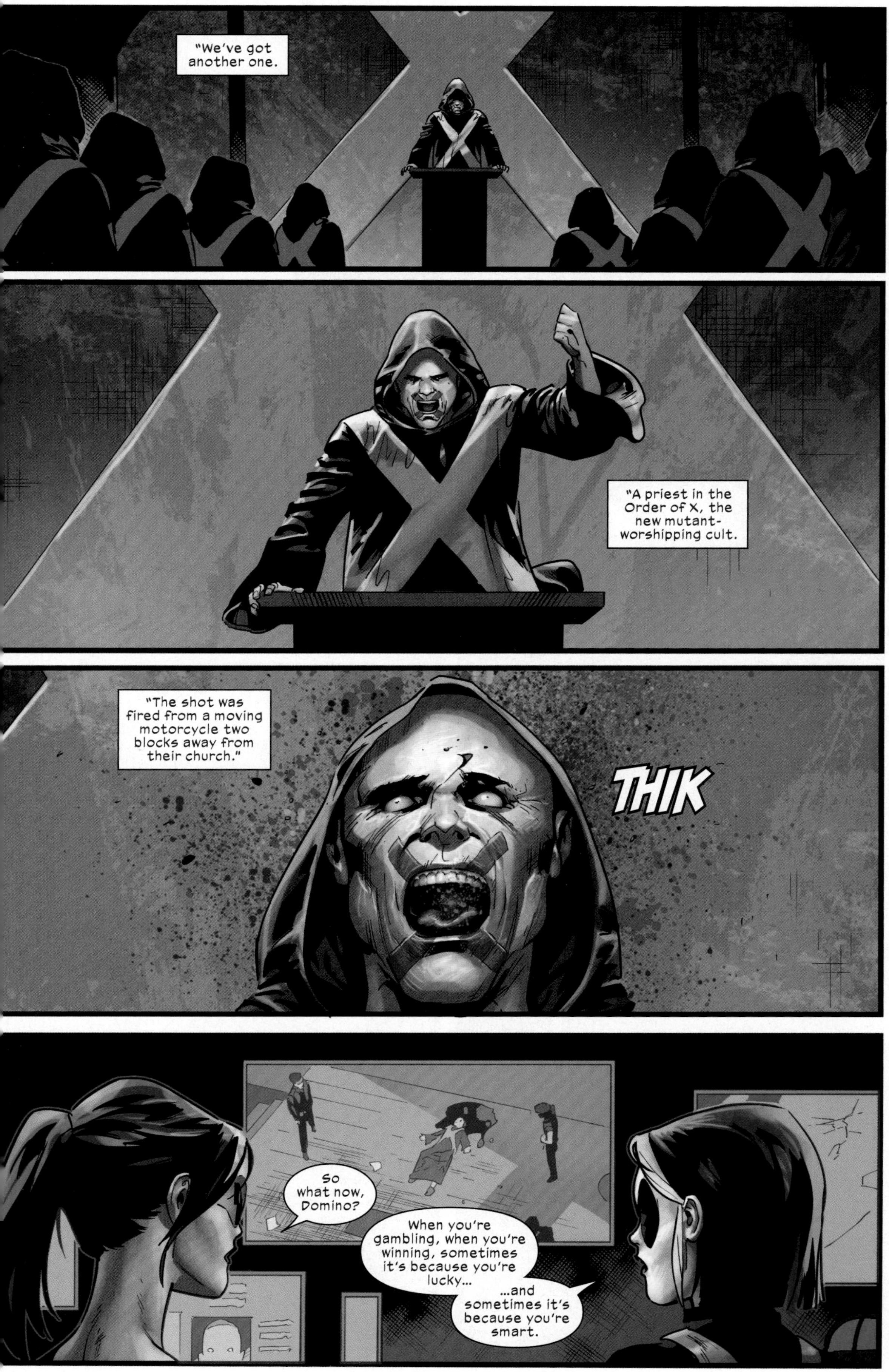
"We've got another one.
"A priest in the Order of X, the new mutant-worshipping cult.
"The shot was fired from a moving motorcycle two blocks away from their church."
THIK
So what now, Domino?
When you're gambling, when you're winning, sometimes it's because you're lucky...
...and sometimes it's because you're smart.

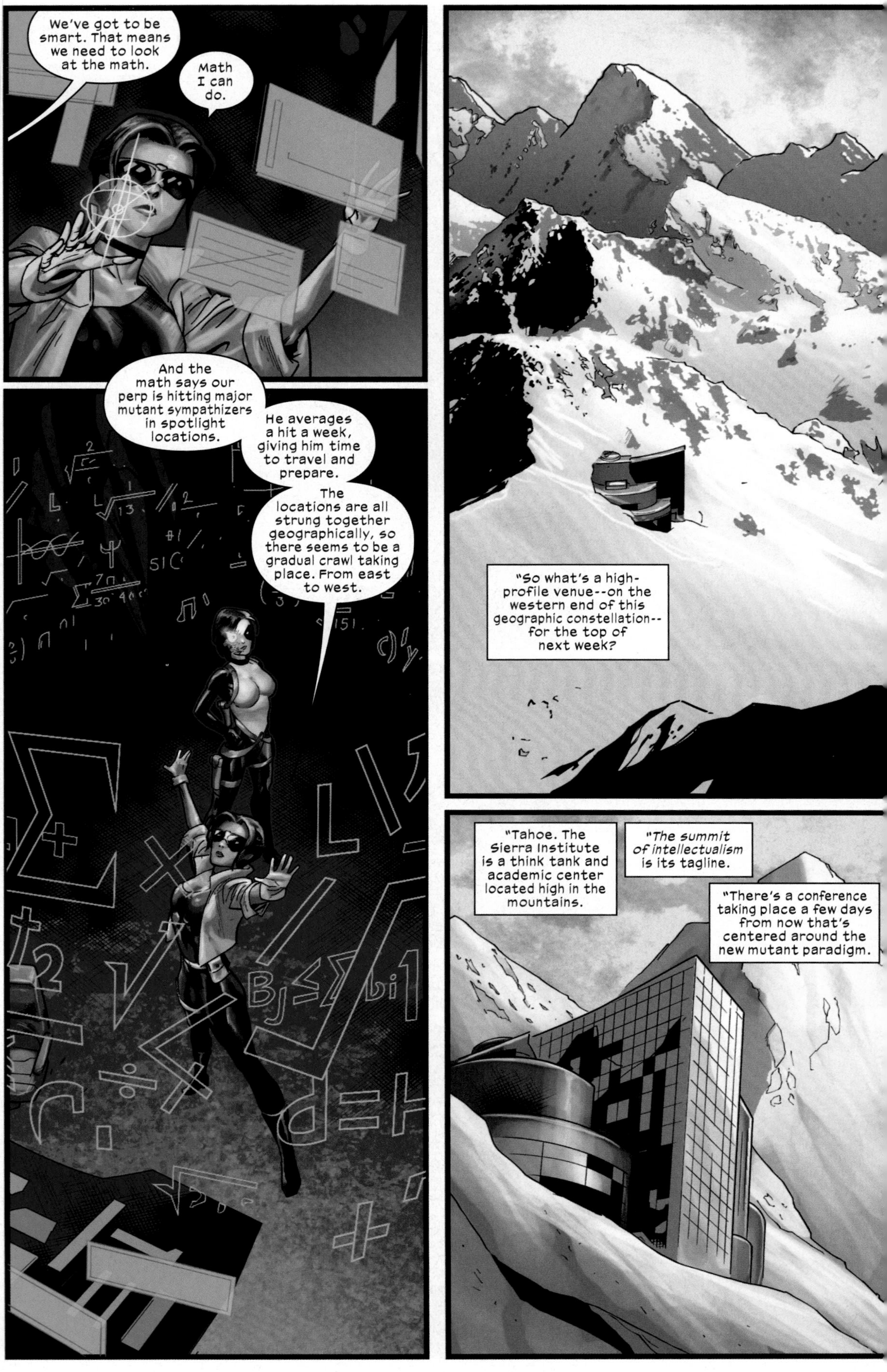
We've got to be smart. That means we need to look at the math.
Math I can do.
And the math says our perp is hitting major mutant sympathizers in spotlight locations.
He averages a hit a week, giving him time to travel and prepare.
The locations are all strung together geographically, so there seems to be a gradual crawl taking place. From east to west.
"So what's a high-profile venue--on the western end of this geographic constellation--for the top of next week?
"Tahoe. The Sierra Institute is a think tank and academic center located high in the mountains.
"*The summit of intellectualism* is its tagline.
"There's a conference taking place a few days from now that's centered around the new mutant paradigm.

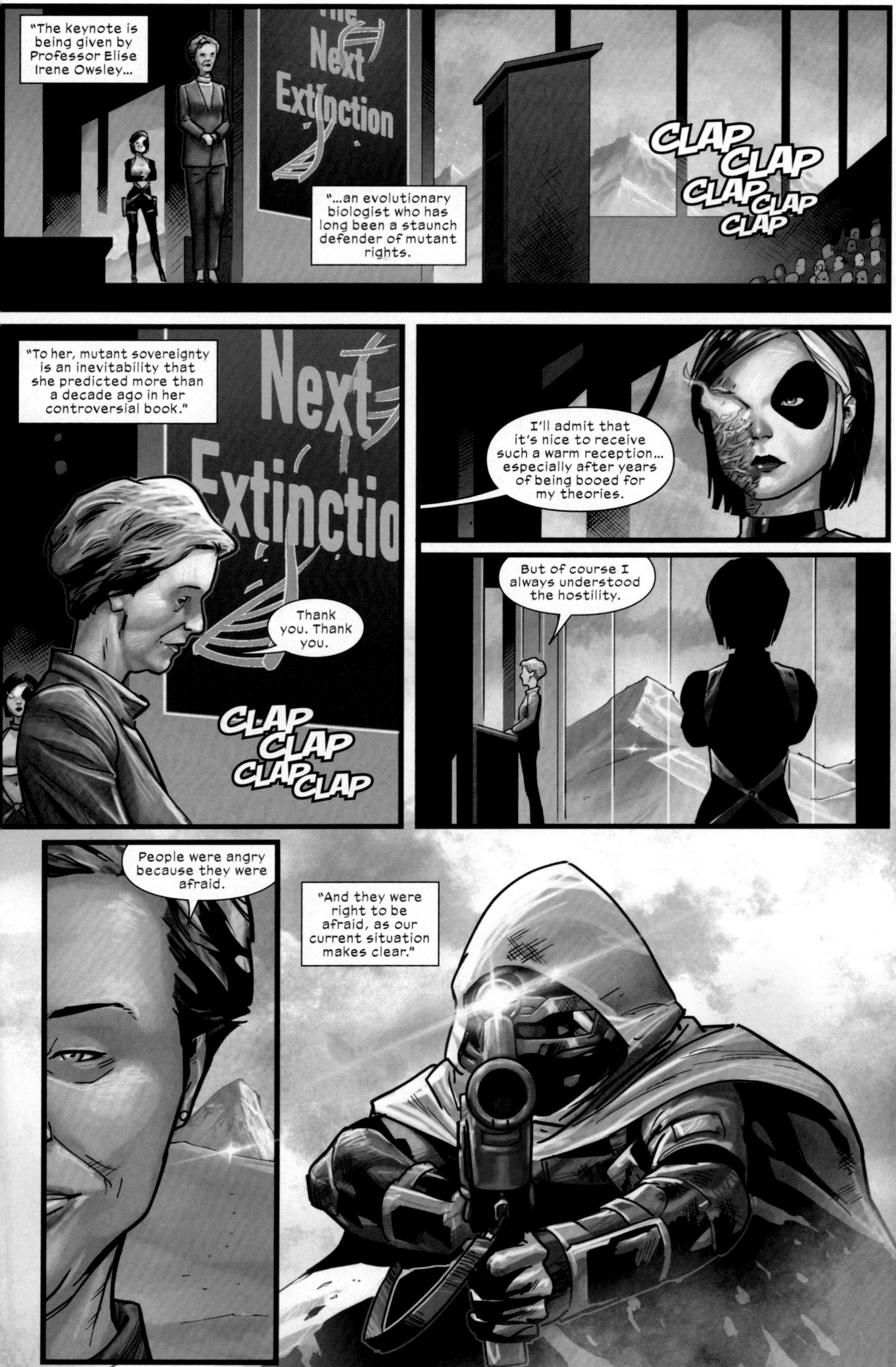
"The keynote is being given by Professor Elise Irene Owsley...
The Next Extinction
"...an evolutionary biologist who has long been a staunch defender of mutant rights.
CLAP CLAP CLAP CLAP CLAP
"To her, mutant sovereignty is an inevitability that she predicted more than a decade ago in her controversial book."
Next Extinctio
Thank you. Thank you.
CLAP CLAP CLAP CLAP
I'll admit that it's nice to receive such a warm reception... especially after years of being booed for my theories.
But of course I always understood the hostility.
People were angry because they were afraid.
"And they were right to be afraid, as our current situation makes clear."

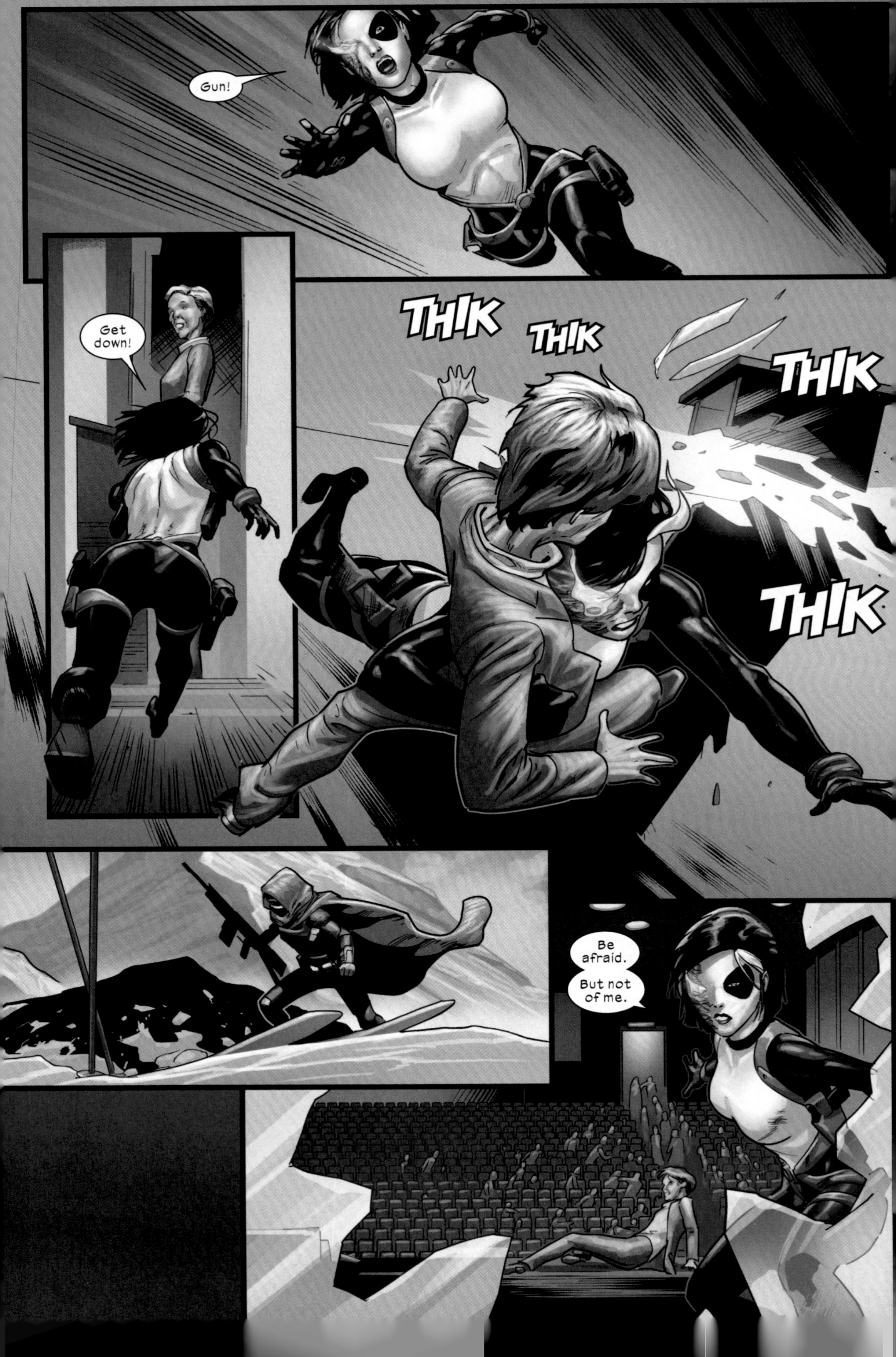
Gun!
Get down!
THIK
THIK
THIK
THIK
Be afraid.
But not of me.

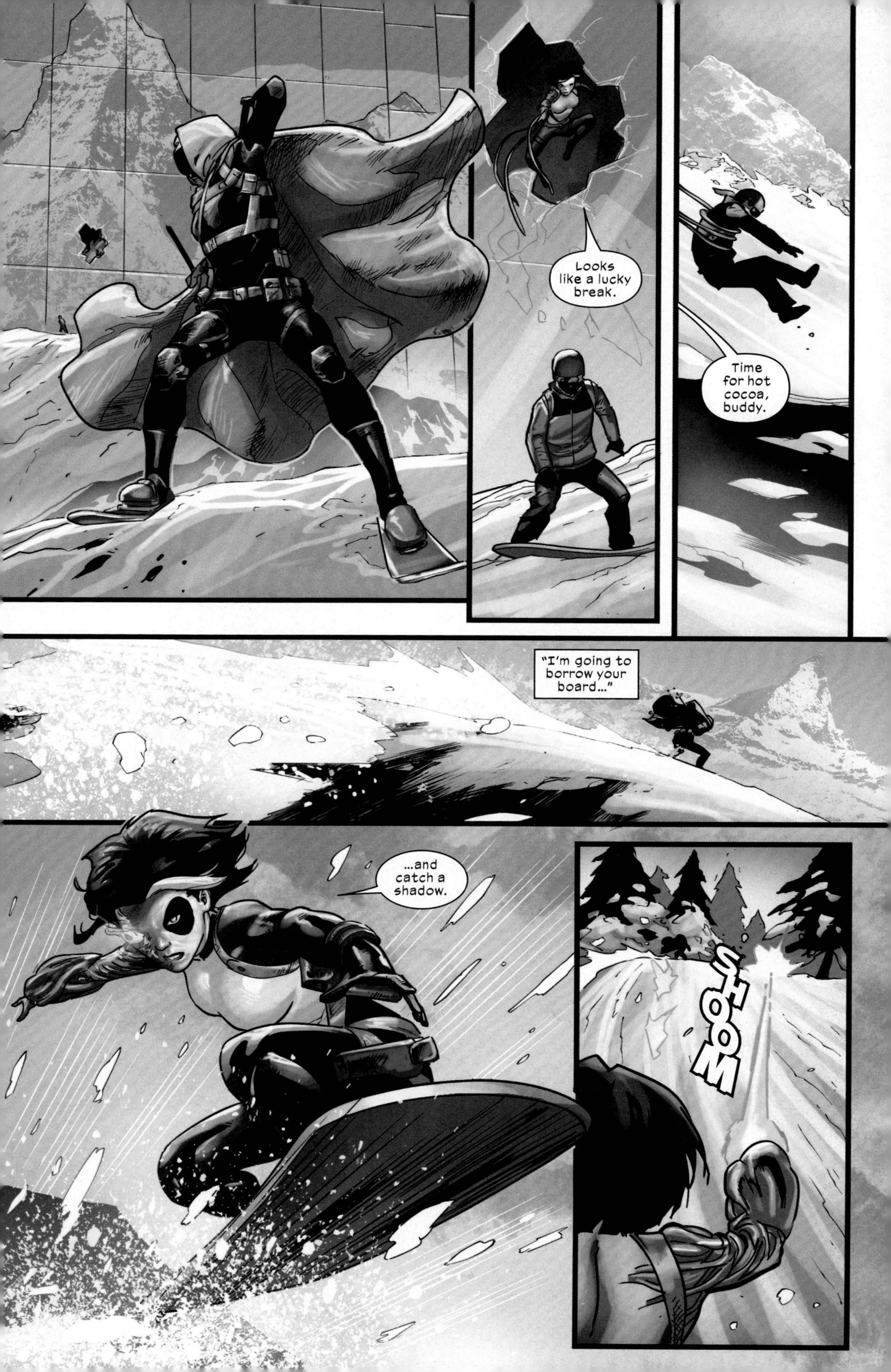
Looks like a lucky break.
Time for hot cocoa, buddy.
"I'm going to borrow your board..."
...and catch a shadow.
SHOOM

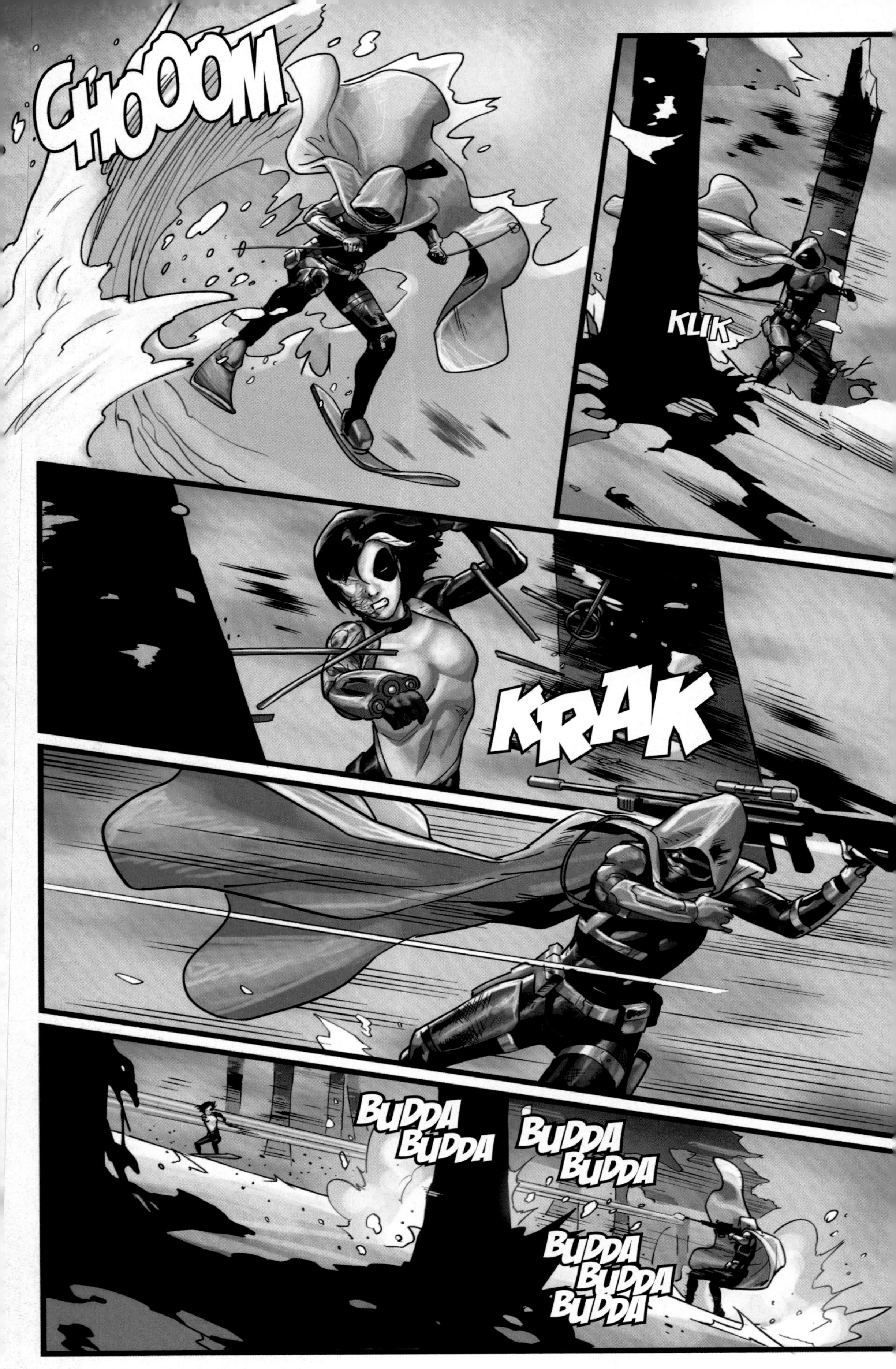
CHOOOM
KLIK
KRAK
BUDDA BUDDA
BUDDA BUDDA
BUDDA BUDDA BUDDA

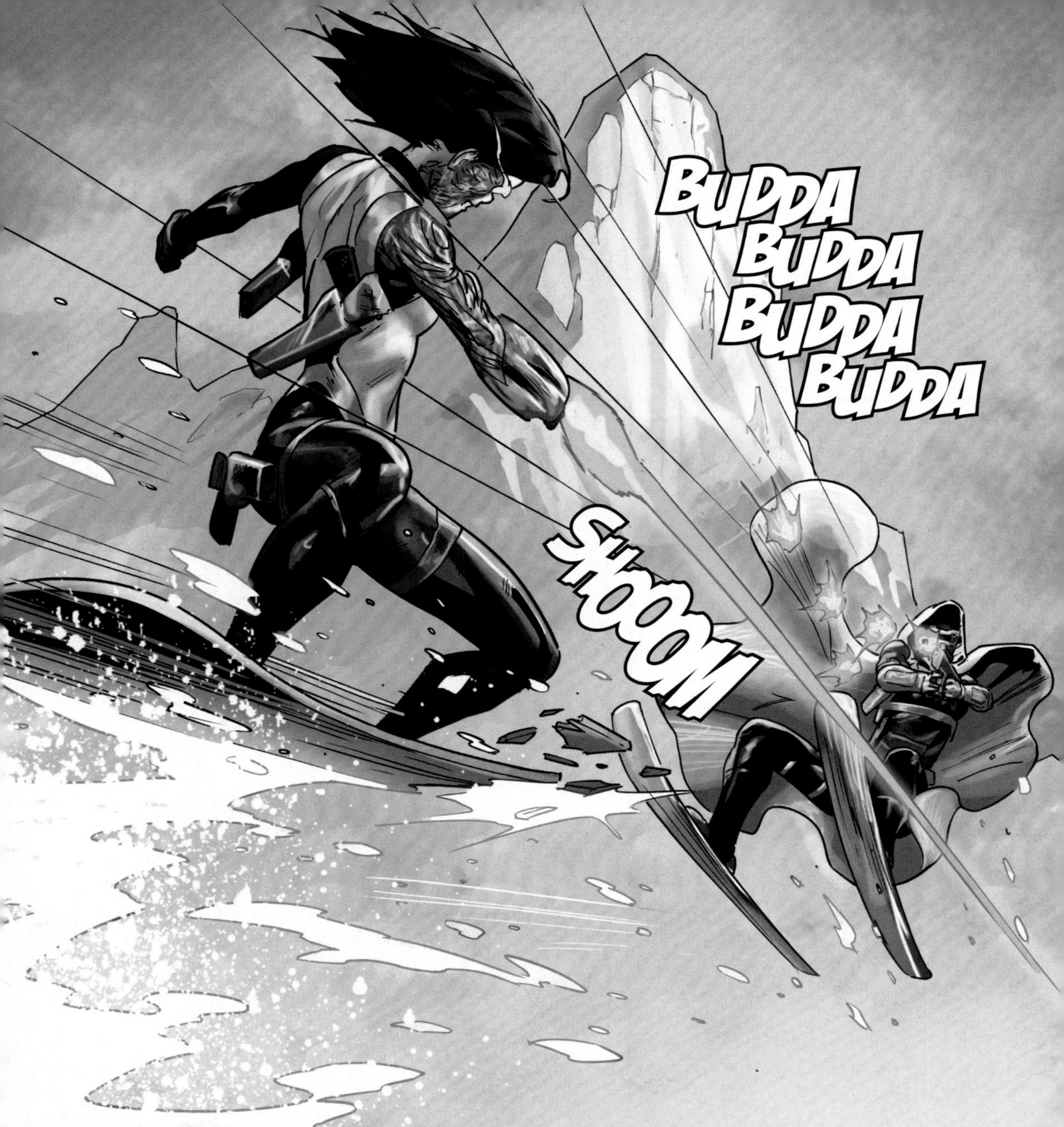
BUDDA
BUDDA
BUDDA
BUDDA
SHOOOM
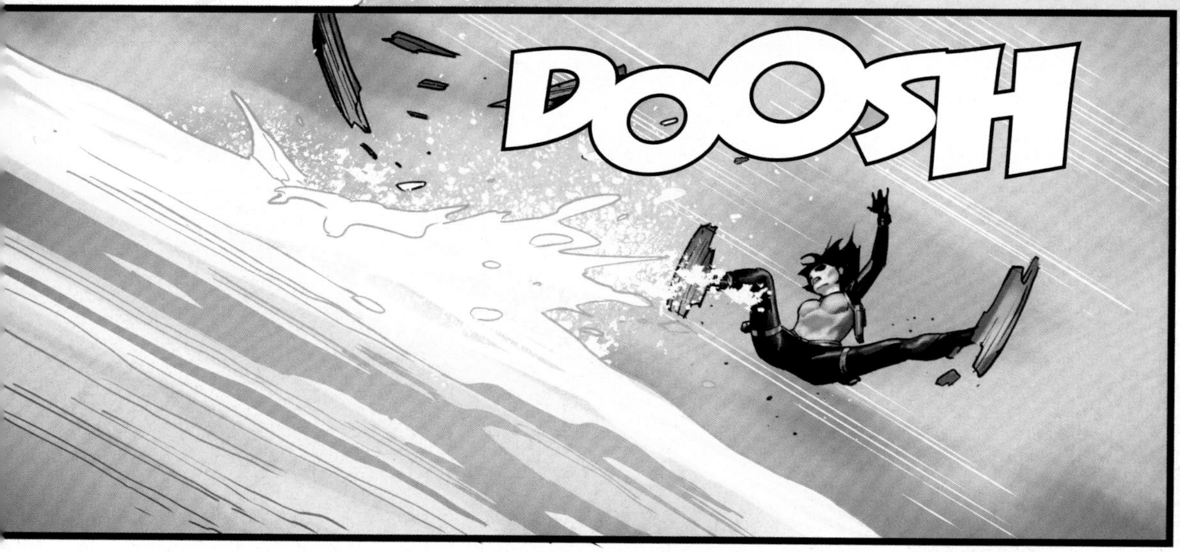
DOOSH

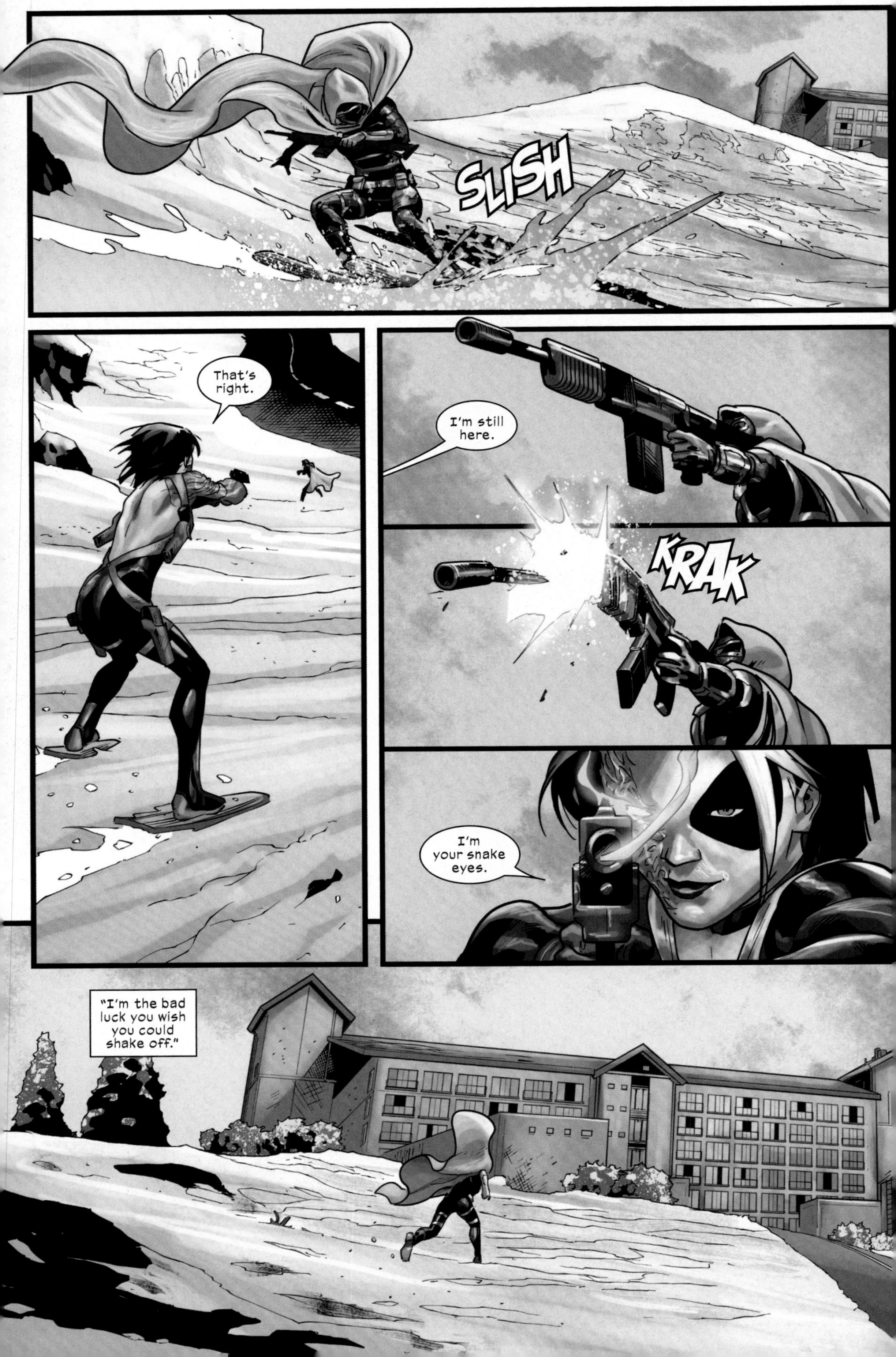
SLISH
That's right.
I'm still here.
KRAK
I'm your snake eyes.
"I'm the bad luck you wish you could shake off."

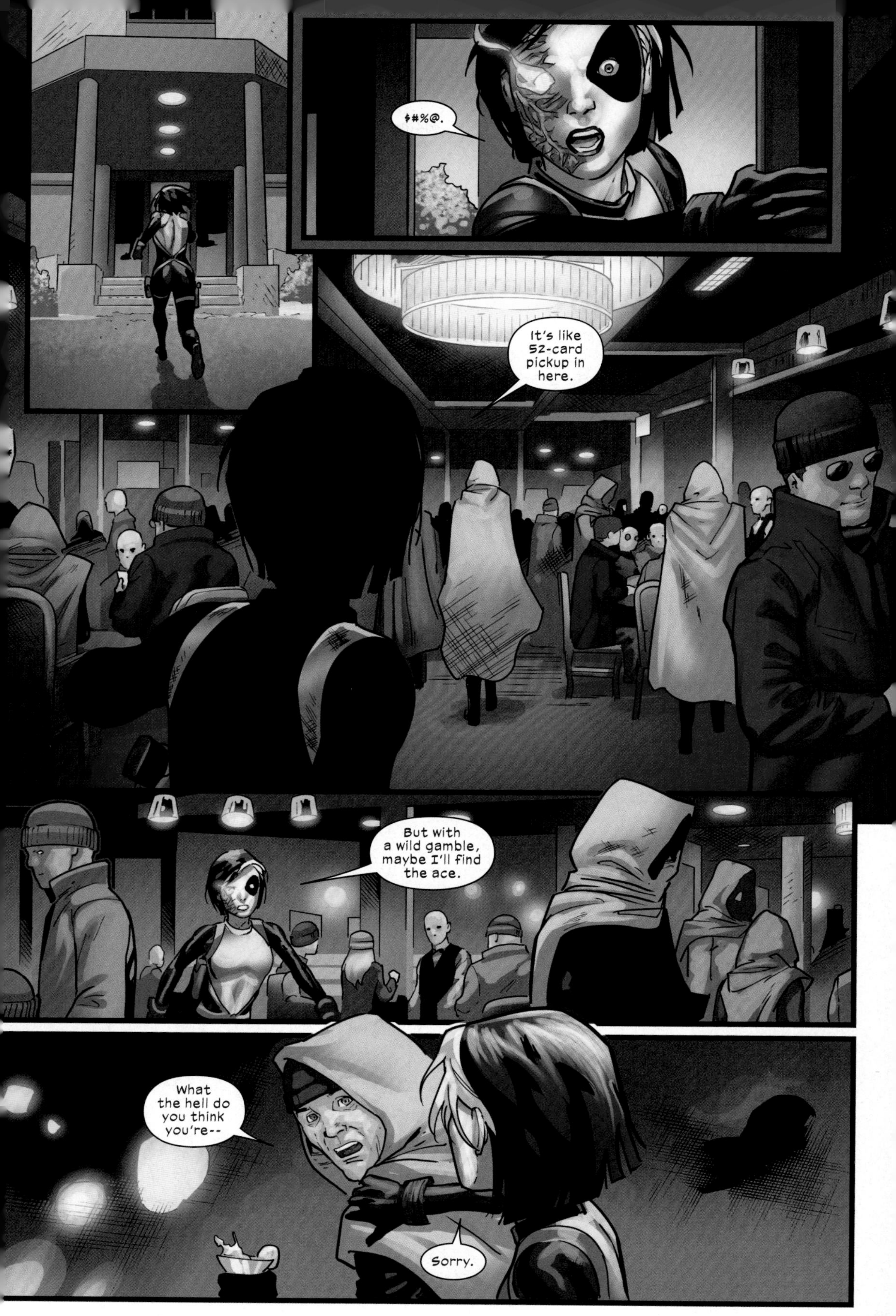
$#%@.
It's like 52-card pickup in here.
But with a wild gamble, maybe I'll find the ace.
What the hell do you think you're--
Sorry.

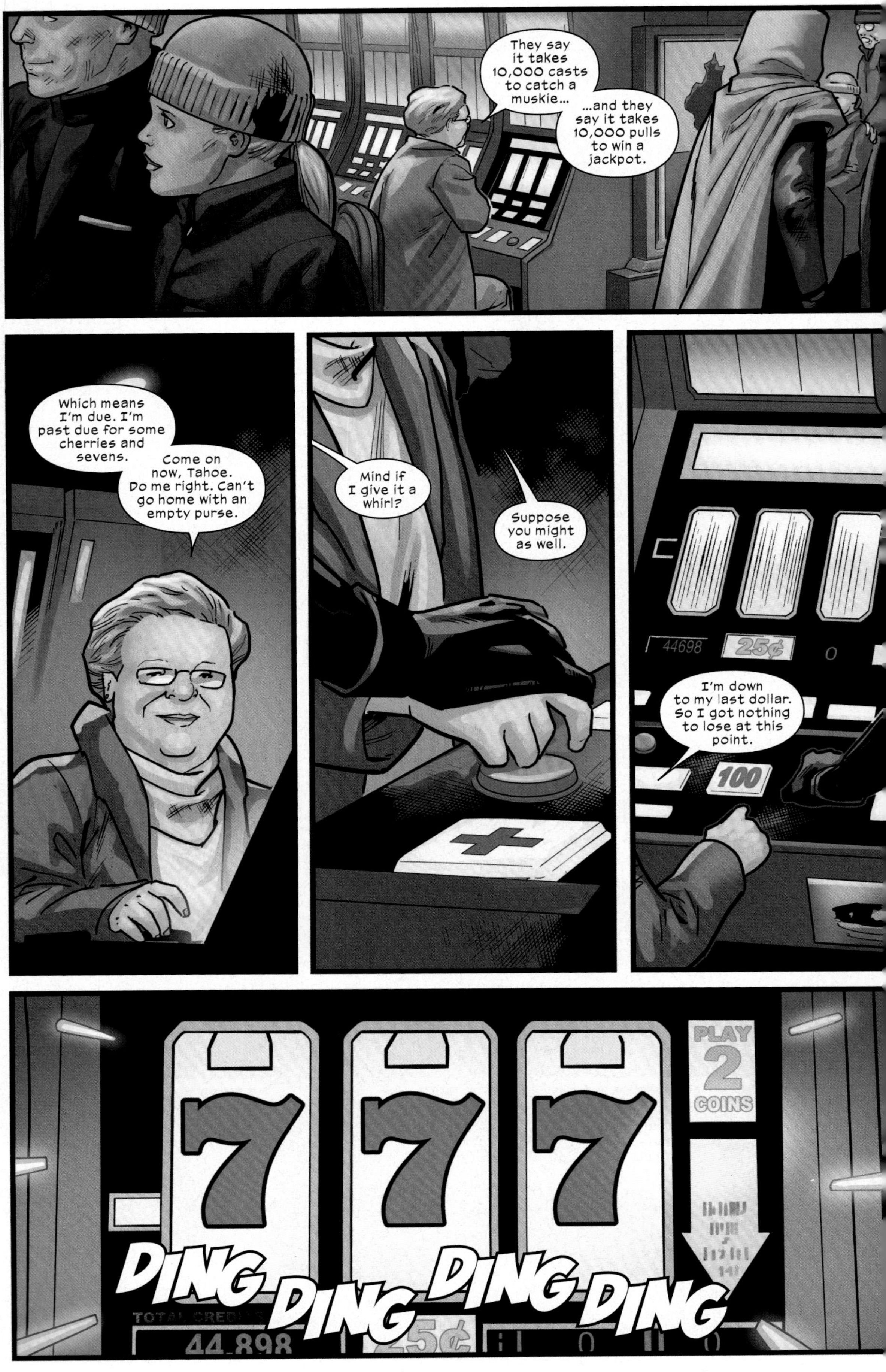
They say it takes 10,000 casts to catch a muskie...
...and they say it takes 10,000 pulls to win a jackpot.
Which means I'm due. I'm past due for some cherries and sevens.
Come on now, Tahoe. Do me right. Can't go home with an empty purse.
Mind if I give it a whirl?
Suppose you might as well.
44698
25¢
I'm down to my last dollar. So I got nothing to lose at this point.
100
PLAY 2 COINS
DING DING DING DING
44,898
25¢

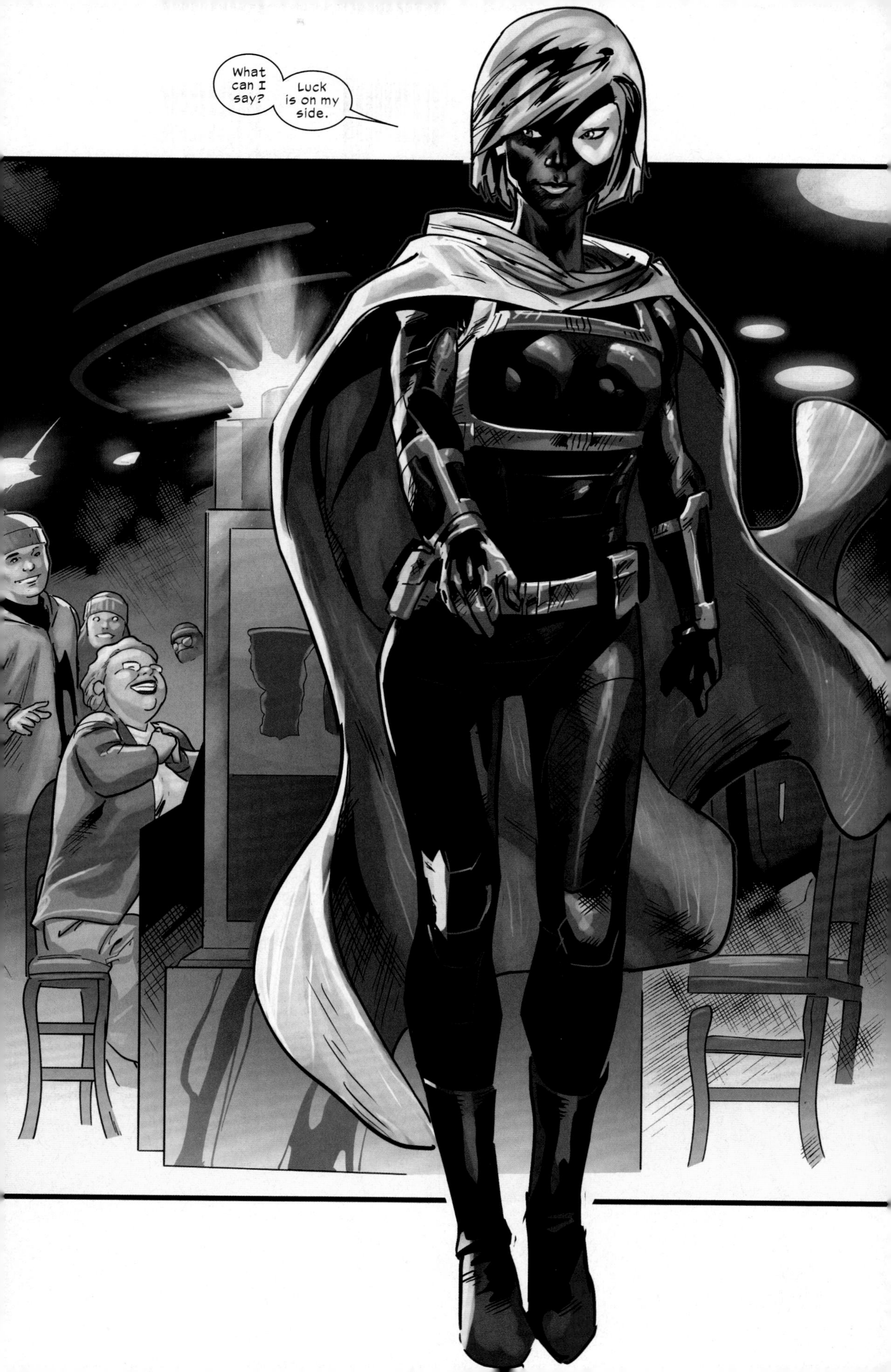
What can I say?
Luck is on my side.

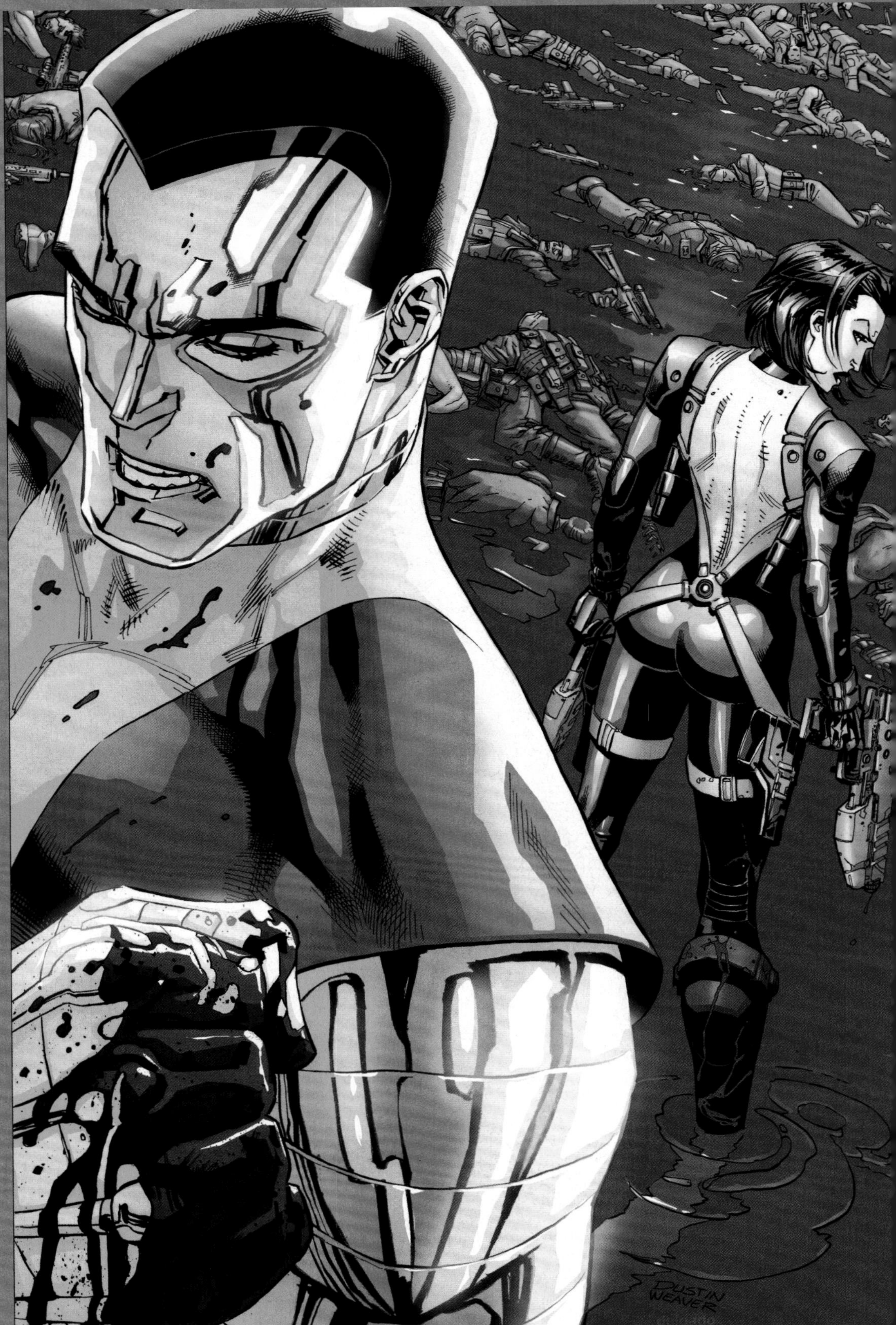
DUSTIN
WEAVER

Game of Dominoes

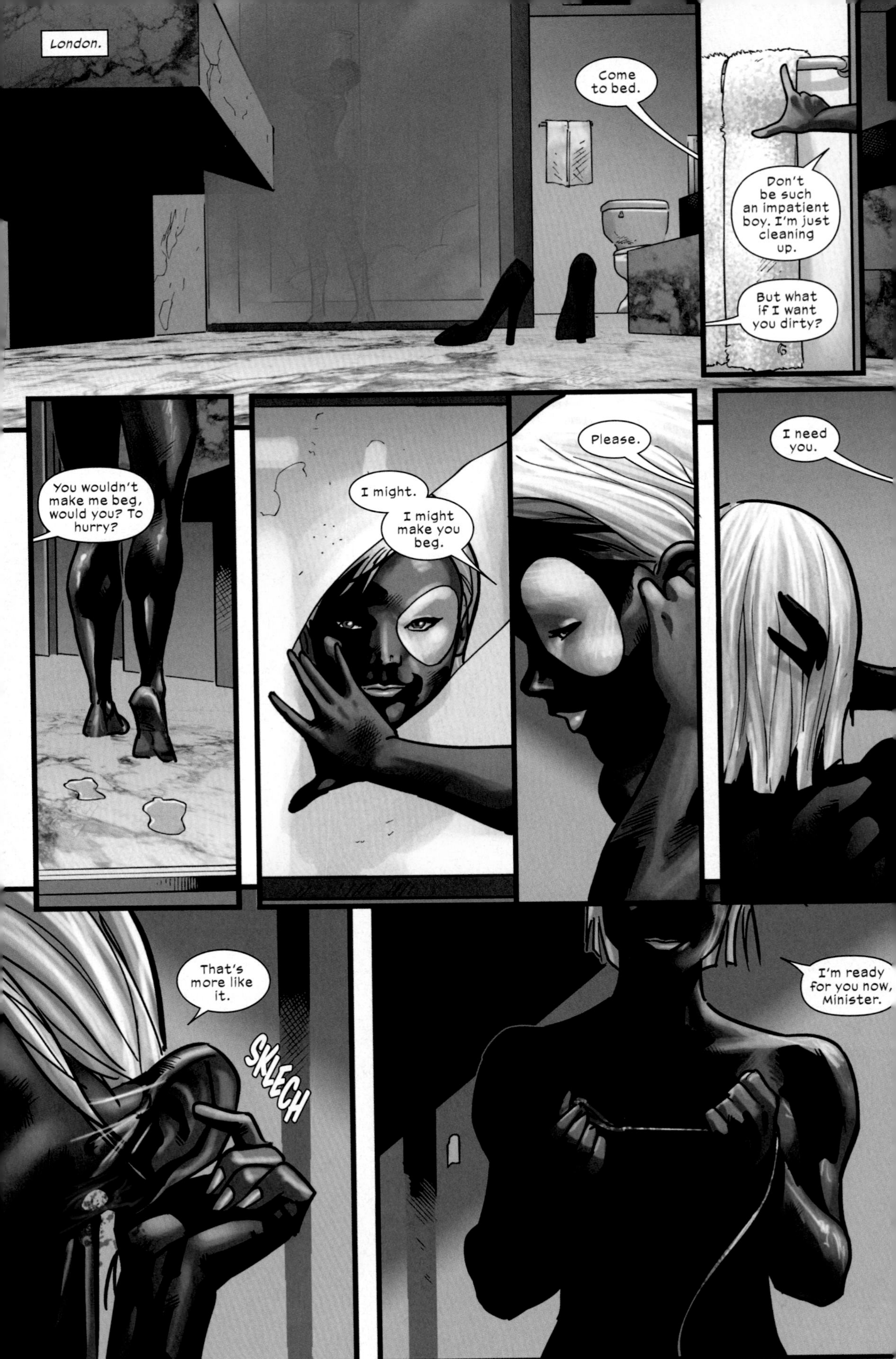
London.
Come to bed.
Don't be such an impatient boy. I'm just cleaning up.
But what if I want you dirty?
You wouldn't make me beg, would you? To hurry?
I might.
I might make you beg.
Please.
I need you.
That's more like it.
SKLECH
I'm ready for you now, Minister.

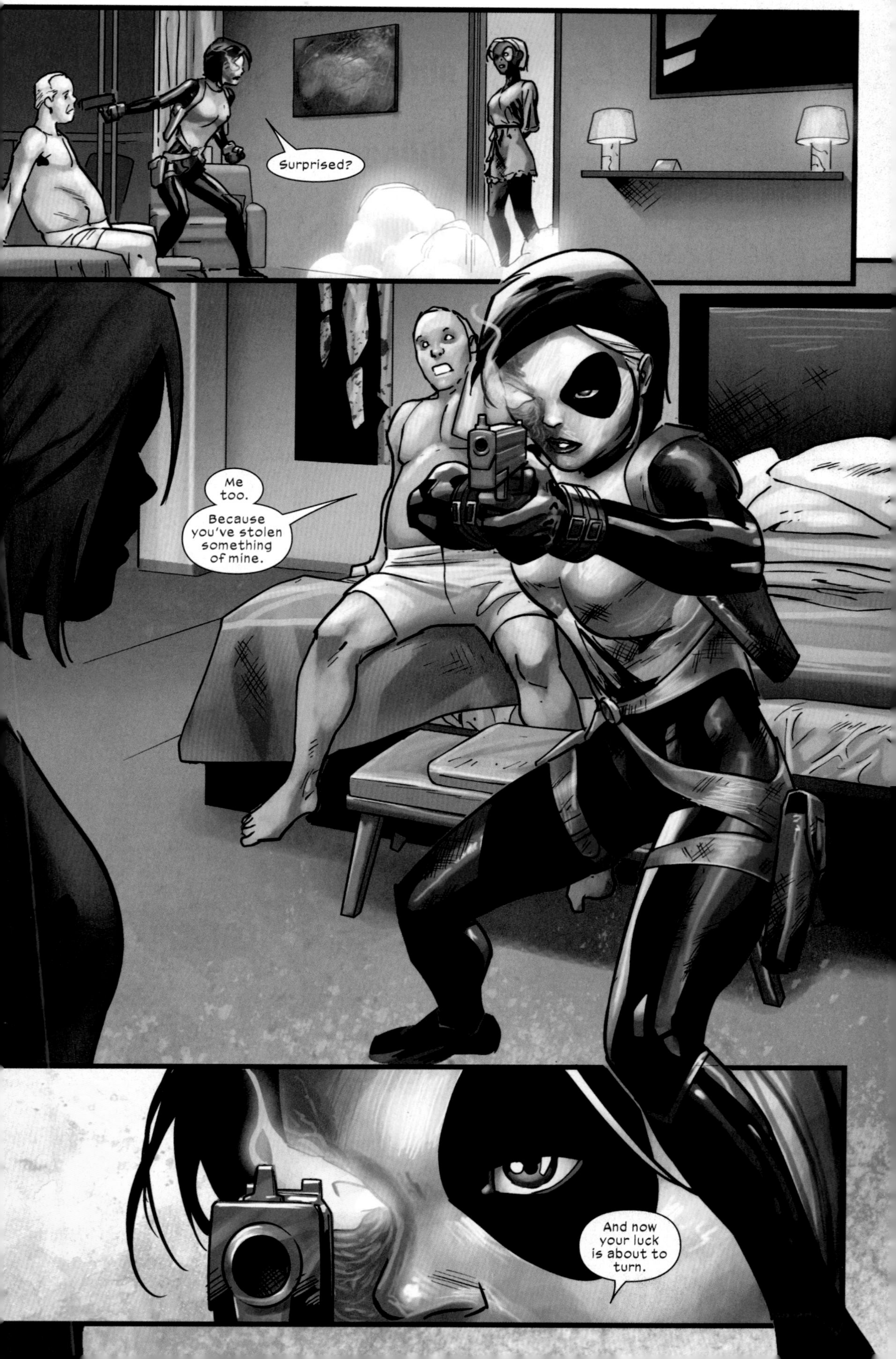
Surprised?
Me too.
Because you've stolen something of mine.
And now your luck is about to turn.

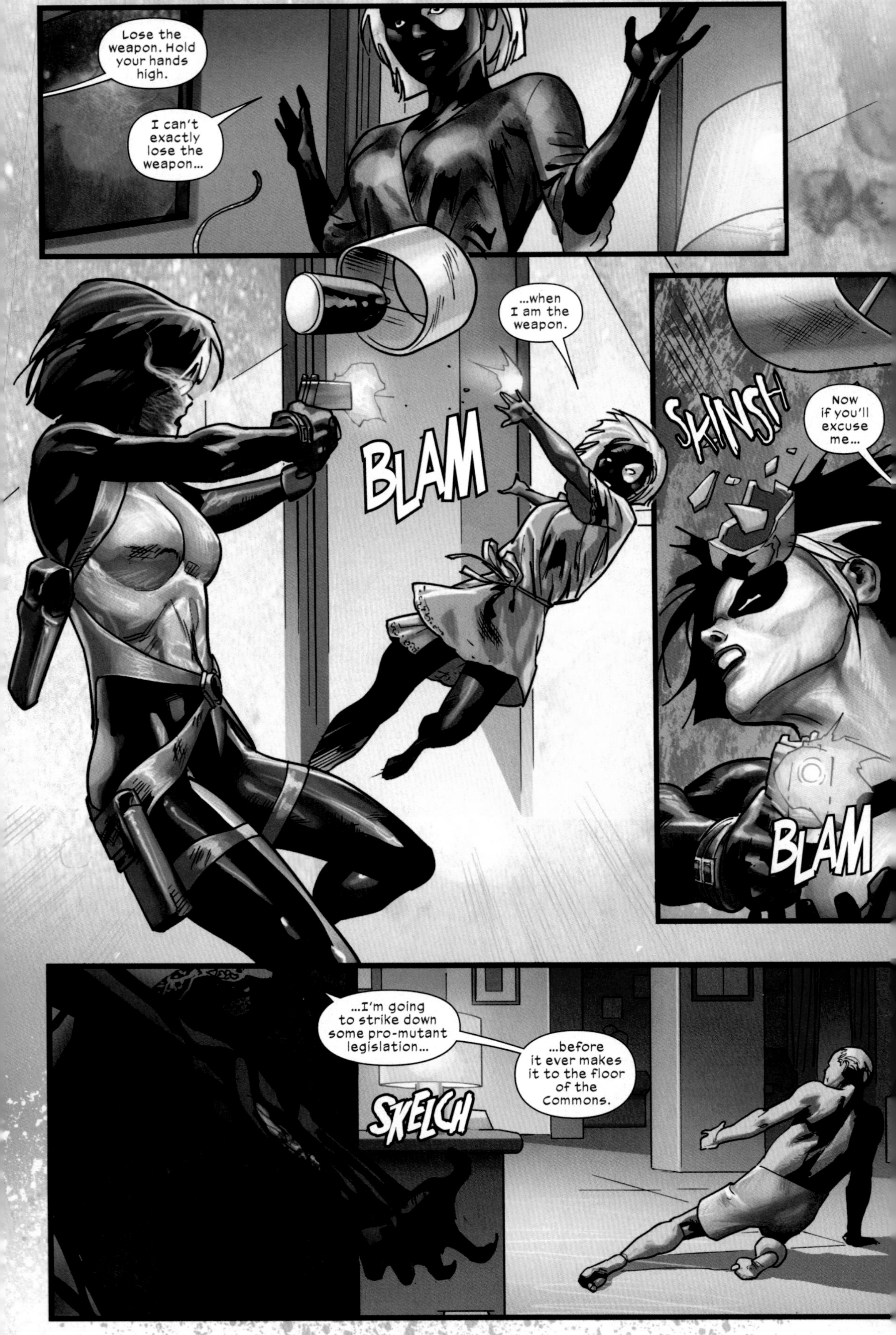
Lose the weapon. Hold your hands high.
I can't exactly lose the weapon...
...when I am the weapon.
BLAM
SKINSH
Now if you'll excuse me...
BLAM
...I'm going to strike down some pro-mutant legislation...
...before it ever makes it to the floor of the Commons.
SKELCH

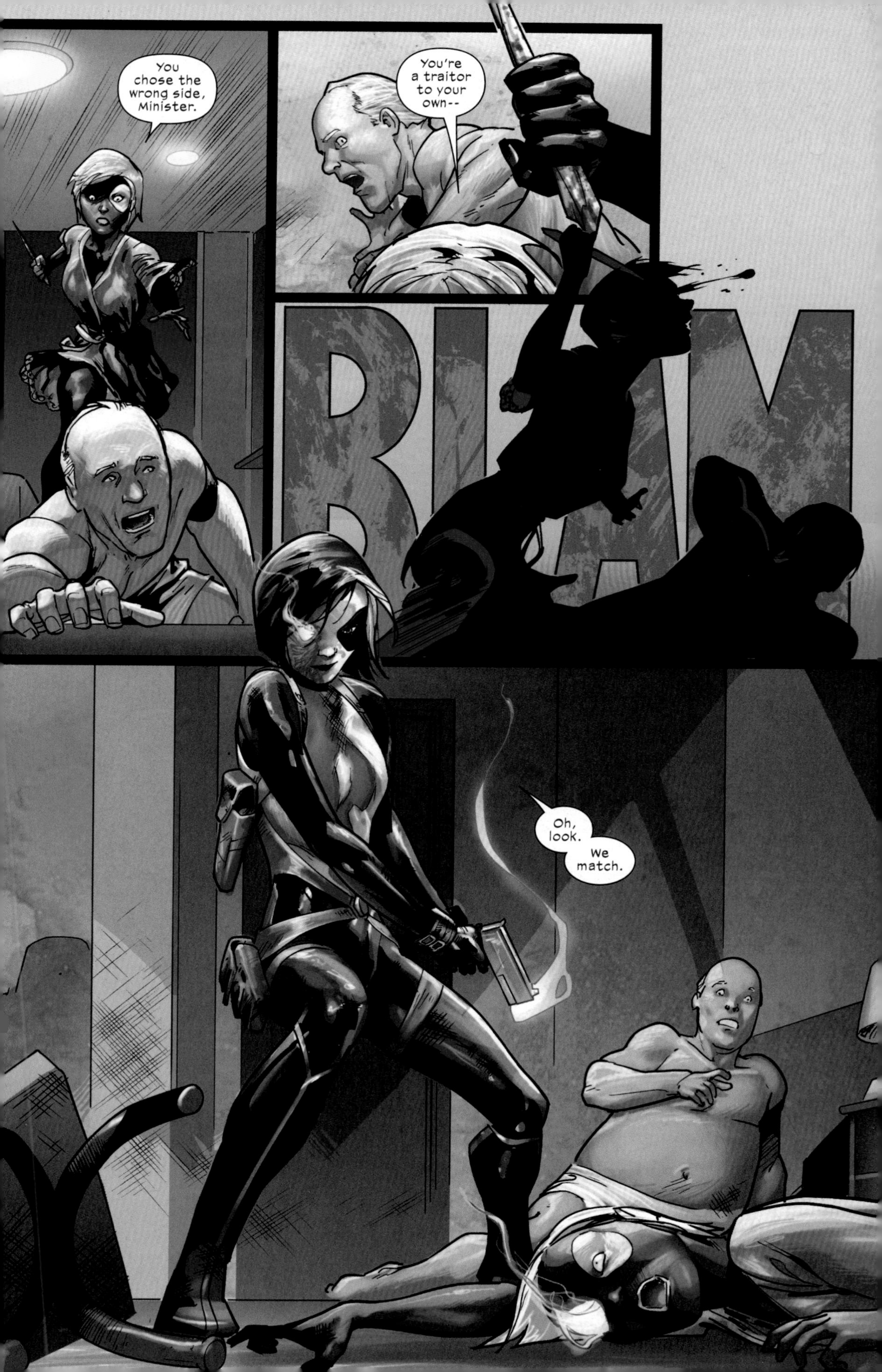
You chose the wrong side, Minister.
You're a traitor to your own--
BLAM
Oh, look. We match.

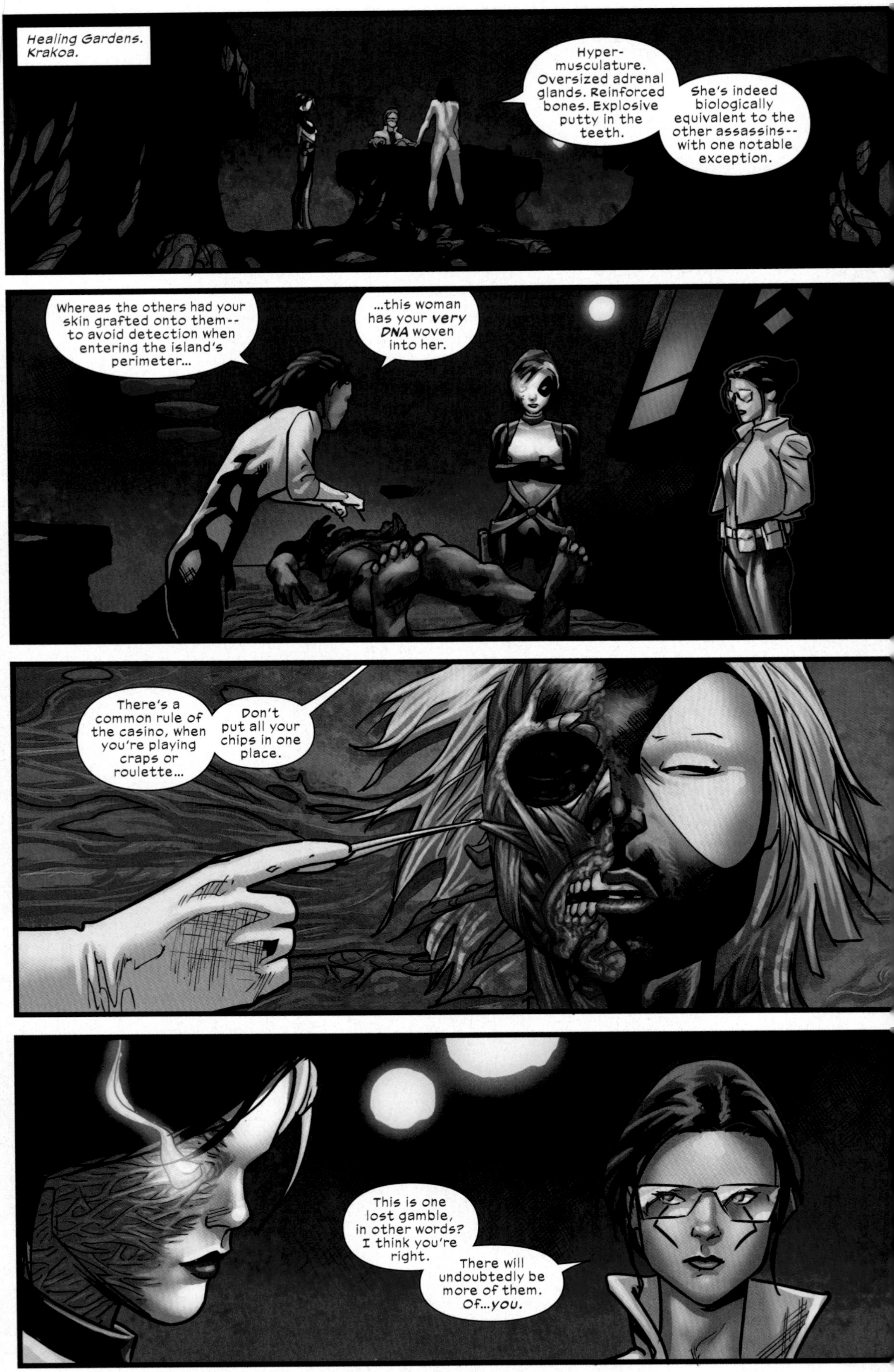

Healing Gardens. Krakoa.
Hyper-musculature. Oversized adrenal glands. Reinforced bones. Explosive putty in the teeth.
She's indeed biologically equivalent to the other assassins--with one notable exception.
Whereas the others had your skin grafted onto them--to avoid detection when entering the island's perimeter...
...this woman has your *very DNA* woven into her.
There's a common rule of the casino, when you're playing craps or roulette...
Don't put all your chips in one place.
This is one lost gamble, in other words? I think you're right.
There will undoubtedly be more of them. Of...*you*.

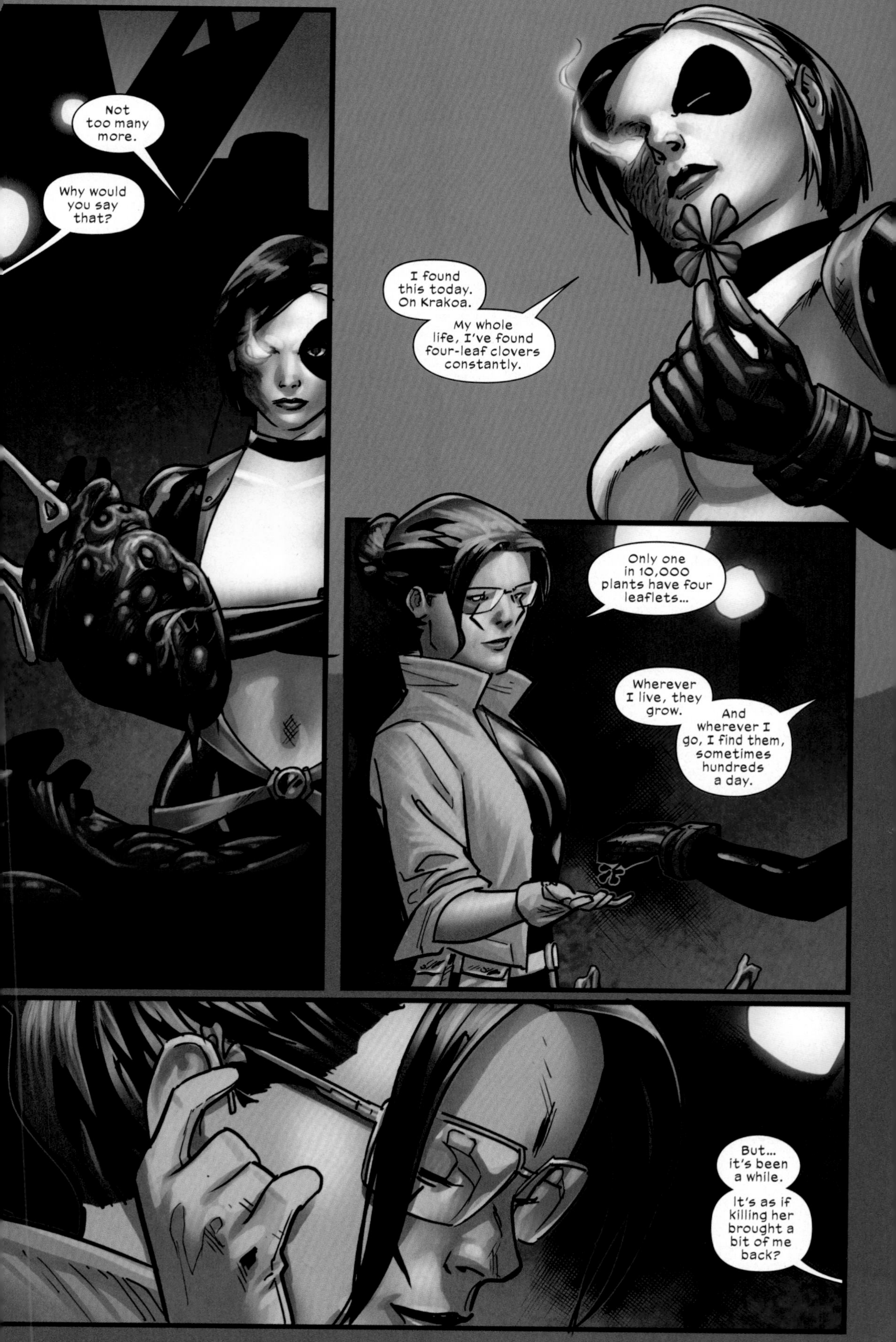
Not too many more.
Why would you say that?
I found this today. On Krakoa.
My whole life, I've found four-leaf clovers constantly.
Only one in 10,000 plants have four leaflets...
Wherever I live, they grow.
And wherever I go, I find them, sometimes hundreds a day.
But... it's been a while.
It's as if killing her brought a bit of me back?

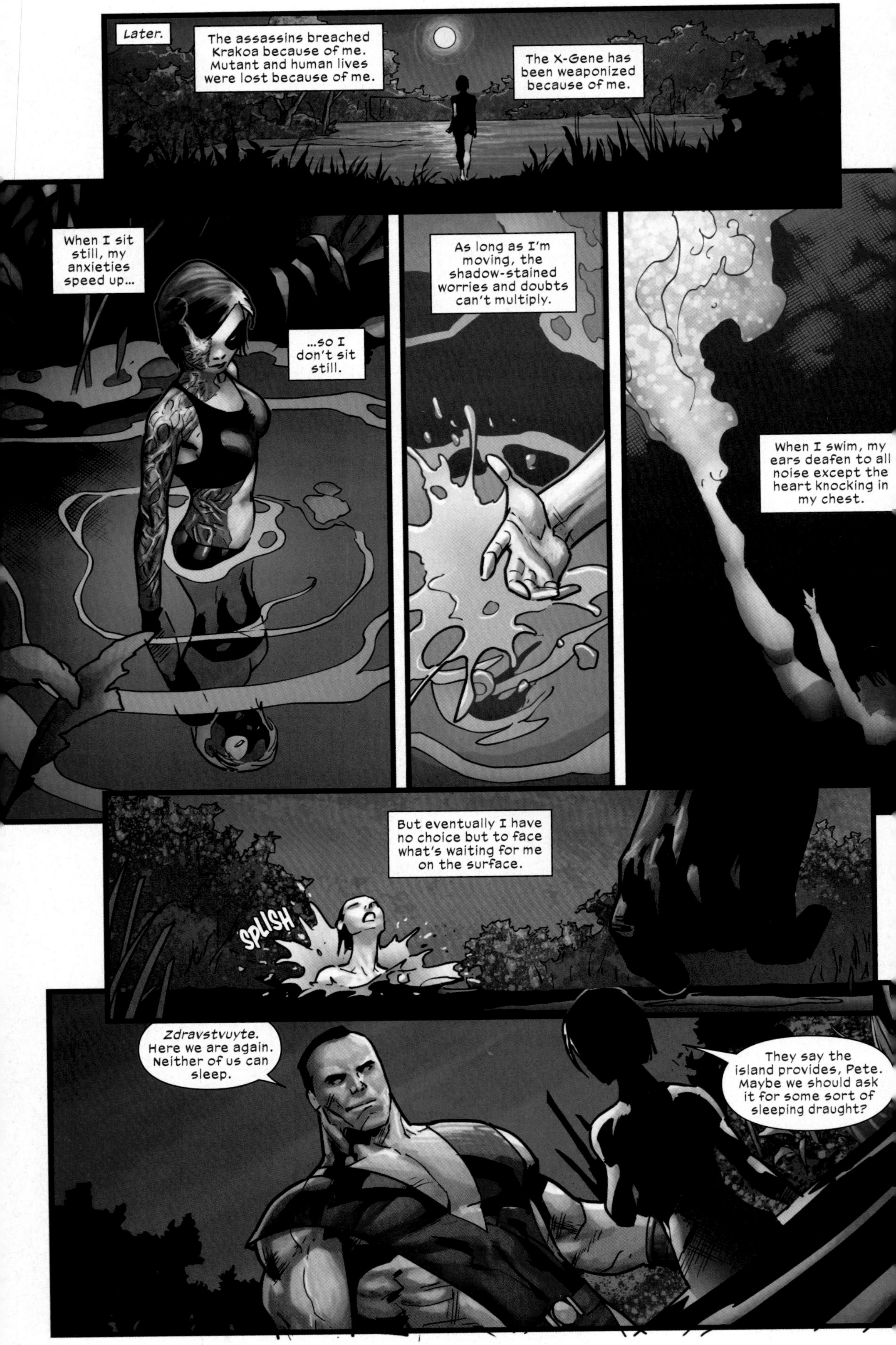
Later.
The assassins breached Krakoa because of me. Mutant and human lives were lost because of me.
The X-Gene has been weaponized because of me.
When I sit still, my anxieties speed up...
...so I don't sit still.
As long as I'm moving, the shadow-stained worries and doubts can't multiply.
When I swim, my ears deafen to all noise except the heart knocking in my chest.
But eventually I have no choice but to face what's waiting for me on the surface.
SPLISH
Zdravstvuyte. Here we are again. Neither of us can sleep.
They say the island provides, Pete. Maybe we should ask it for some sort of sleeping draught?

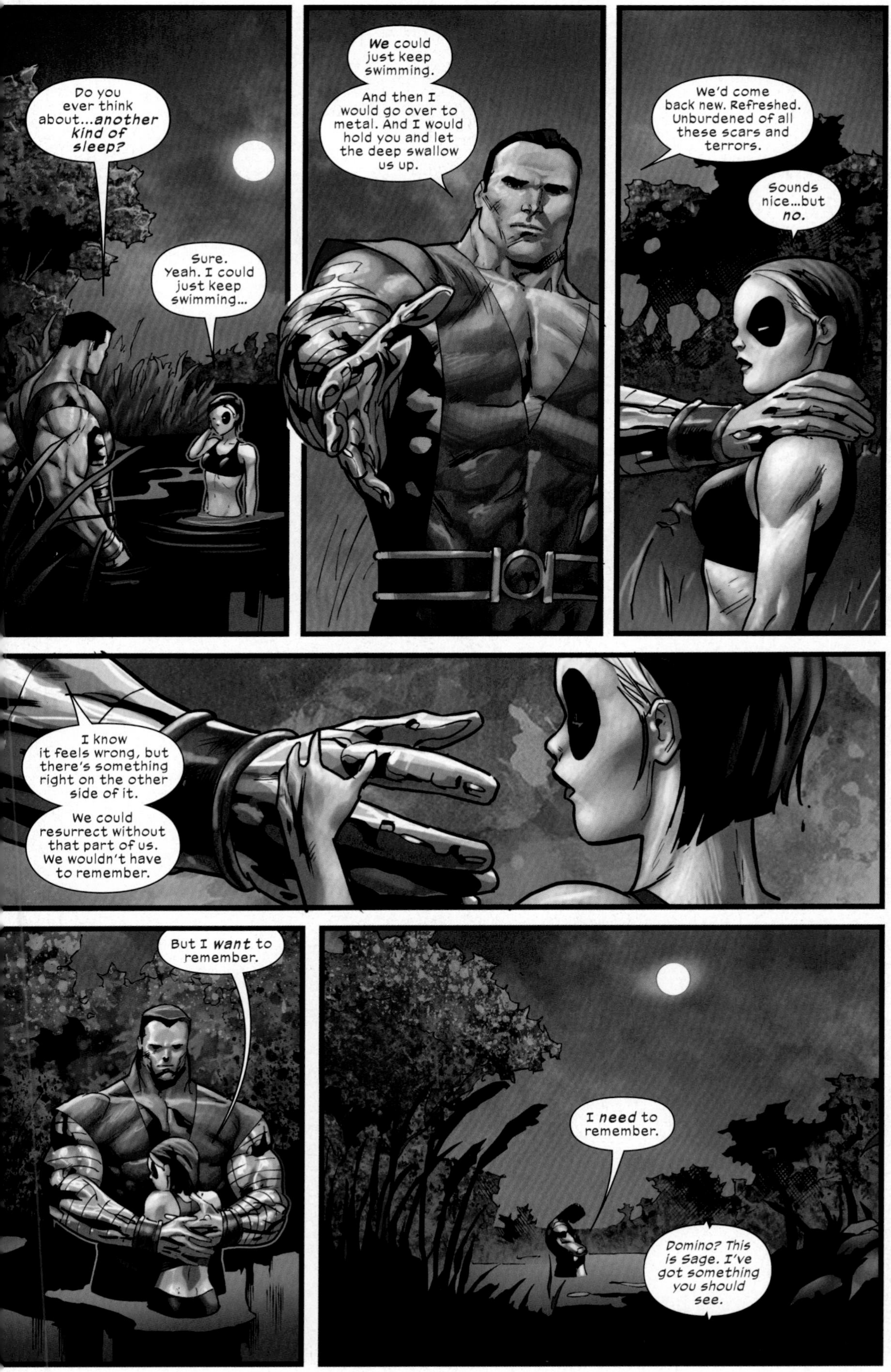

Do you ever think about...*another kind of sleep?*
Sure. Yeah. I could just keep swimming...
We could just keep swimming.
And then I would go over to metal. And I would hold you and let the deep swallow us up.
We'd come back new. Refreshed. Unburdened of all these scars and terrors.
Sounds nice...but *no.*
I know it feels wrong, but there's something right on the other side of it.
We could resurrect without that part of us. We wouldn't have to remember.
But I *want* to remember.
I *need* to remember.
Domino? This is Sage. I've got something you should see.

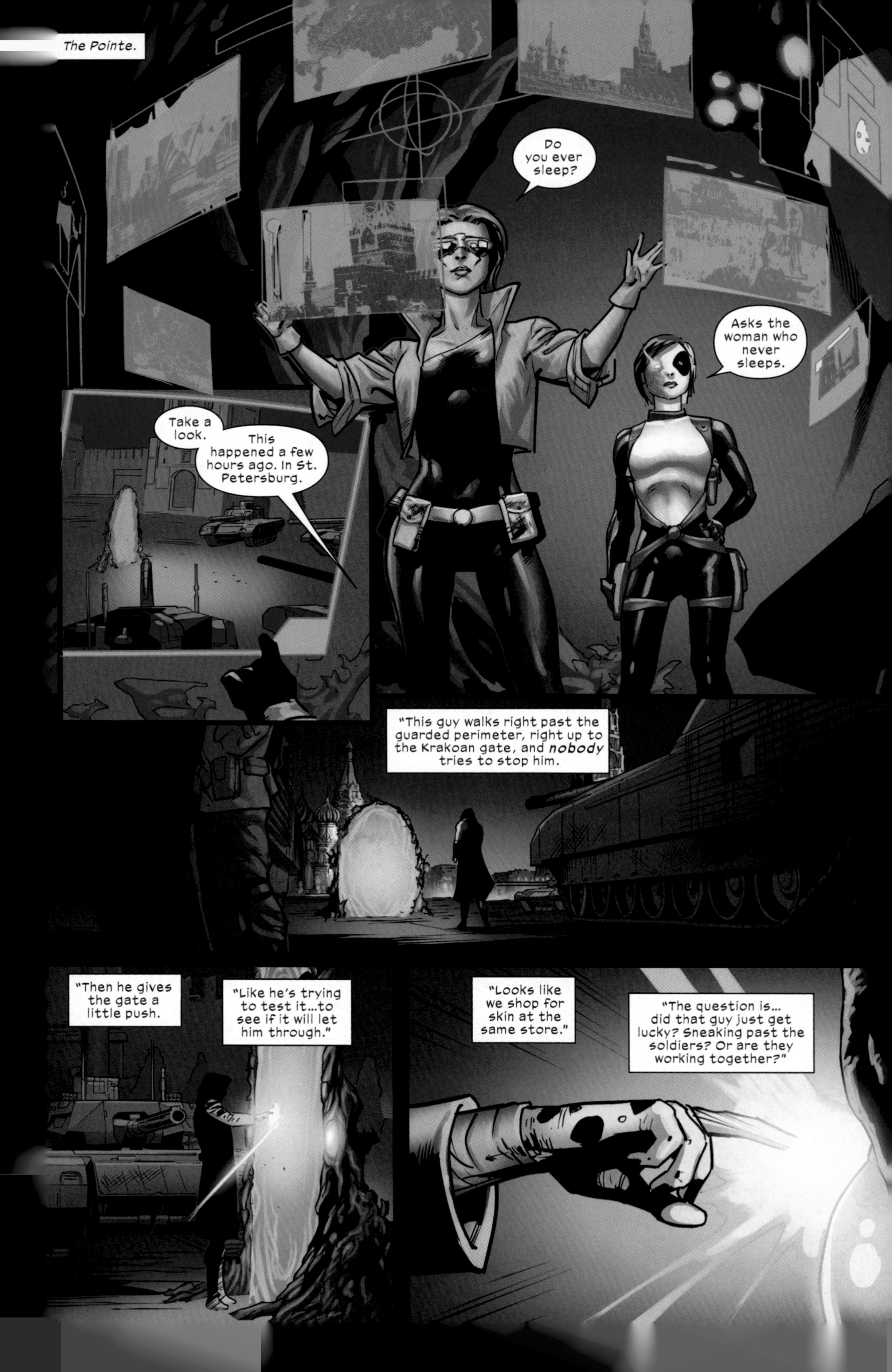
The Pointe.
Do you ever sleep?
Asks the woman who never sleeps.
Take a look.
This happened a few hours ago. In St. Petersburg.
"This guy walks right past the guarded perimeter, right up to the Krakoan gate, and *nobody* tries to stop him.
"Then he gives the gate a little push.
"Like he's trying to test it...to see if it will let him through."
"Looks like we shop for skin at the same store."
"The question is... did that guy just get lucky? Sneaking past the soldiers? Or are they working together?"

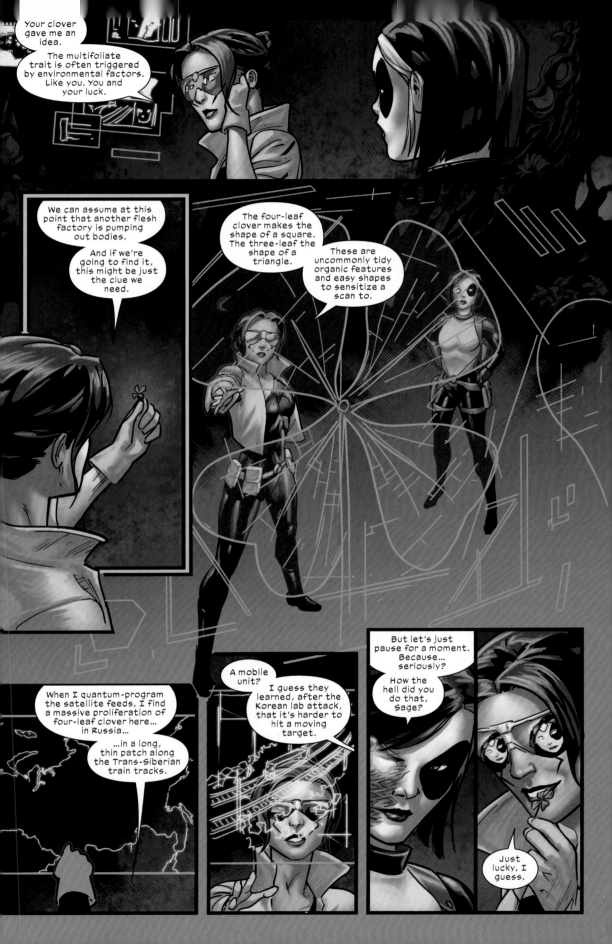

Your clover gave me an idea.

The multifoliate trait is often triggered by environmental factors. Like you. You and your luck.

We can assume at this point that another flesh factory is pumping out bodies.

And if we're going to find it, this might be just the clue we need.

The four-leaf clover makes the shape of a square. The three-leaf the shape of a triangle.

These are uncommonly tidy organic features and easy shapes to sensitize a scan to.

When I quantum-program the satellite feeds, I find a massive proliferation of four-leaf clover here... in Russia...

...in a long, thin patch along the Trans-Siberian train tracks.

A mobile unit?

I guess they learned, after the Korean lab attack, that it's harder to hit a moving target.

But let's just pause for a moment. Because... seriously?

How the hell did you do that, Sage?

Just lucky, I guess.

QUIET COUNCIL AGENDA: "SOCIAL VENUE"

The authority of the Council has agreed that Krakoa would benefit from a gathering place for its citizens.

Impact statement:

This will encourage a sense of community, social play, stress relief and mutant reproduction.*

Recommendations:

Feedback has been solicited for the council's consideration. Some notable suggestions are included below.

1. Gambit strongly advocates for a treetop casino. His quote in favor of this: "*Poo-yie*, I thought you'd never ask. I know a thing or three about gambling, me. This one time, back in Louisiana, me and T-Boy, we turned this river barge into quite the slick operation. You could throw down cards or you could fix a plate and drink a drink or *aborder* the night away."

2. Apocalypse tried to dismiss the proposal as "frivolous. Base. Irrelevant."

3. Forge put forward a 500-page architectural draft for a juice bar and gym that he suggests we call HOT SQUATS. He has used his bio-tech to develop exercise equipment -- including big balls filled with saltwater -- that will, in his words, "Get you ripped as ▇▇▇ You want the world to follow us? Give them a hot ass to chase."

4. Black Tom's opinion was solicited. He said, "Oh, we already built that." When he was asked to elaborate on what exactly he -- or we? -- built, he said, "The thing you're talking about. We built it." Questions followed about the when and what and the where and how of it all -- to which he responded, "We always do our best thinking when we're on the throne. So this morning, after tea, we're dropping a deuce, understand? And there it is in our heads, the whole glorious vision, and once it's in our heads, it's as good as done." He was again asked to elaborate and said, "The Green Lagoon, of course. The world's greatest tiki bar. Come on. Let us show you."

* Bylaw: MAKE MORE MUTANTS

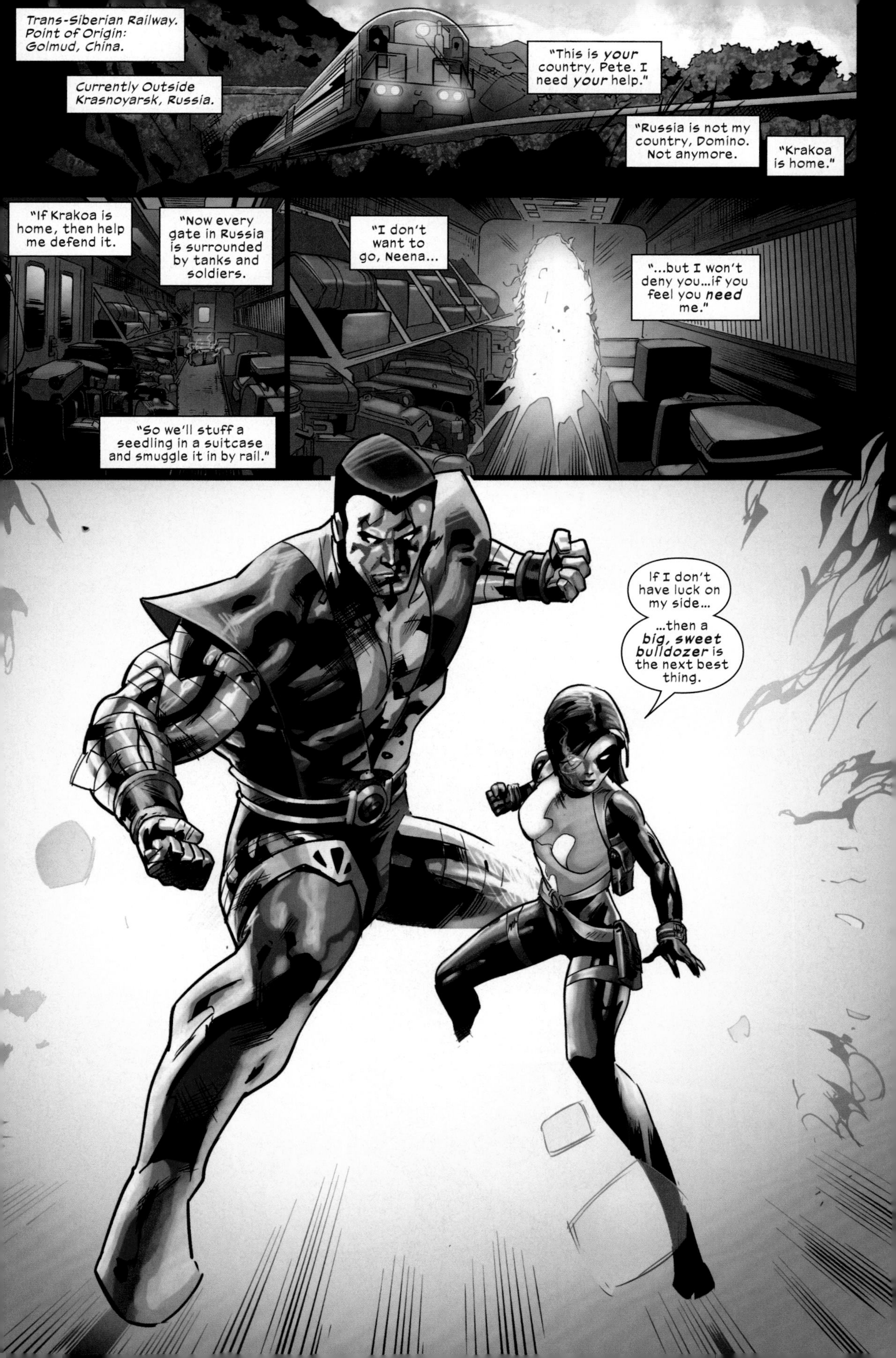
Trans-Siberian Railway.
Point of Origin:
Golmud, China.
Currently Outside
Krasnoyarsk, Russia.
"This is *your* country, Pete. I need *your* help."
"Russia is not my country, Domino. Not anymore.
"Krakoa is home."
"If Krakoa is home, then help me defend it.
"Now every gate in Russia is surrounded by tanks and soldiers.
"So we'll stuff a seedling in a suitcase and smuggle it in by rail."
"I don't want to go, Neena...
"...but I won't deny you...if you feel you *need* me."
If I don't have luck on my side...
...then a ***big, sweet bulldozer*** is the next best thing.

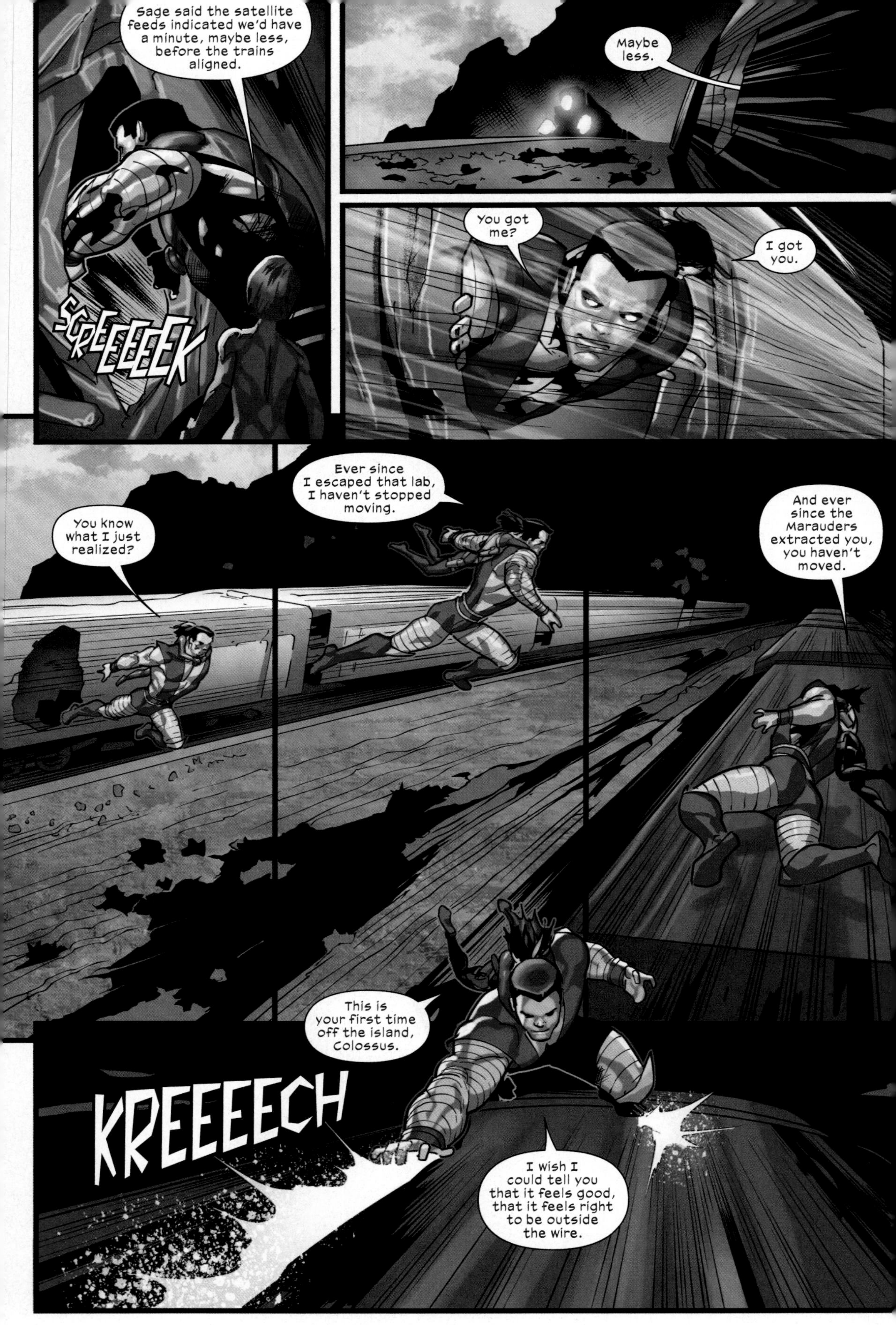
Sage said the satellite feeds indicated we'd have a minute, maybe less, before the trains aligned.
SCREEEEEEK
Maybe less.
You got me?
I got you.
You know what I just realized?
Ever since I escaped that lab, I haven't stopped moving.
And ever since the Marauders extracted you, you haven't moved.
This is your first time off the island, Colossus.
KREEEEECH
I wish I could tell you that it feels good, that it feels right to be outside the wire.

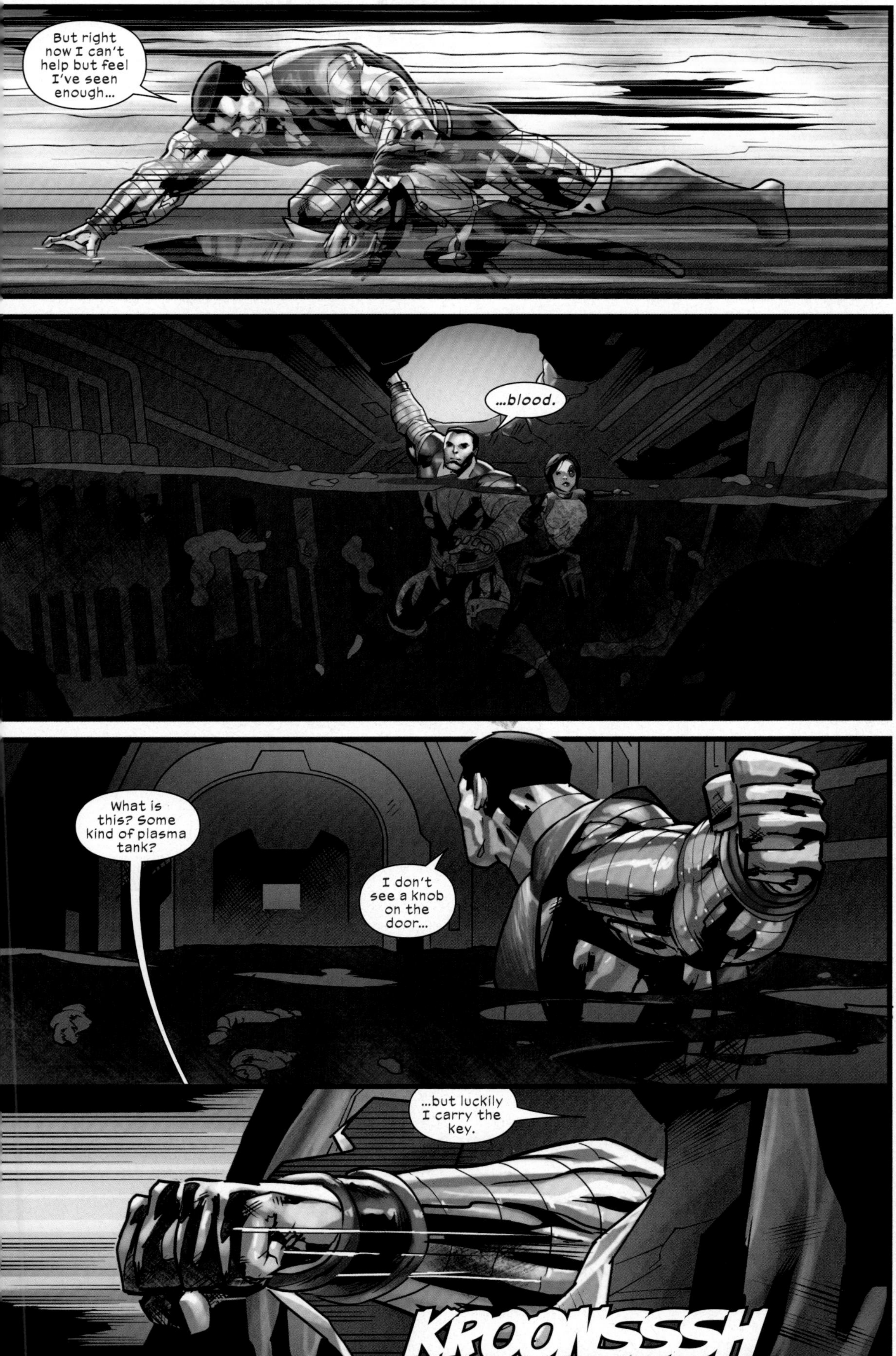
But right now I can't help but feel I've seen enough...
...blood.
What is this? Some kind of plasma tank?
I don't see a knob on the door...
...but luckily I carry the key.
KROONSSSH

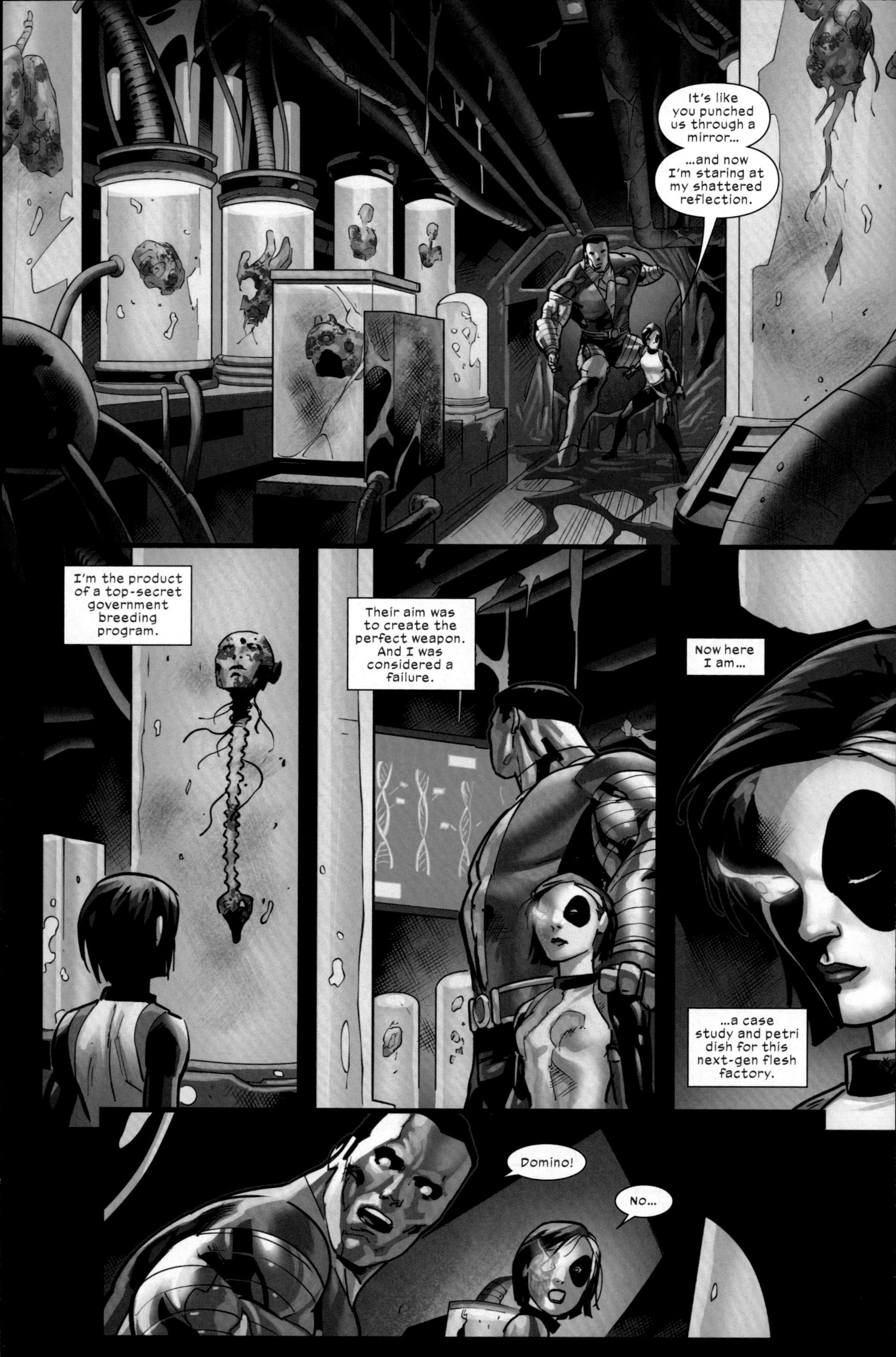
It's like you punched us through a mirror...
...and now I'm staring at my shattered reflection.
I'm the product of a top-secret government breeding program.
Their aim was to create the perfect weapon. And I was considered a failure.
Now here I am...
...a case study and petri dish for this next-gen flesh factory.
Domino!
No...

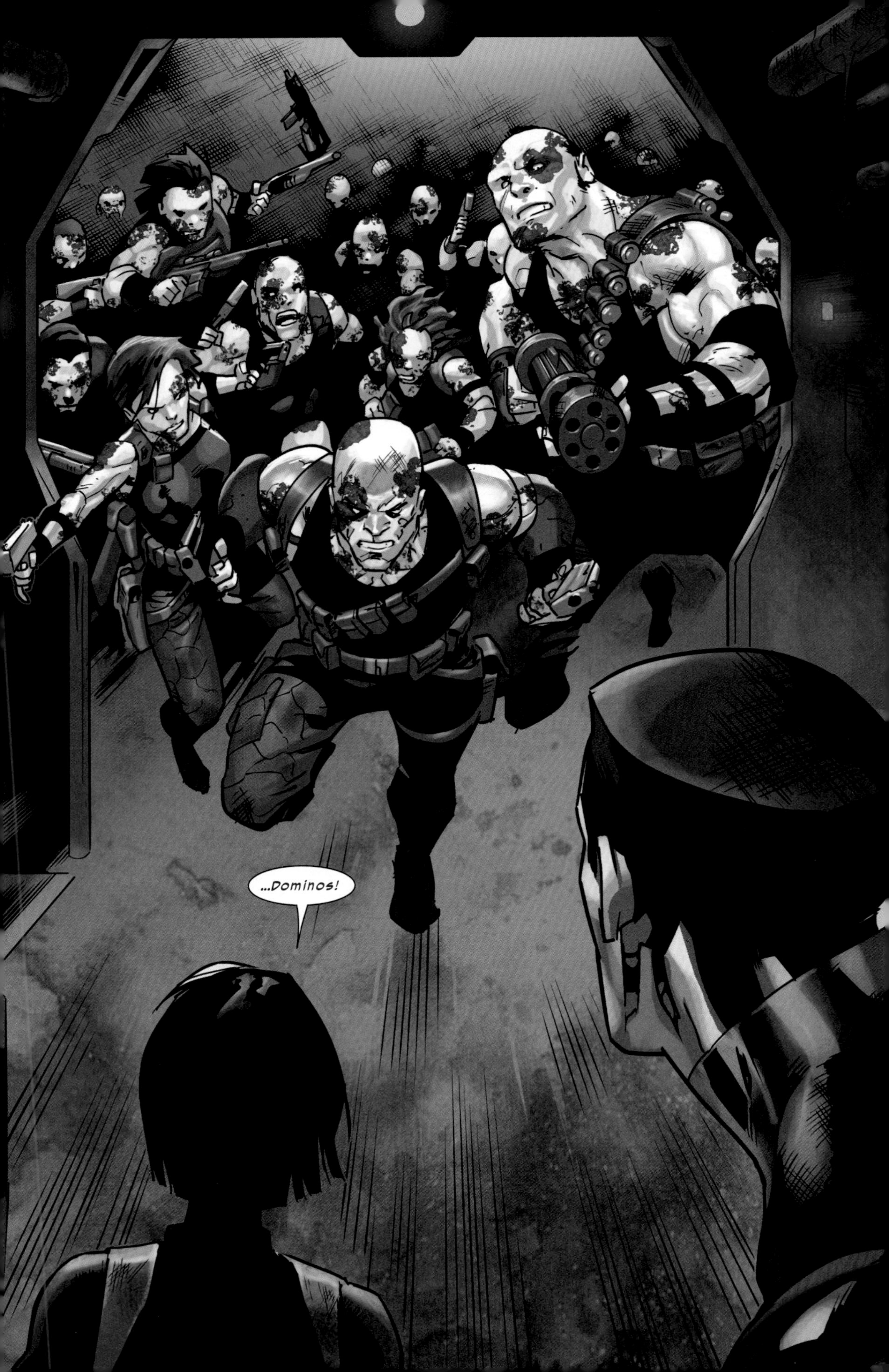
...Dominos!

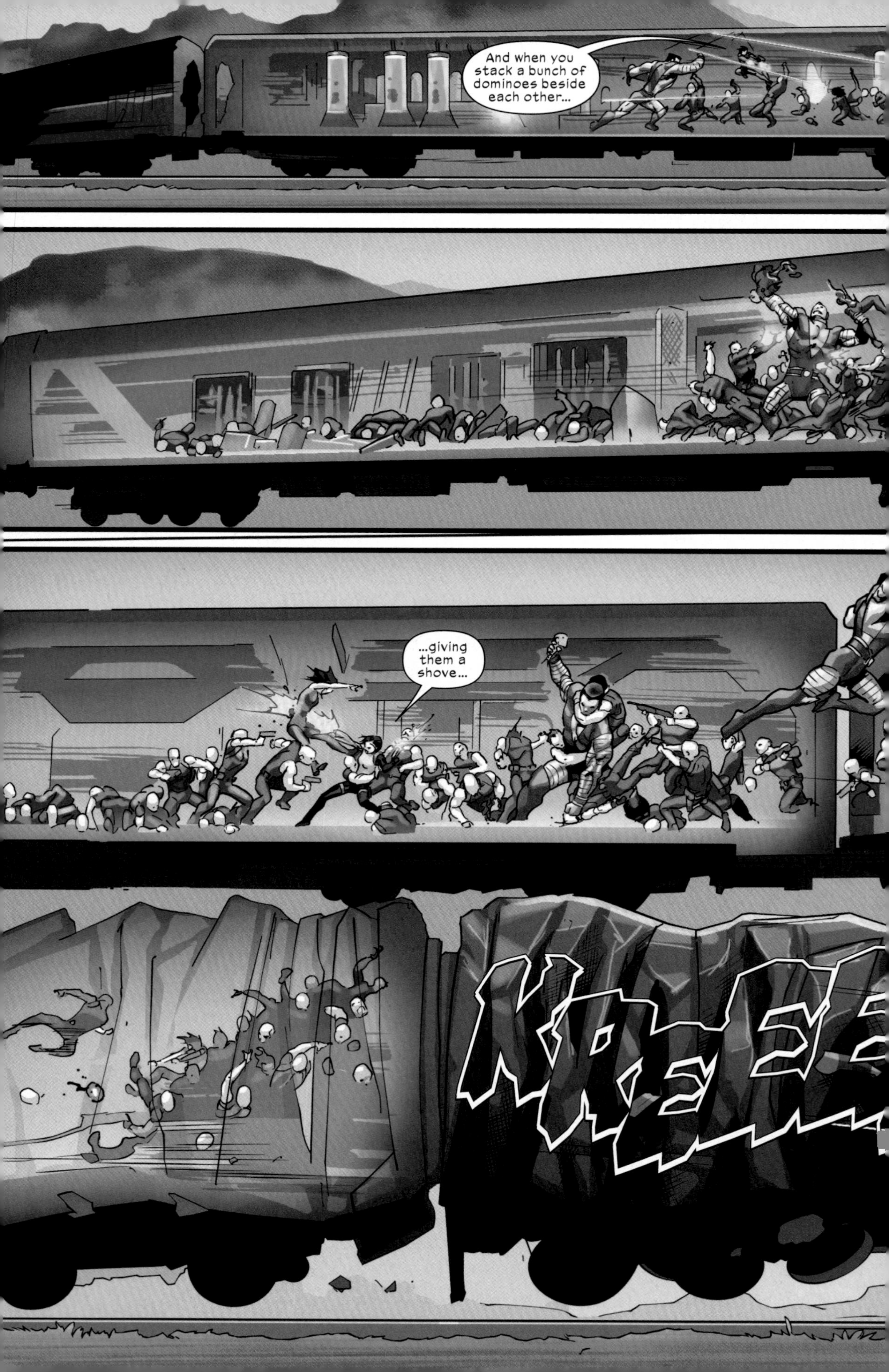

And when you stack a bunch of dominoes beside each other...
...giving them a shove...

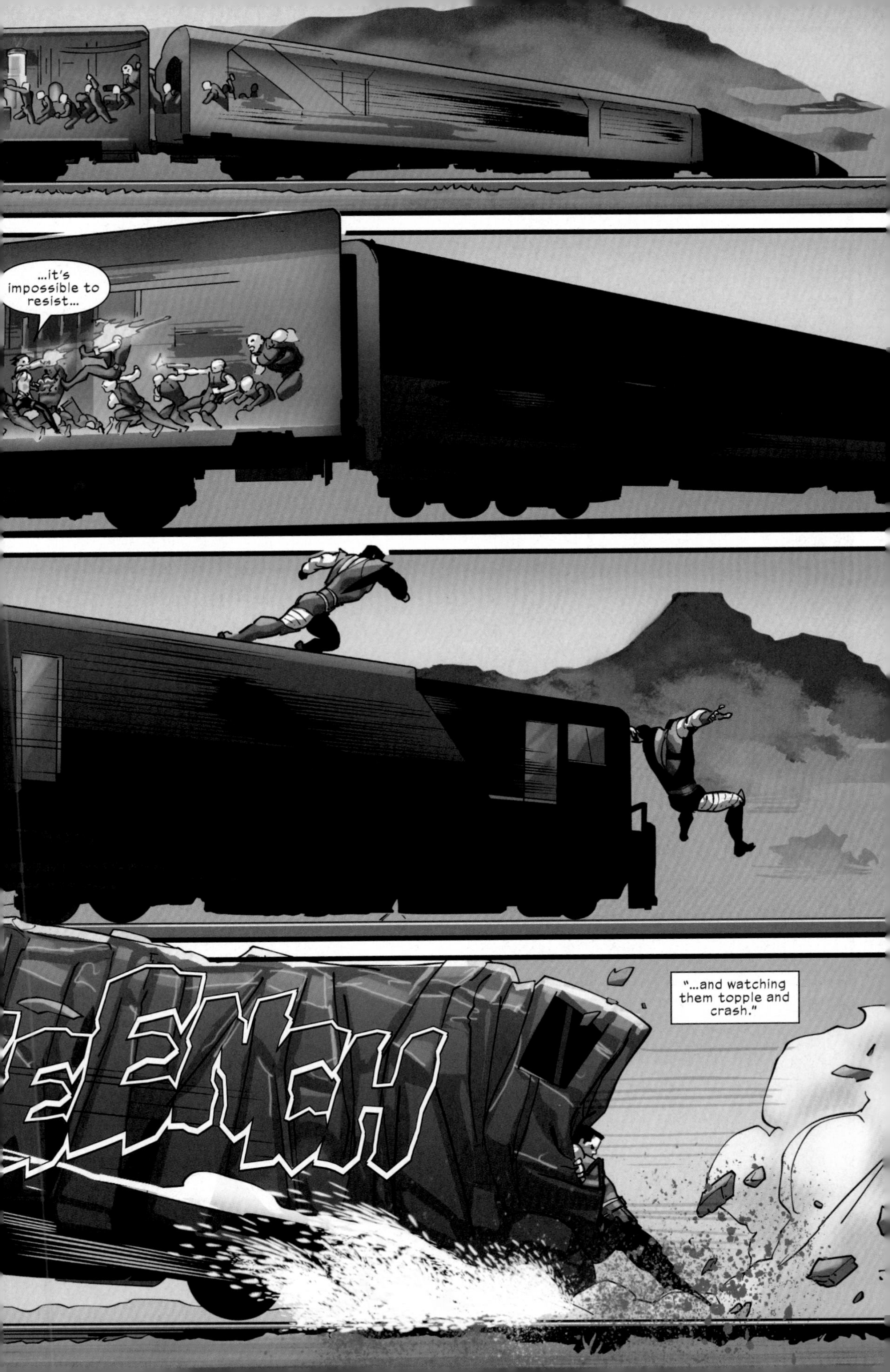
...it's impossible to resist...
"...and watching them topple and crash."

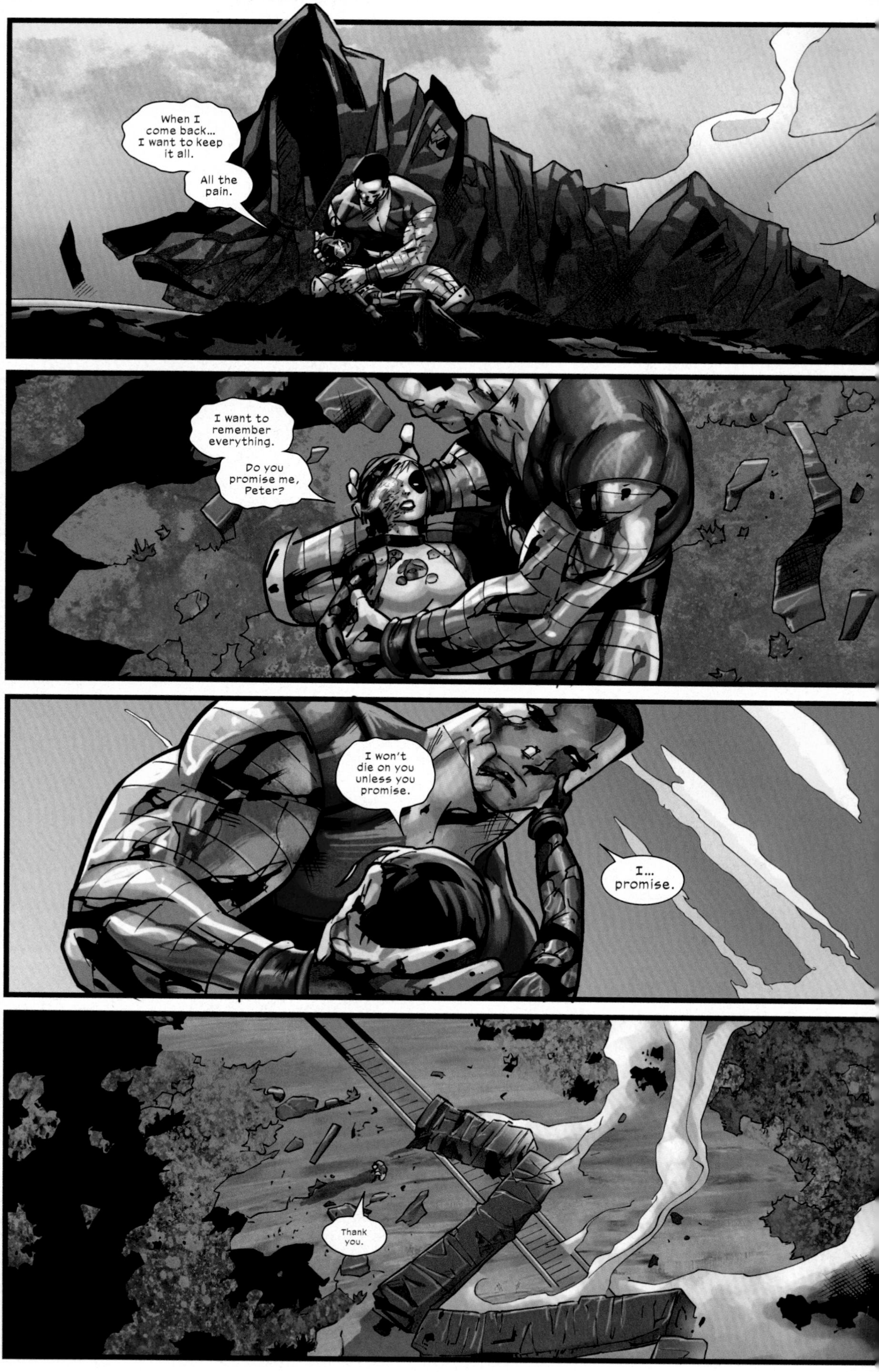

When I come back... I want to keep it all.
All the pain.
I want to remember everything.
Do you promise me, Peter?
I won't die on you unless you promise.
I... promise.
Thank you.

BEAST'S LOGBOOK:
THE MAN WITH THE PEACOCK TATTOO

When held captive in South Korea, Domino was heavily sedated, compromising her memory of the experience.

Her mind recalls an indeterminate mess of sensations. Bright lights burning her vision. A cold steel table grinding into her spine. The lick of scalpels on her skin. The hot flood of blood. Tanks bubbling. Flesh cauterizing. Voices whispering.

But one element remains concrete and constant: the Man with the Peacock Tattoo.

Her vision of him has been telepathically confirmed by Jean, who mind-scanned one of the dying assassins and conjured his visage.

They know little beyond his cream suit and the design inked into the back of his hand. He wore a mask, which I suspect to be made of labradorite.

Labradorite occurs in Newfoundland, Finland, Genosha and Russia. It is said to be a stone with a magic connection to transformation and protection.

He appears to be the head of a shadow organization united against mutantkind. The flesh factory in which Domino was housed -- and the experiments she endured -- indicates an attempt to cheat evolution and create Super-Soldier competition.

Which is the same threatening calculus of Orchis.

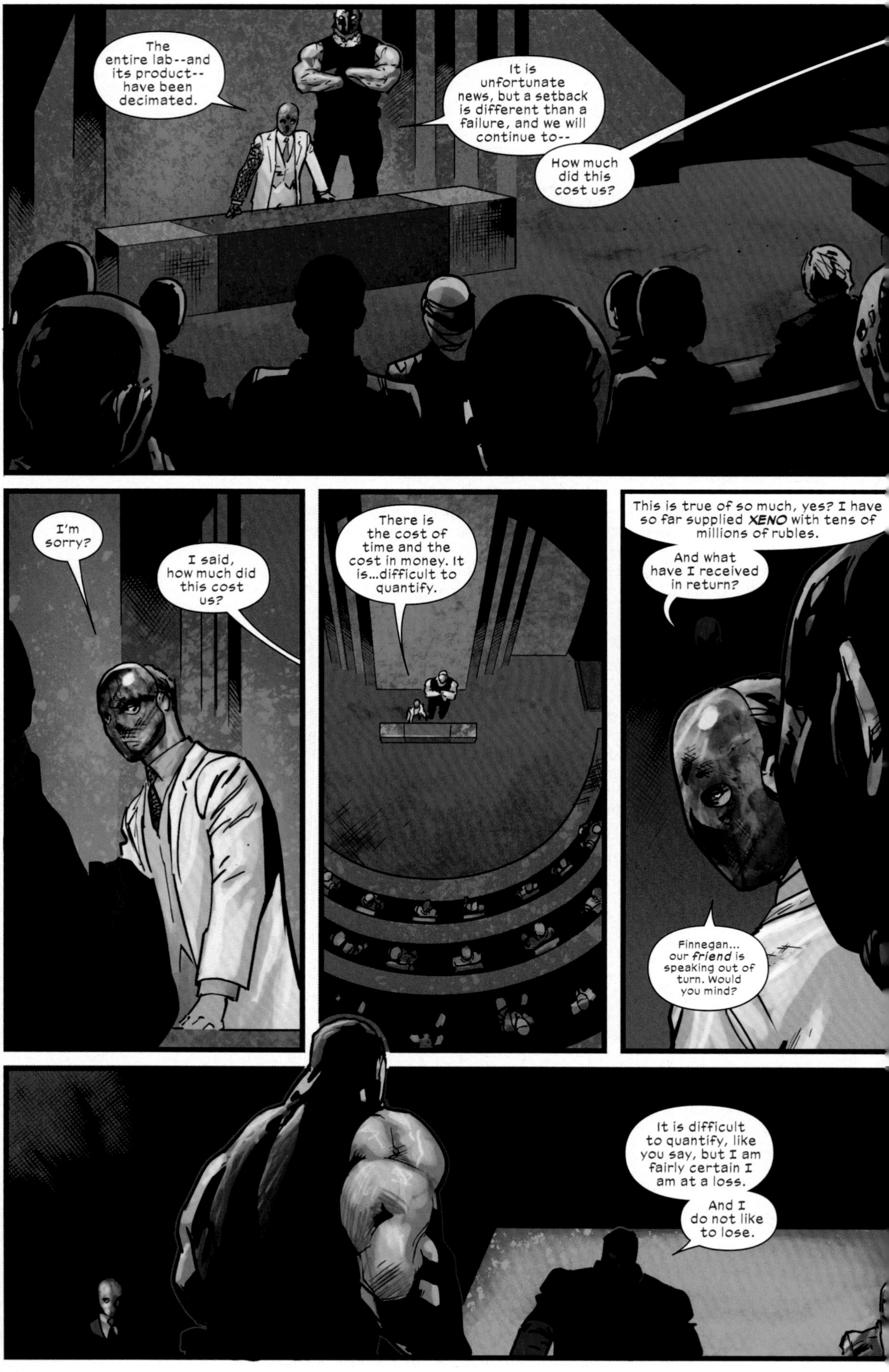
The entire lab--and its product--have been decimated.
It is unfortunate news, but a setback is different than a failure, and we will continue to--
How much did this cost us?
I'm sorry?
I said, how much did this cost us?
There is the cost of time and the cost in money. It is...difficult to quantify.
This is true of so much, yes? I have so far supplied XENO with tens of millions of rubles.
And what have I received in return?
Finnegan... our friend is speaking out of turn. Would you mind?
It is difficult to quantify, like you say, but I am fairly certain I am at a loss.
And I do not like to lose.

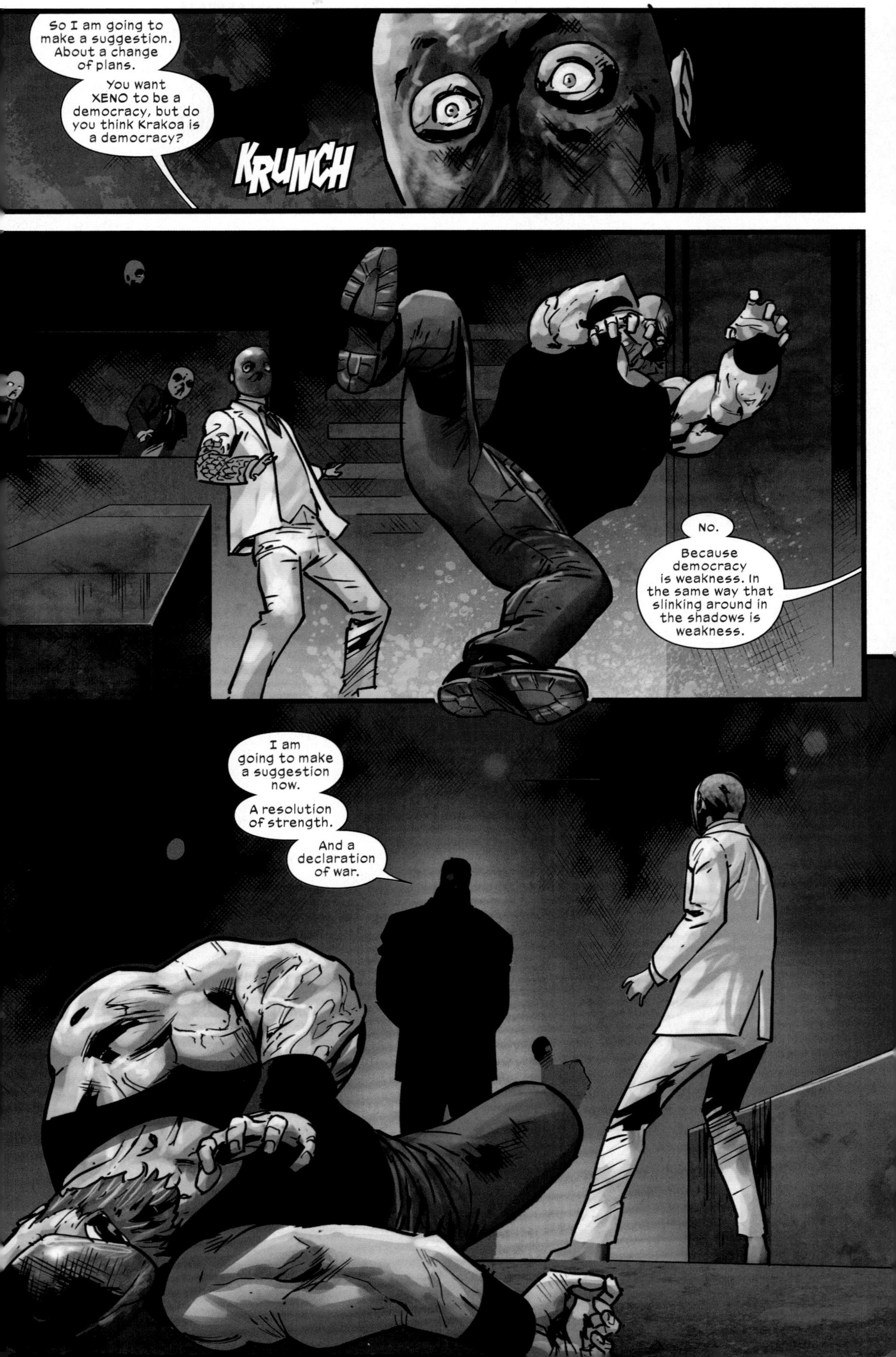
So I am going to make a suggestion. About a change of plans.
You want XENO to be a democracy, but do you think Krakoa is a democracy?
KRUNCH
No.
Because democracy is weakness. In the same way that slinking around in the shadows is weakness.
I am going to make a suggestion now.
A resolution of strength.
And a declaration of war.

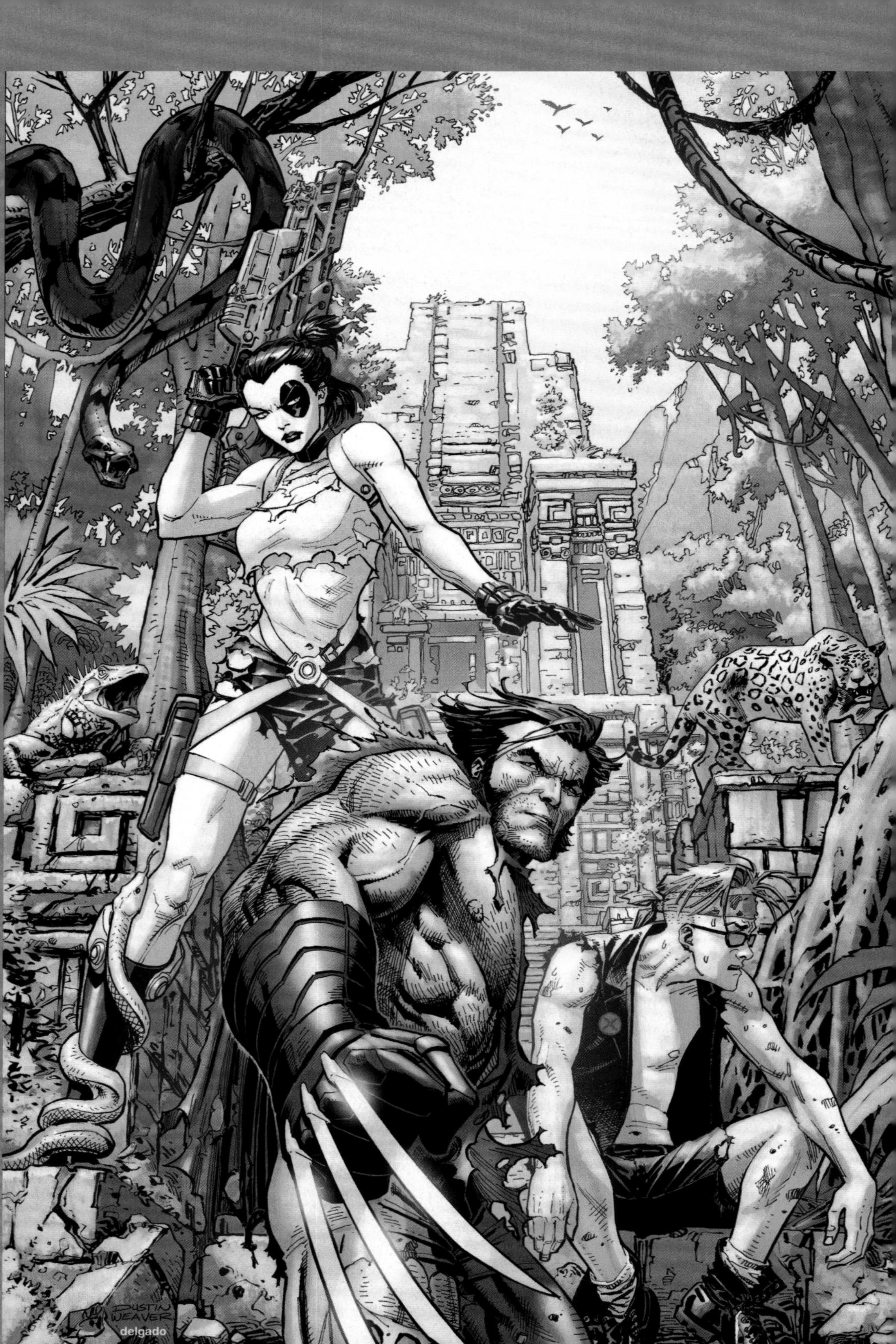
DUSTIN WEAVER
delgado

The Moral Jungle

[dawn_of_x]

[kra_]
[koa_]

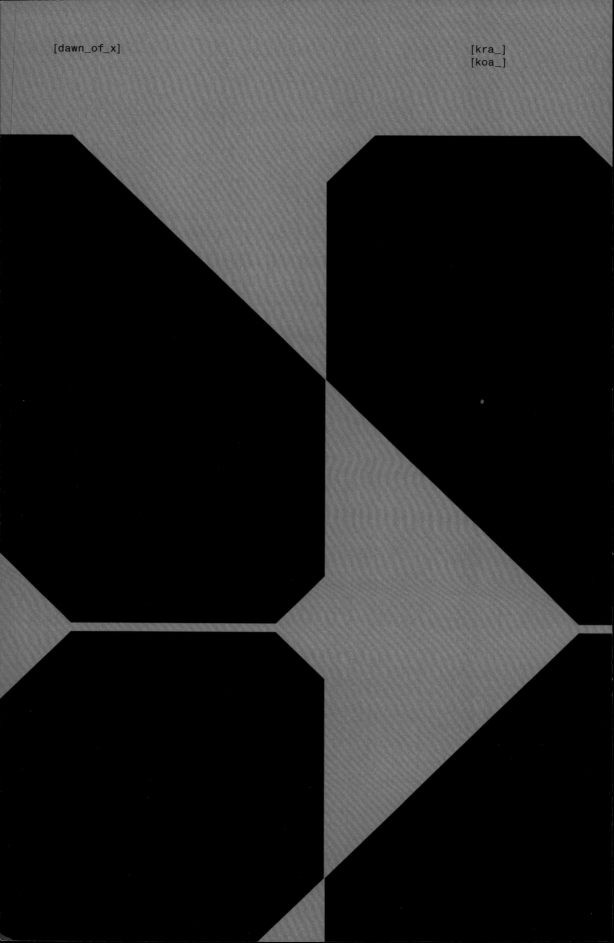

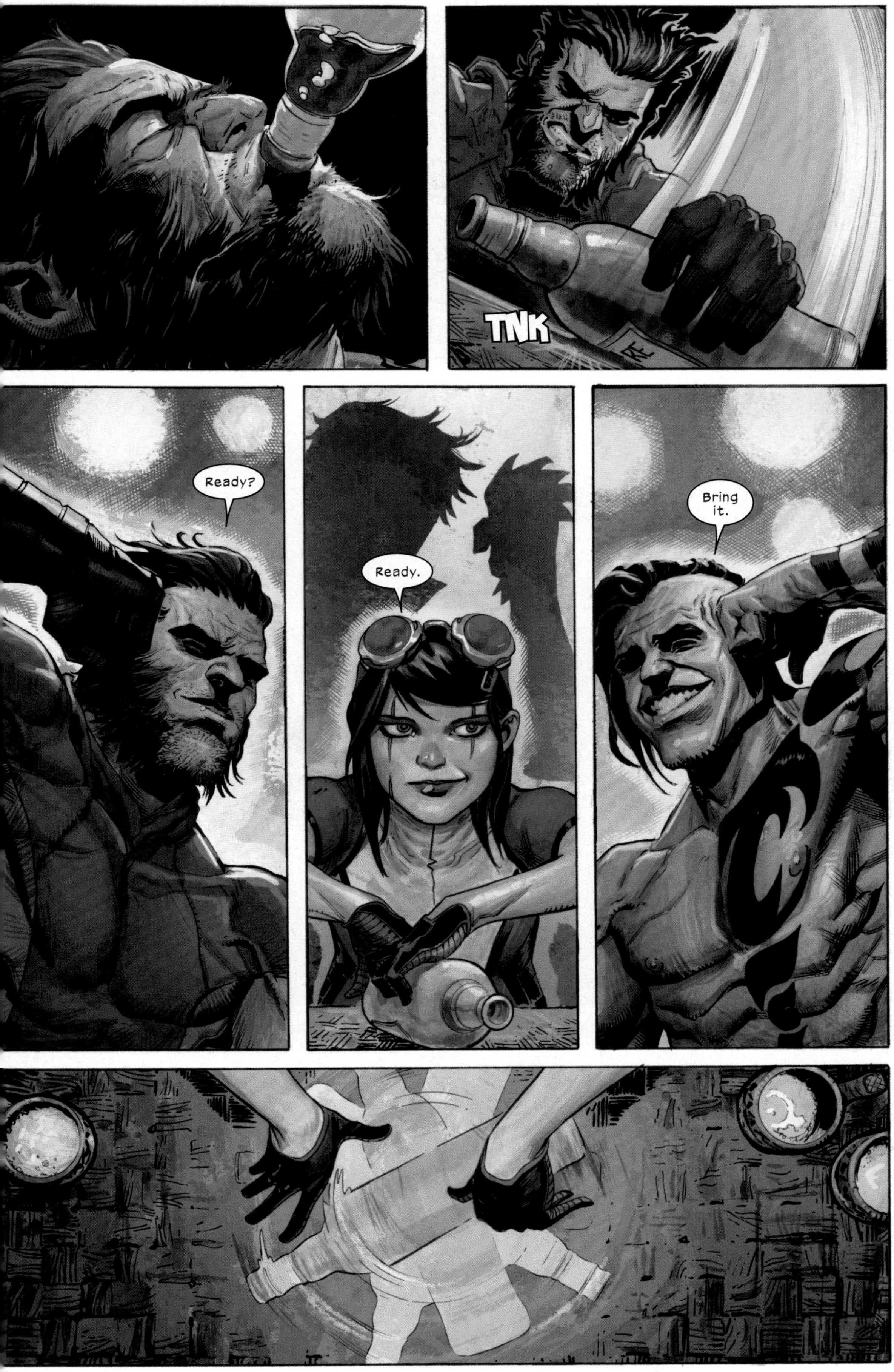
TNK
Ready?
Ready.
Bring it.

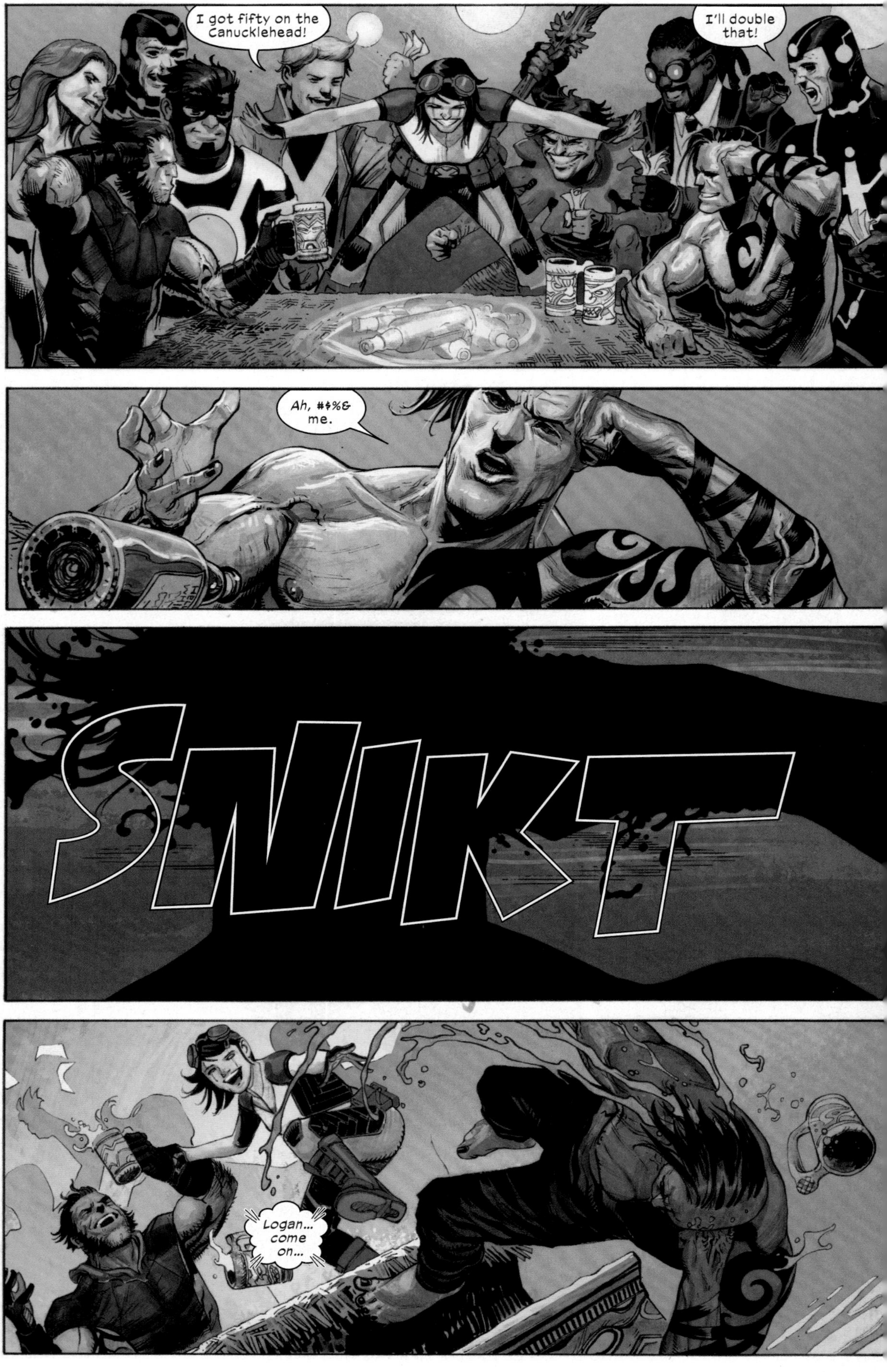
I got fifty on the Canucklehead!
I'll double that!
Ah, #$%& me.
SNIKT
Logan... come on...

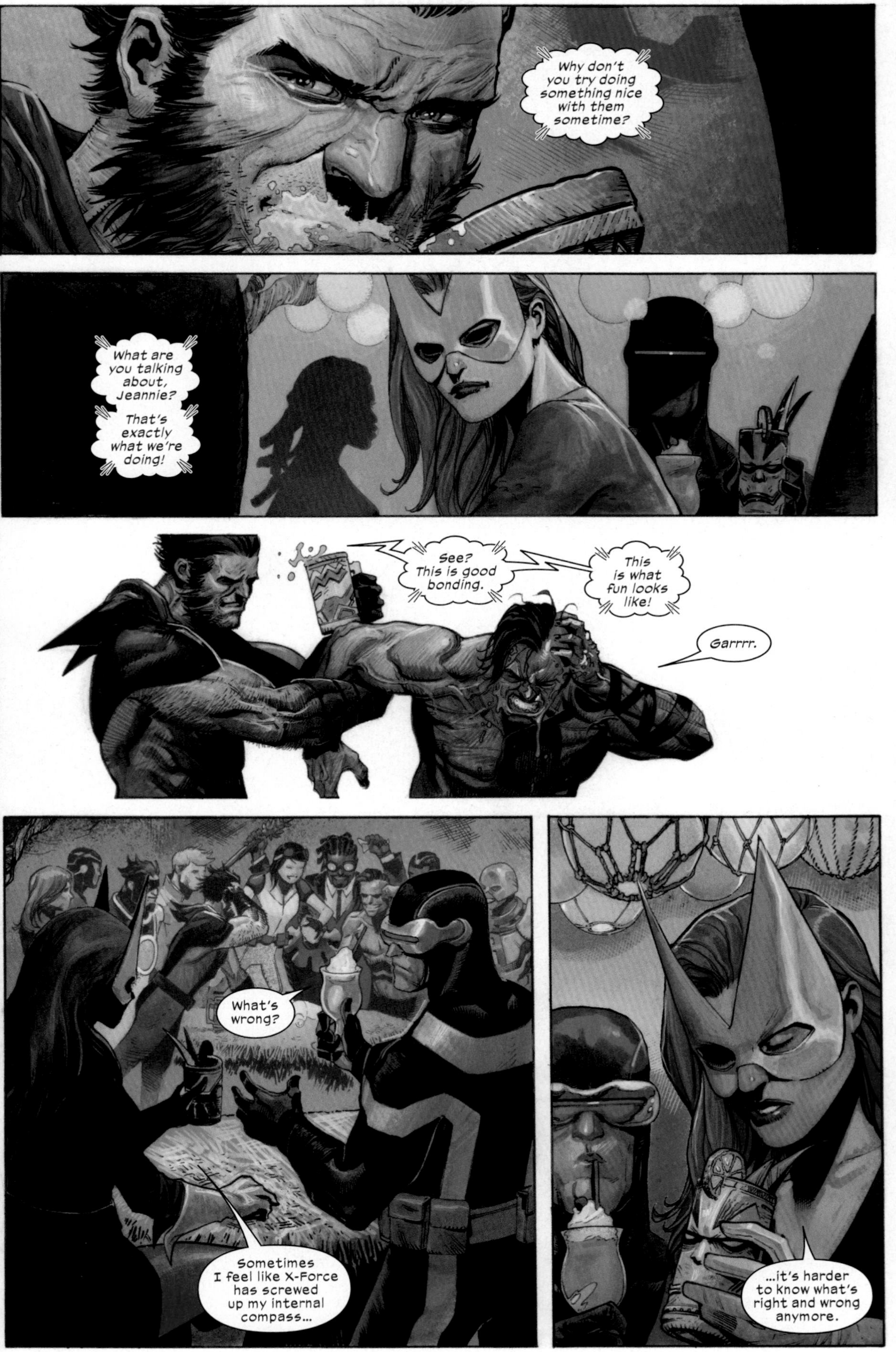
Why don't you try doing something nice with them sometime?
What are you talking about, Jeannie?
That's exactly what we're doing!
See? This is good bonding.
This is what fun looks like!
Garrrr.
What's wrong?
Sometimes I feel like X-Force has screwed up my internal compass...
...it's harder to know what's right and wrong anymore.

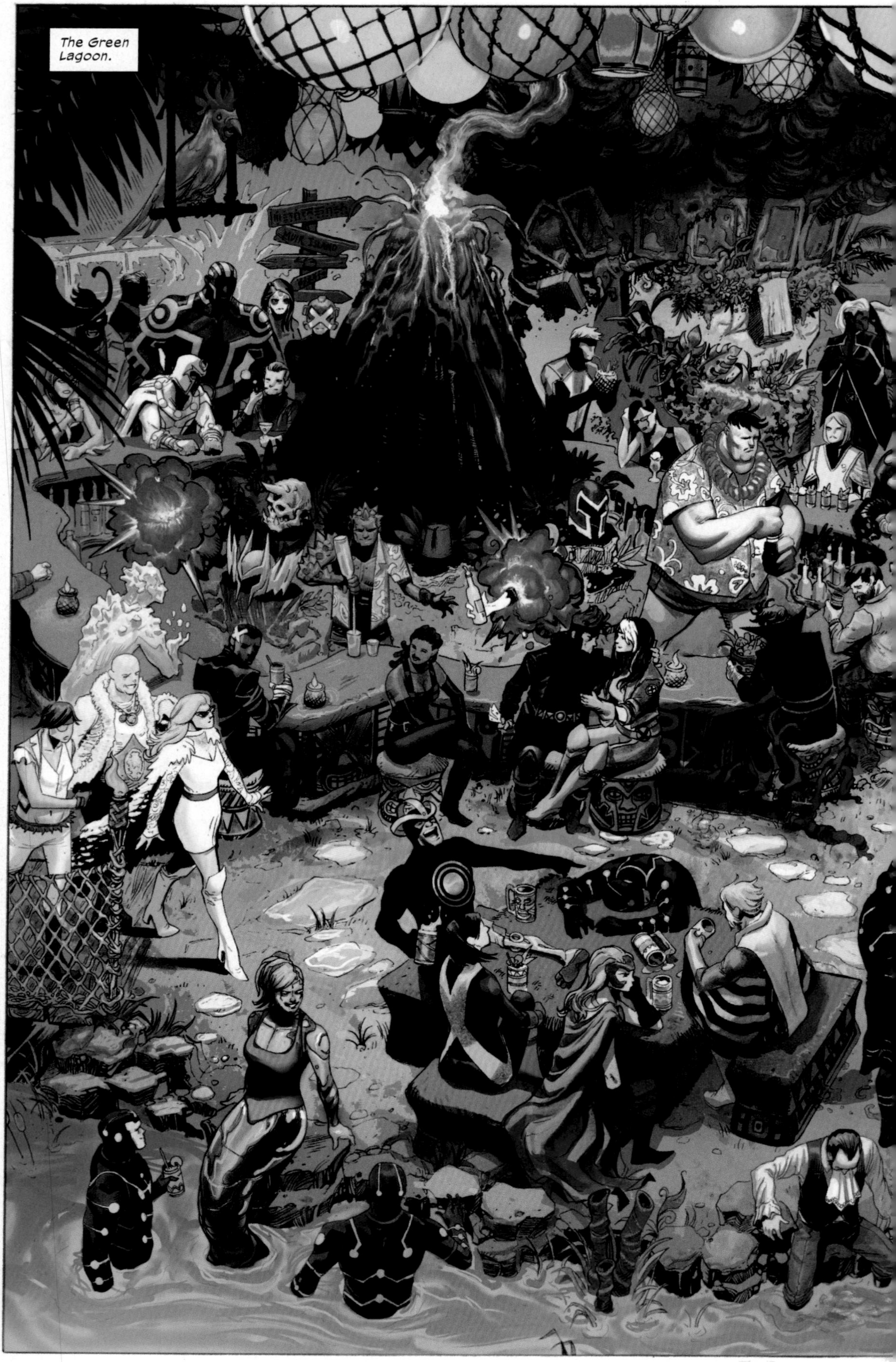
The Green Lagoon.

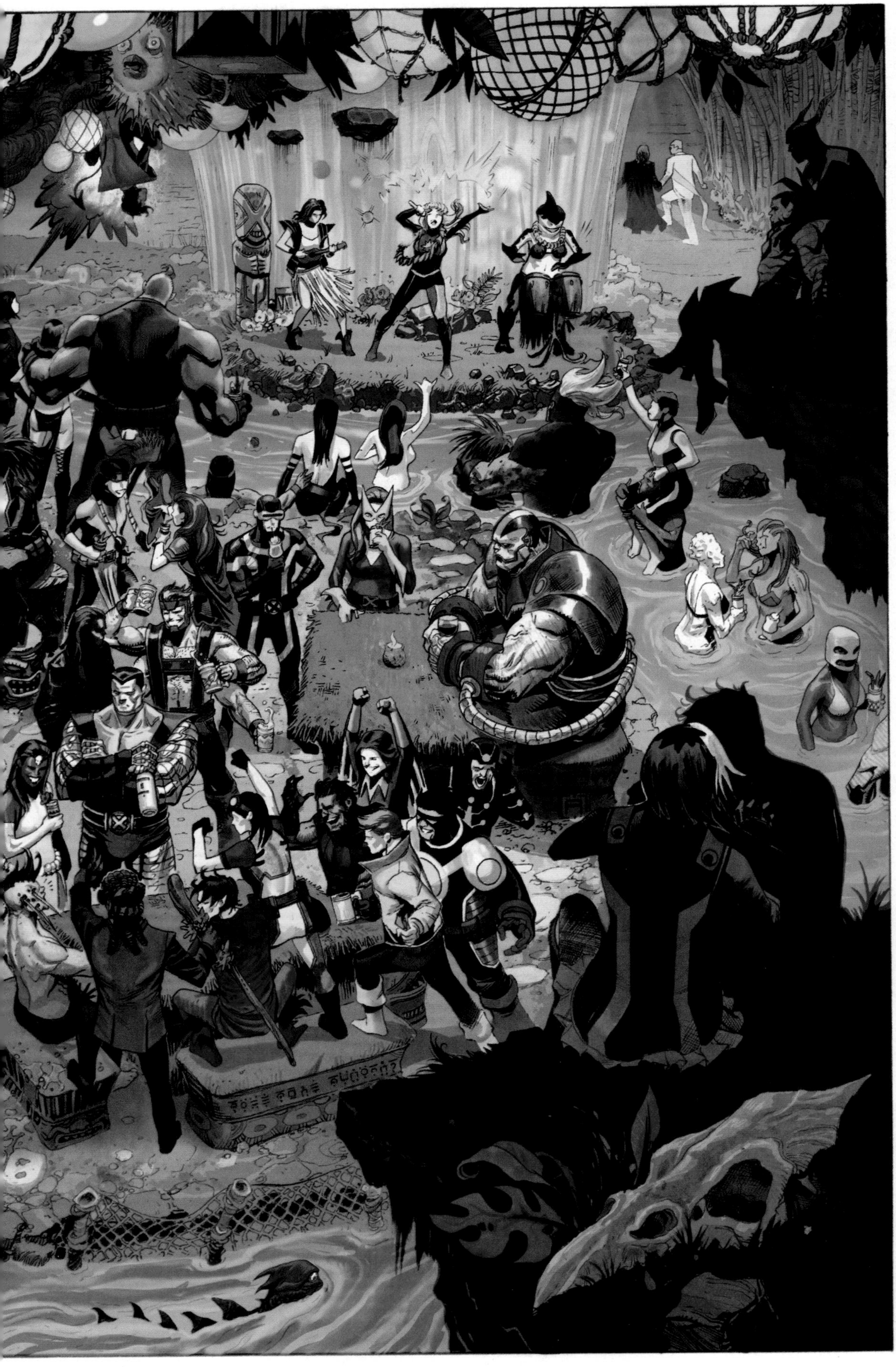

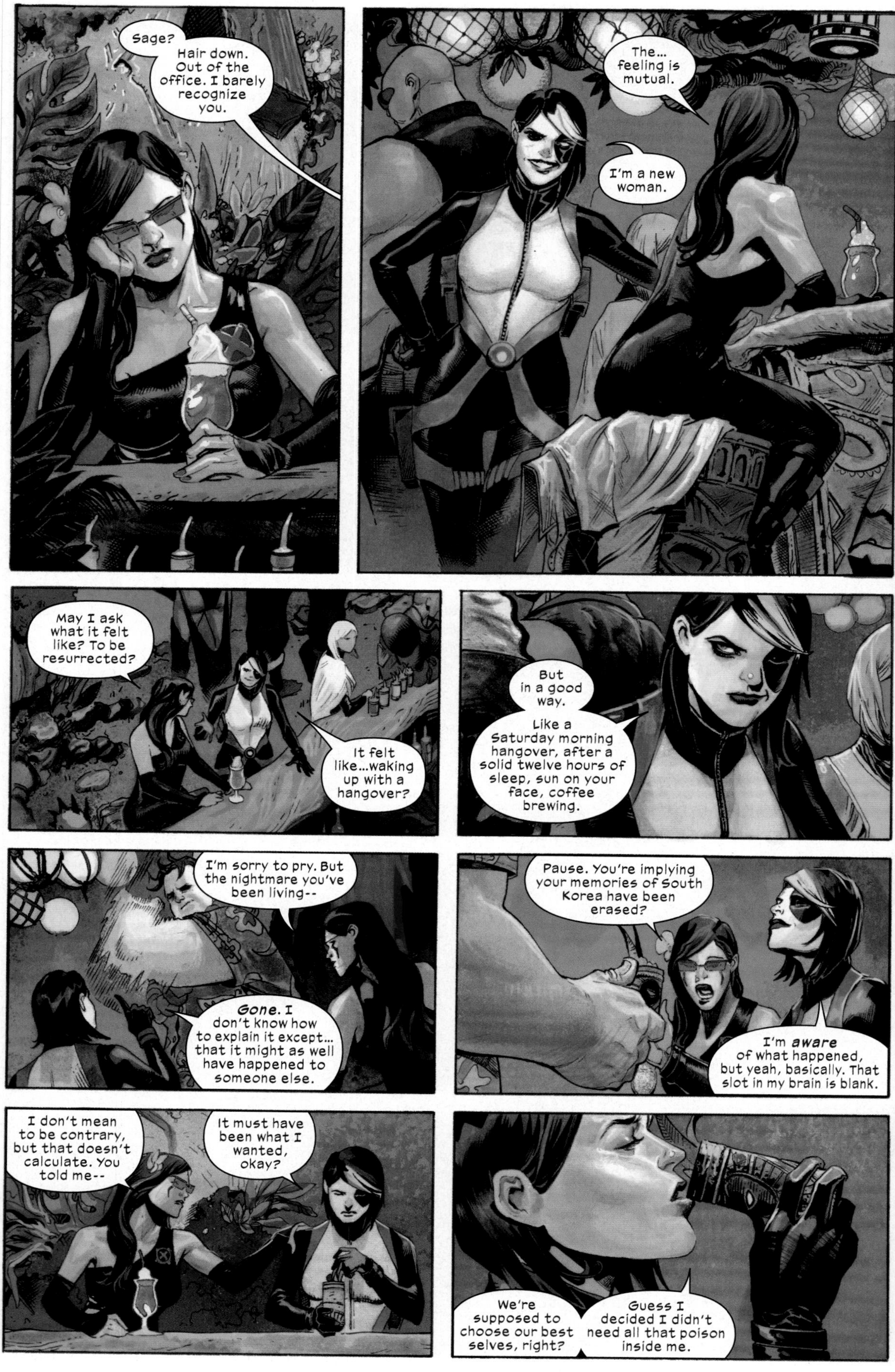

Sage?
Hair down. Out of the office. I barely recognize you.
The... feeling is mutual.
I'm a new woman.
May I ask what it felt like? To be resurrected?
It felt like...waking up with a hangover?
But in a good way.
Like a Saturday morning hangover, after a solid twelve hours of sleep, sun on your face, coffee brewing.
I'm sorry to pry. But the nightmare you've been living--
Gone. I don't know how to explain it except... that it might as well have happened to someone else.
Pause. You're implying your memories of South Korea have been erased?
I'm *aware* of what happened, but yeah, basically. That slot in my brain is blank.
I don't mean to be contrary, but that doesn't calculate. You told me--
It must have been what I wanted, okay?
We're supposed to choose our best selves, right?
Guess I decided I didn't need all that poison inside me.

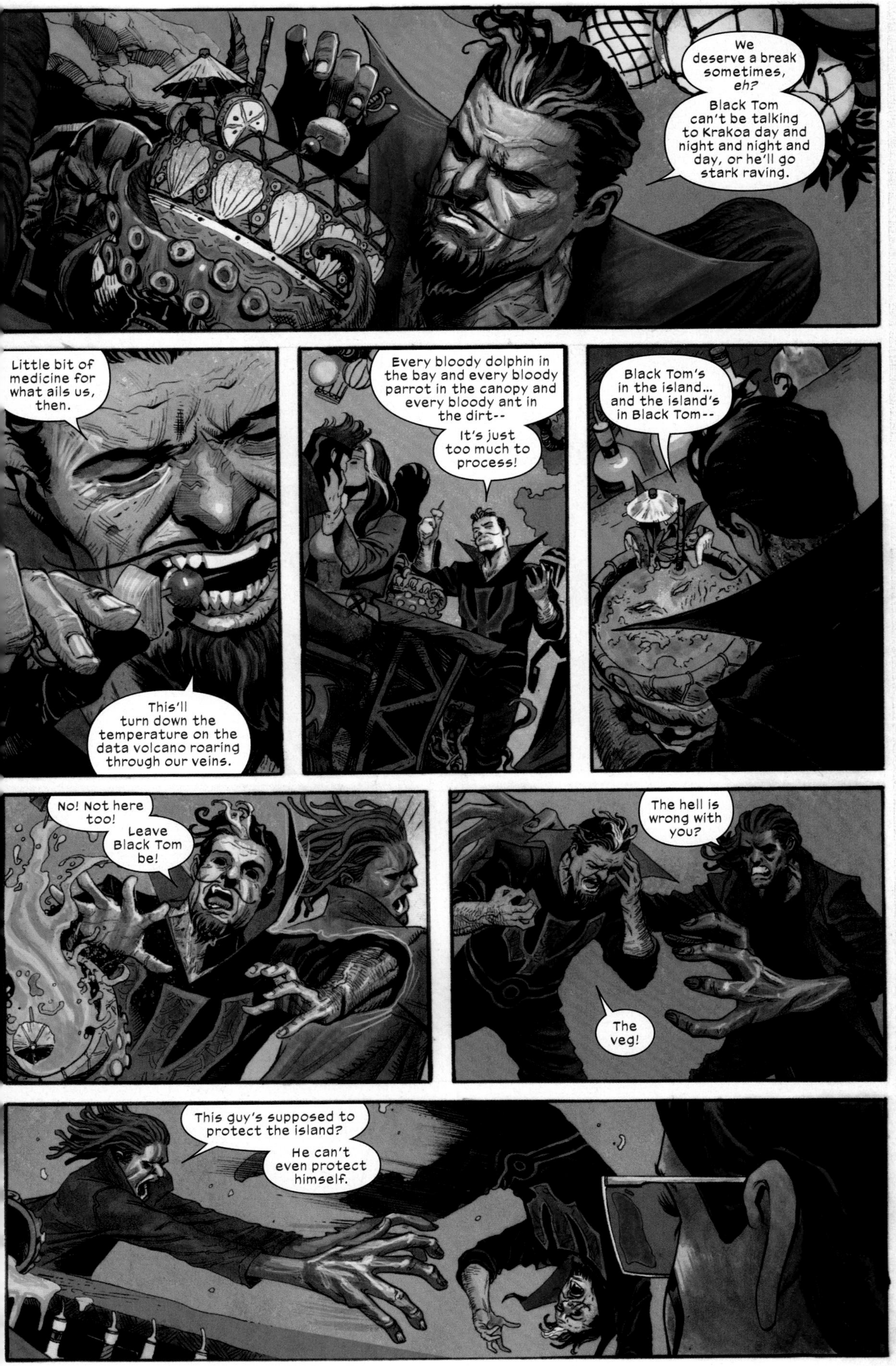
We deserve a break sometimes, *eh?*
Black Tom can't be talking to Krakoa day and night and night and day, or he'll go stark raving.
Little bit of medicine for what ails us, then.
This'll turn down the temperature on the data volcano roaring through our veins.
Every bloody dolphin in the bay and every bloody parrot in the canopy and every bloody ant in the dirt--
It's just too much to process!
Black Tom's in the island... and the island's in Black Tom--
No! Not here too!
Leave Black Tom be!
The hell is wrong with you?
The veg!
This guy's supposed to protect the island?
He can't even protect himself.

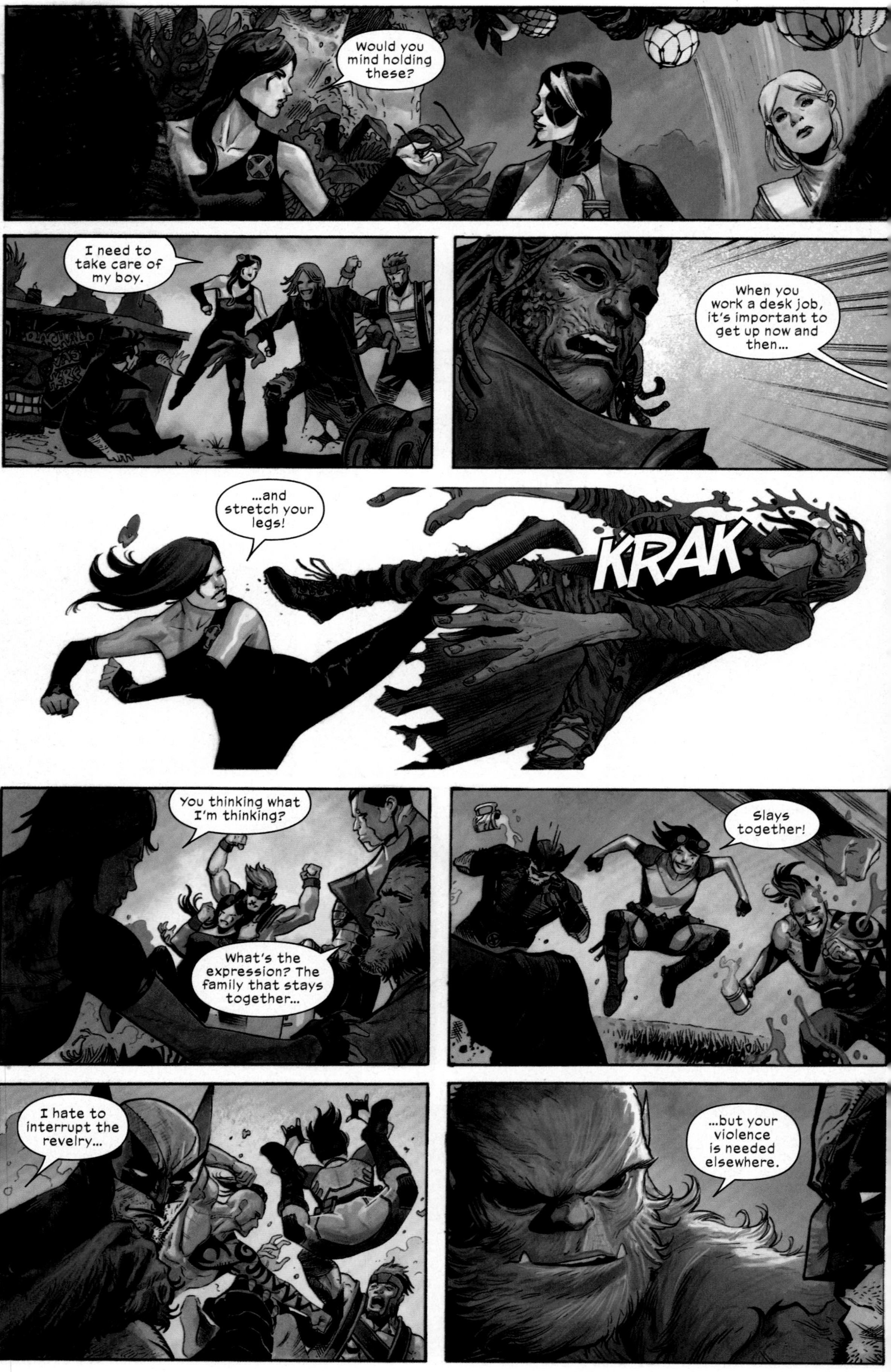

Would you mind holding these?
I need to take care of my boy.
When you work a desk job, it's important to get up now and then...
...and stretch your legs!
KRAK
You thinking what I'm thinking?
What's the expression? The family that stays together...
Slays together!
I hate to interrupt the revelry...
...but your violence is needed elsewhere.

BEAST'S LOGBOOK:
THE TROUBLE WITH TERRA VERDE

THEN:

The South American country initially held off on signing the treaty because of the time and finances so far invested in telefloronics, a neuro-responsive green tech they hoped would boom their impoverished economy and make them into a global player. The president more than once cited the nation of Wakanda as an aspirational model.

The declaration of mutant sovereignty -- and the introduction of Krakoan tech to the marketplace -- nullified all their efforts and investments.

With his country in crippling debt, the president had no choice but to sign with the mutants. But an insurgency rose up against him. The group of militants -- consisting of the scientists who had given their lives to the study and development of telefloronics -- call themselves MUERTE VERDE, the Green Death. They activated their telefloronic prototypes and made themselves into symbiotes -- both flesh and botanical -- living weapons.

The president's son was among them.

NOW:

Several months ago, X-Force staged a stealth assault on Terra Verde. The telefloronic threat was believed to be overcome.

But now the country has gone dark. All communication with the government and military has abruptly cut off.

And not just that, but the news stations and periodicals are no longer broadcasting or publishing. Phones and emails go unanswered. No radio or digital signals have been detected.

Last week, a satellite view of the country at night displayed galaxies of light clustered around towns and cities.

But as of this evening, the view is completely black.

I couldn't possibly have had anything to do with this, but a part of me is anxious as to what the team might discover.

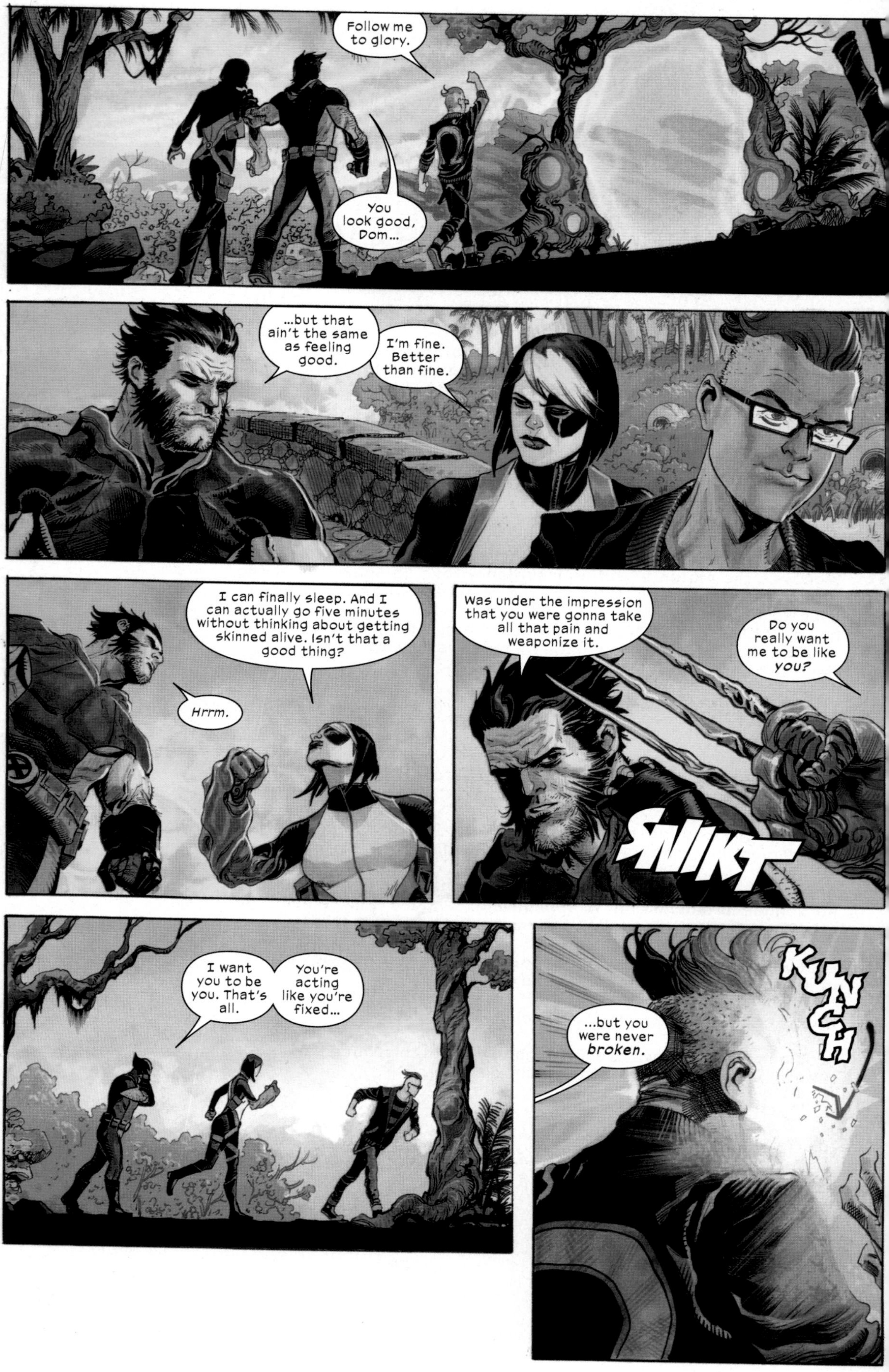
Follow me to glory.
You look good, Dom...
...but that ain't the same as feeling good.
I'm fine. Better than fine.
I can finally sleep. And I can actually go five minutes without thinking about getting skinned alive. Isn't that a good thing?
Hrrm.
Was under the impression that you were gonna take all that pain and weaponize it.
Do you really want me to be like *you?*
SNIKT
I want you to be you. That's all.
You're acting like you're fixed...
...but you were never *broken*.
KUNCH

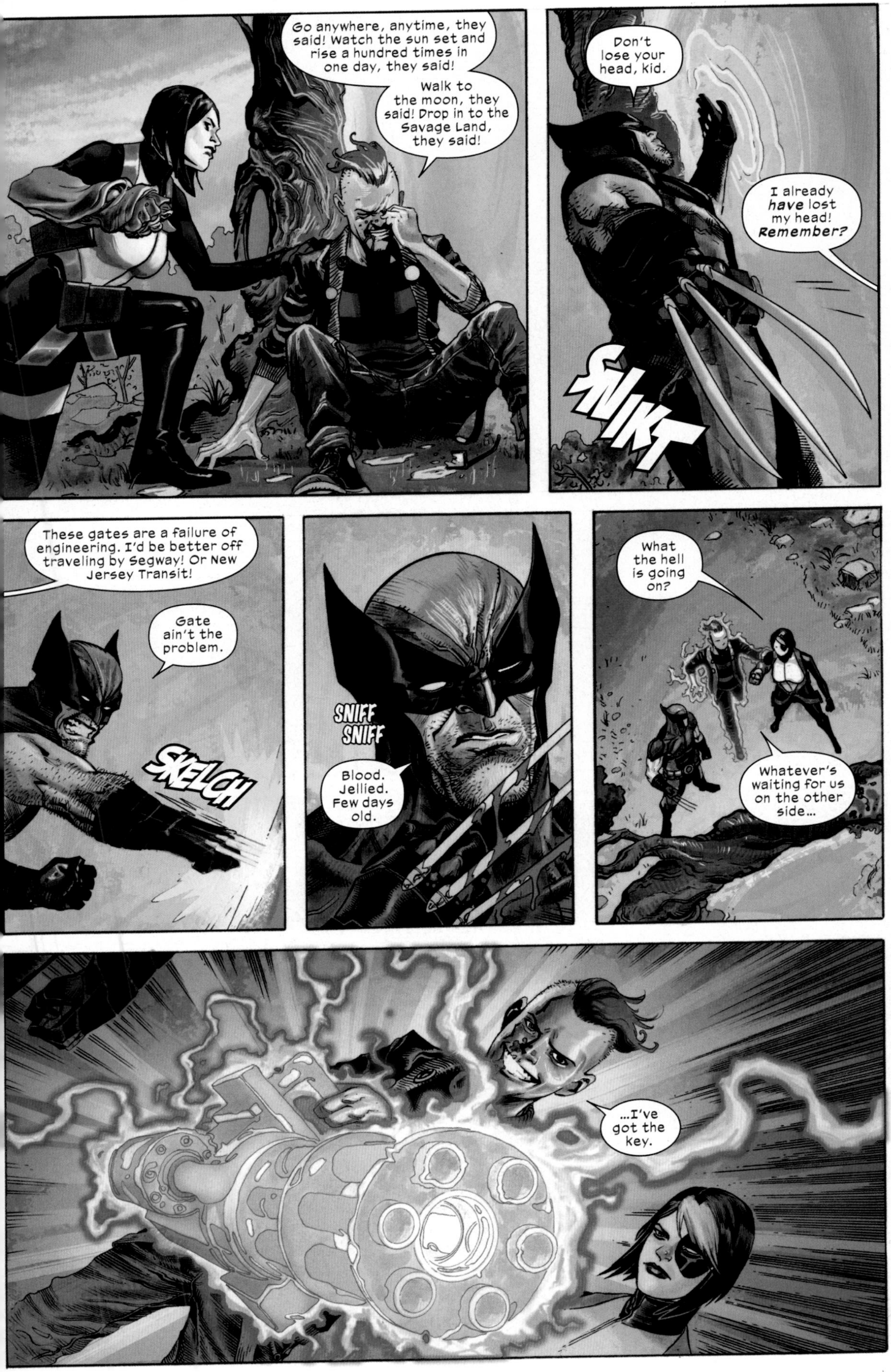
Go anywhere, anytime, they said! Watch the sun set and rise a hundred times in one day, they said!
Walk to the moon, they said! Drop in to the Savage Land, they said!
Don't lose your head, kid.
I already have lost my head! Remember?
SNIKT
These gates are a failure of engineering. I'd be better off traveling by Segway! Or New Jersey Transit!
Gate ain't the problem.
SKELCH
SNIFF SNIFF
Blood. Jellied. Few days old.
What the hell is going on?
Whatever's waiting for us on the other side...
...I've got the key.

Presidential Manor.
Terra Verde.

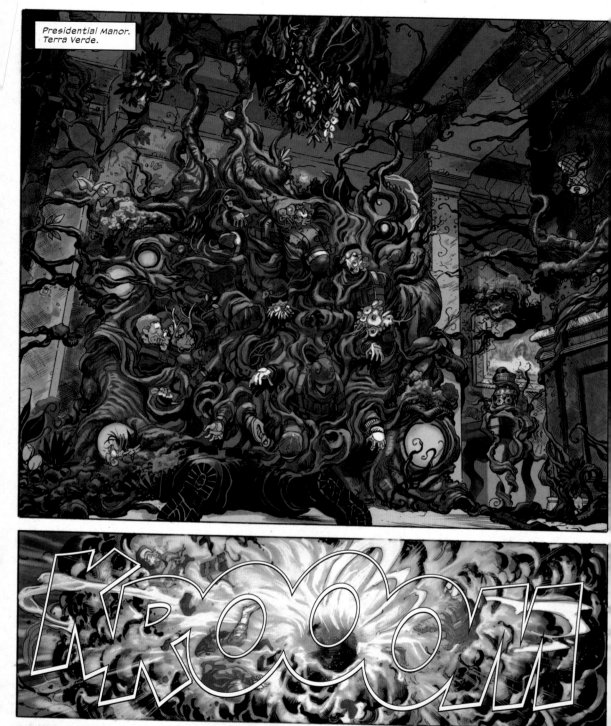

How do you say, "This place looks like a greenhouse puked all over it," in Spanish?

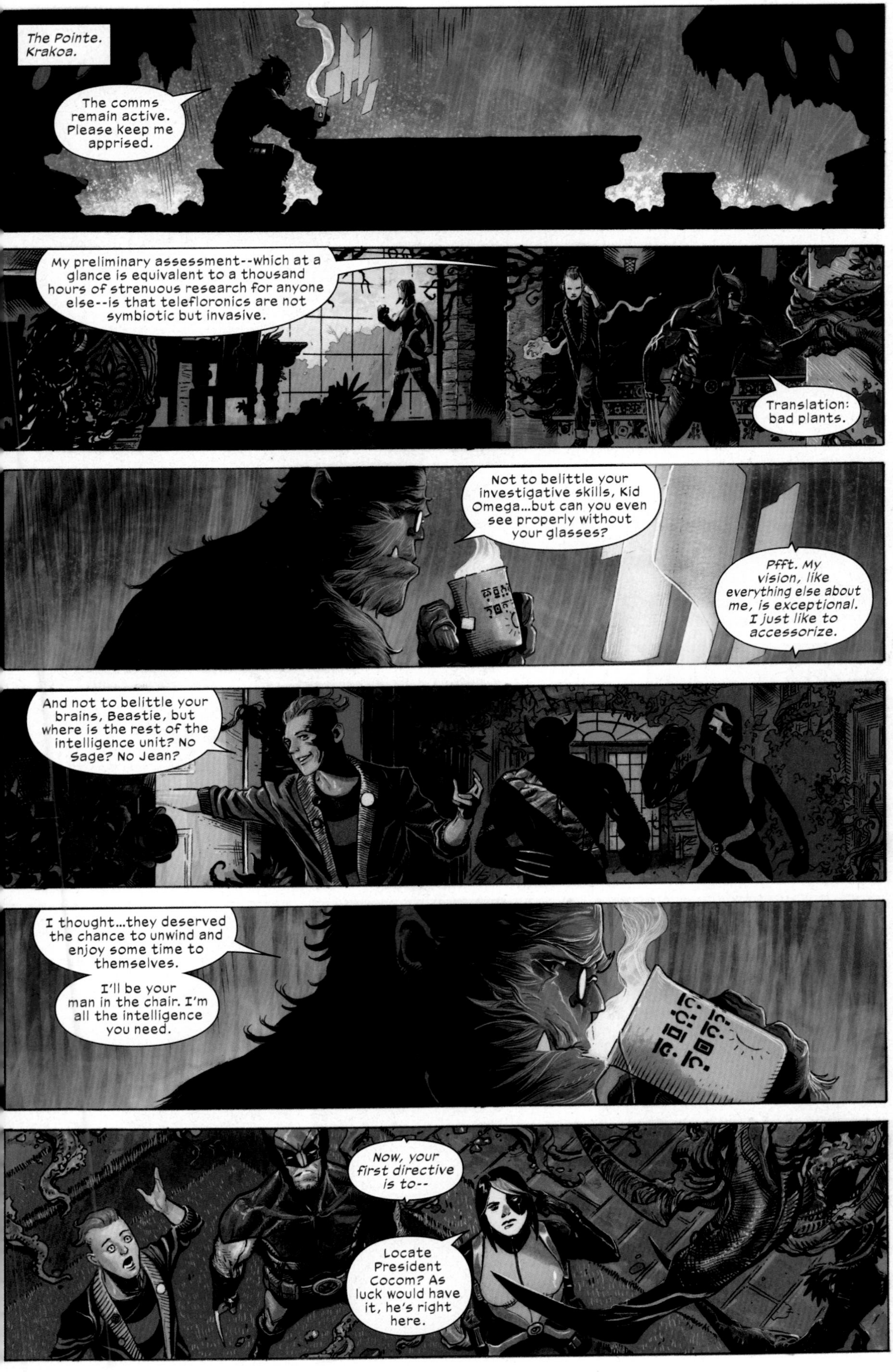
The Pointe. Krakoa.
The comms remain active. Please keep me apprised.
My preliminary assessment--which at a glance is equivalent to a thousand hours of strenuous research for anyone else--is that telefloronics are not symbiotic but invasive.
Translation: bad plants.
Not to belittle your investigative skills, Kid Omega...but can you even see properly without your glasses?
Pfft. My vision, like everything else about me, is exceptional. I just like to accessorize.
And not to belittle your brains, Beastie, but where is the rest of the intelligence unit? No Sage? No Jean?
I thought...they deserved the chance to unwind and enjoy some time to themselves.
I'll be your man in the chair. I'm all the intelligence you need.
Now, your first directive is to--
Locate President Cocom? As luck would have it, he's right here.

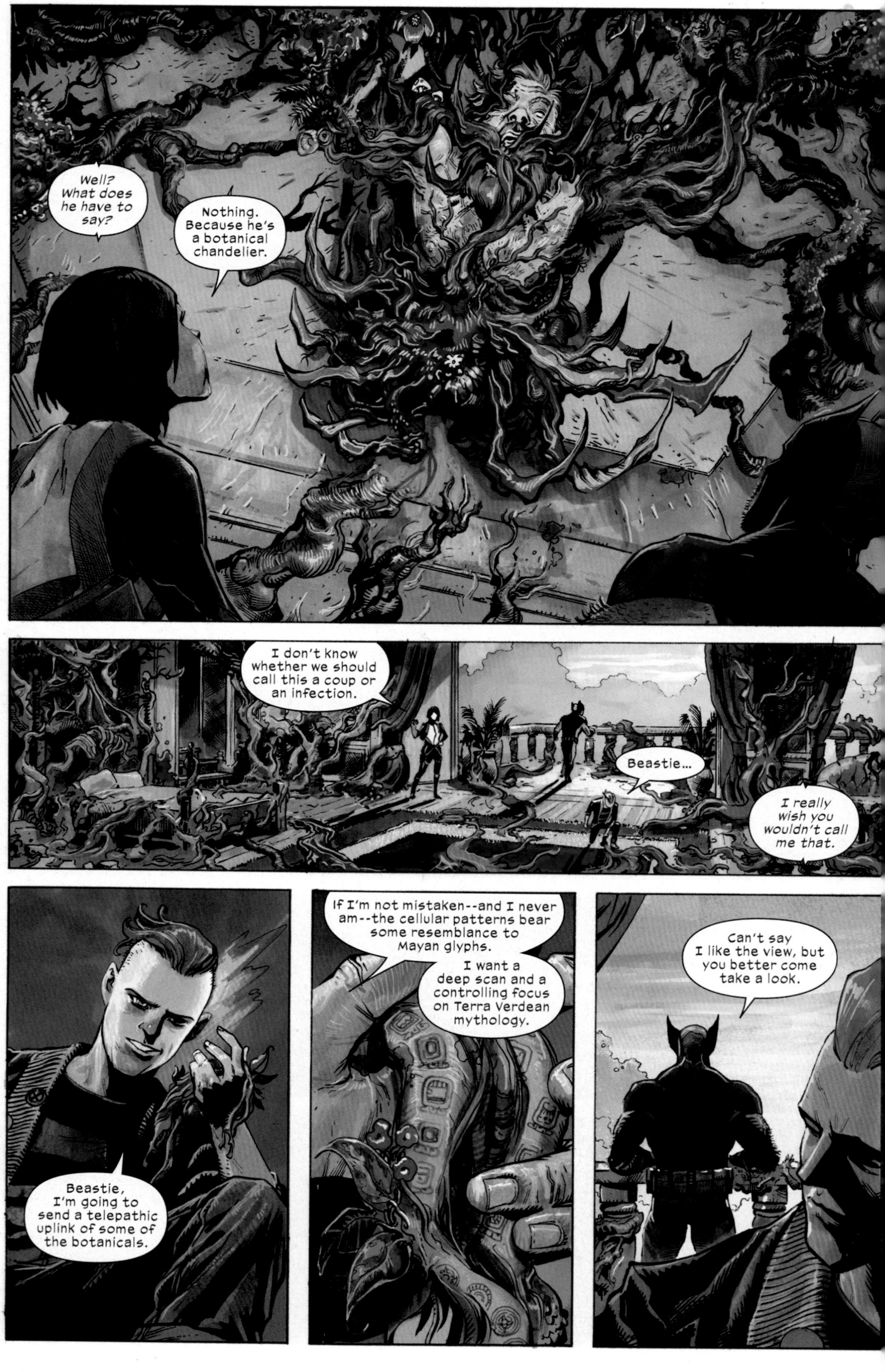
Well? What does he have to say?
Nothing. Because he's a botanical chandelier.
I don't know whether we should call this a coup or an infection.
Beastie...
I really wish you wouldn't call me that.
Beastie, I'm going to send a telepathic uplink of some of the botanicals.
If I'm not mistaken--and I never am--the cellular patterns bear some resemblance to Mayan glyphs.
I want a deep scan and a controlling focus on Terra Verdean mythology.
Can't say I like the view, but you better come take a look.

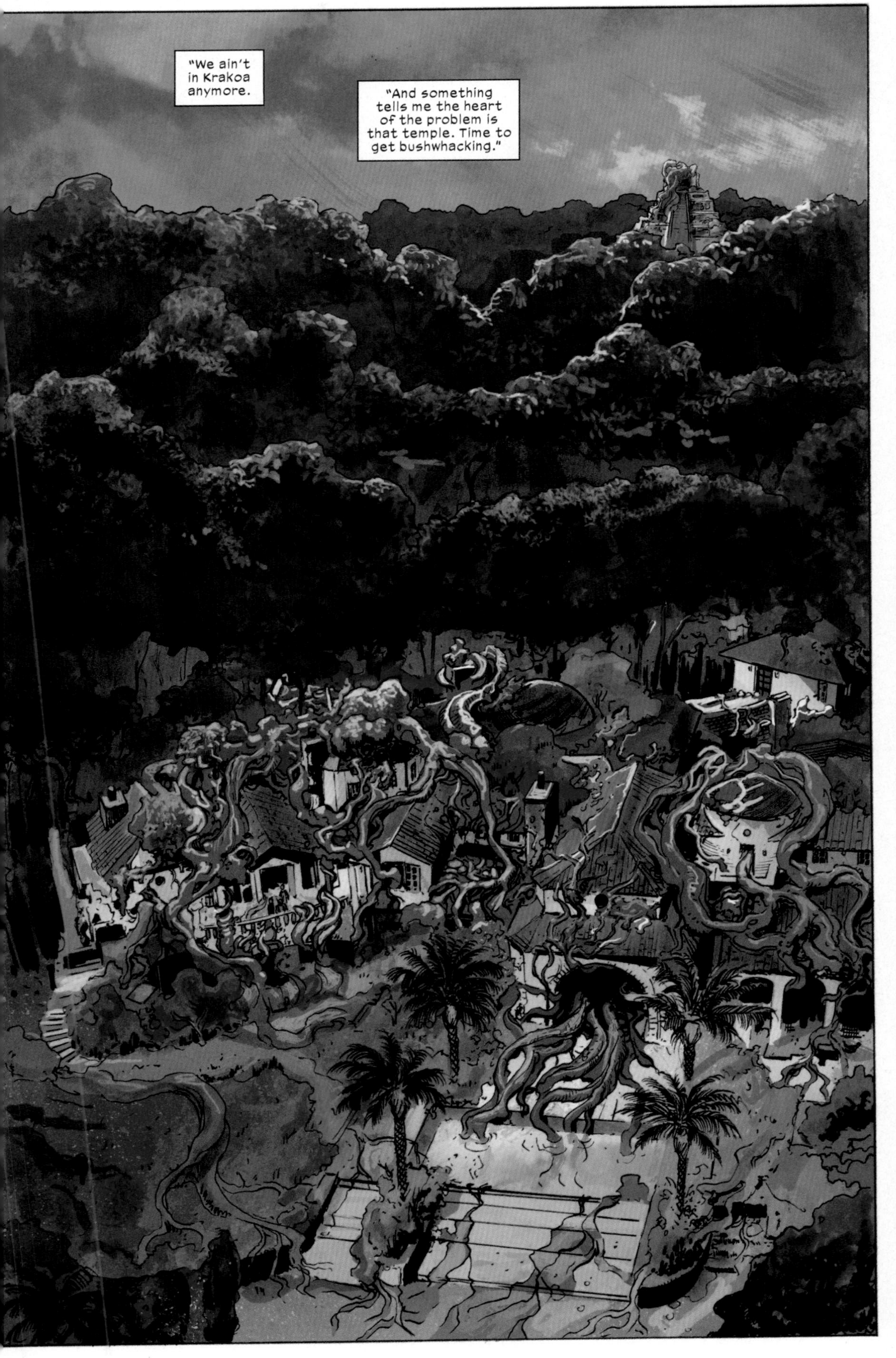
"We ain't in Krakoa anymore.
"And something tells me the heart of the problem is that temple. Time to get bushwhacking."

BEAST'S LOGBOOK: TELFLORONICS AND THE MYTHOLOGY OF TERRA VERDE

The ancient stories of Terra Verde -- interpreted from oral story-tellers and reconstructed from iconography dating back before the 16th century, beyond the Mayans to the time of Olmec -- indicate a departure from the standard myths in one important way.

There is a focus on the personified force of nature. Botanicals are a key element of worship.

Rituals celebrate the connection between humankind and the environment. The standard tropes exist -- such as fertility and erotic strength of flowers, disease and the curative power of herbs -- but Terra Verdeans had their own unique and dark marriage to the Earth.

Sacrifice was a standard instrument of agriculture. The plentitude and even the taste and color of fruit and maize and other crops were determined by death. Flesh and blood were considered essential fertilizers. Heads were hung from sapodilla and passion fruit trees. Fingers were planted in the fields. The slaying and burning of jaguars appeased droughts and blights.

The plants must be sated if they are to be obedient. In this way, Terra Verde bears some resemblance to Krakoa (which requires the consumption of two mutants each year if it is to thrive).

Hieroglyphic stories, some codexes and a skull sculpted with glyphs tell the story of a "maize god" whose caress could make kernels plump and wither depending on his mood.

And then there was the punishing deity known as *ak'* (translation: vine). He is sometimes represented with a tangled ball of vines for a head and sometimes with branches growing out of his back like antlered wings and sometimes both.

A combination of Spanish occupation, Roman Catholic indoctrination, and modernization all but erased these stories and traditions -- but the idea behind telefloronics is deeply ingrained in Terra Verdean culture and history.

In the 16th, 17th, and 18th centuries, the holiest and most respected men and women were those who -- roughly translated -- "spoke to the plants."

And the temple -- known as *Ya'ax* (or The Green) -- was their church and the seat of their power.

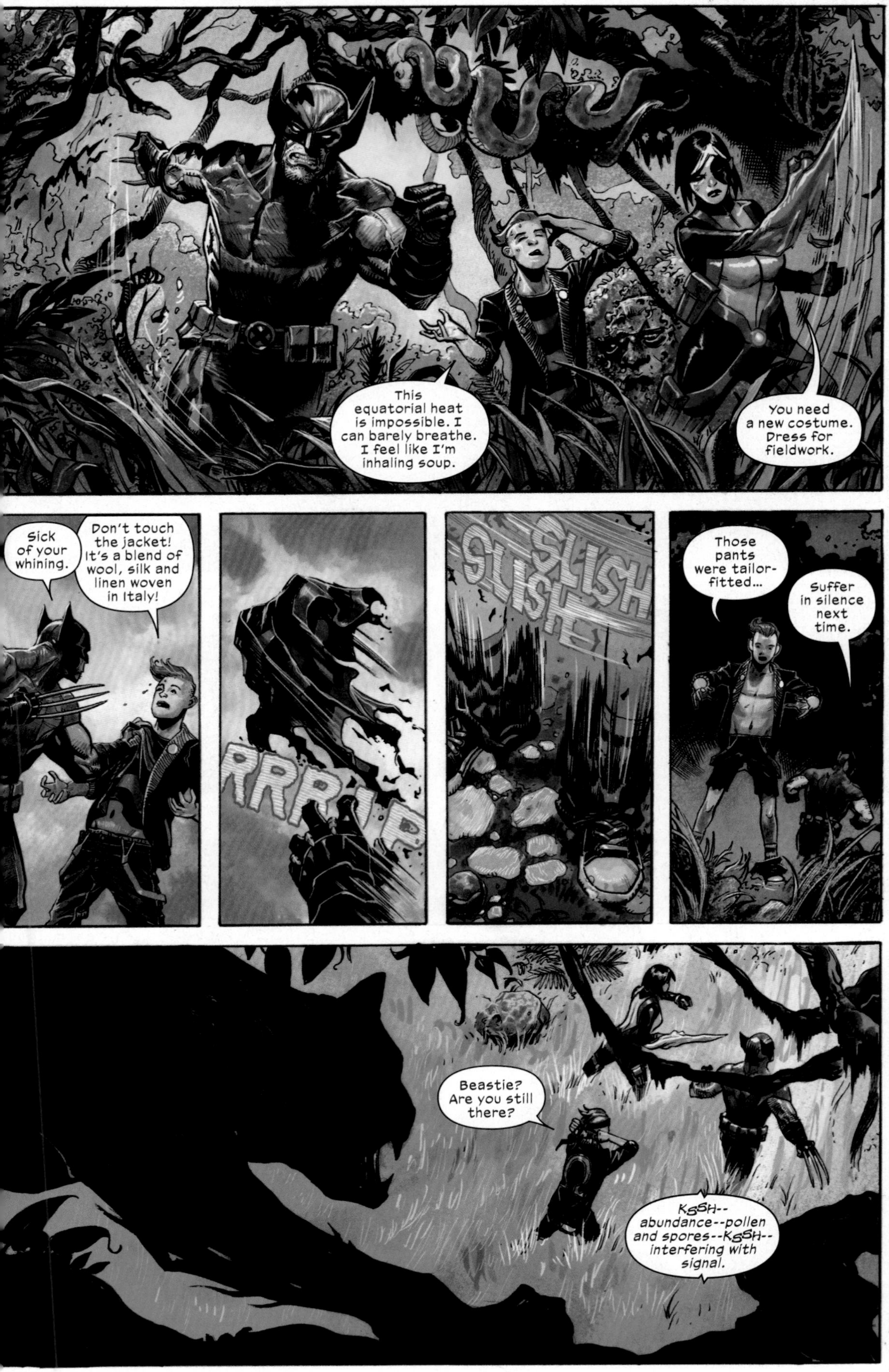
This equatorial heat is impossible. I can barely breathe. I feel like I'm inhaling soup.
You need a new costume. Dress for fieldwork.
Sick of your whining.
Don't touch the jacket! It's a blend of wool, silk and linen woven in Italy!
RRRIP
SLISH
SLISH
Those pants were tailor-fitted...
Suffer in silence next time.
Beastie? Are you still there?
KSSH-- abundance--pollen and spores--KSSH-- interfering with signal.

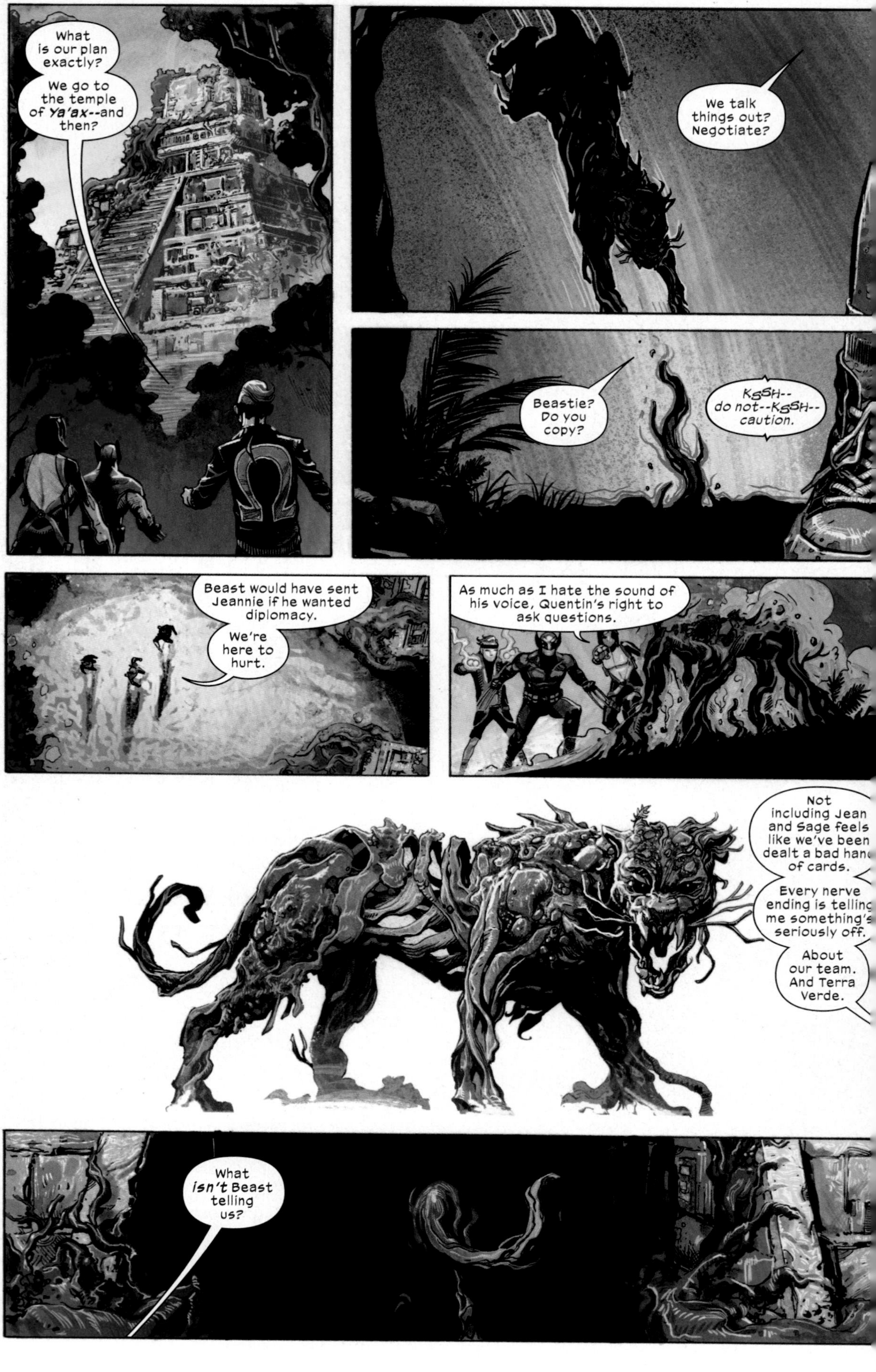
What is our plan exactly?
We go to the temple of *Ya'ax*--and then?
We talk things out? Negotiate?
Beastie? Do you copy?
KSSH-- do not--KSSH-- caution.
Beast would have sent Jeannie if he wanted diplomacy.
We're here to hurt.
As much as I hate the sound of his voice, Quentin's right to ask questions.
Not including Jean and Sage feels like we've been dealt a bad han of cards.
Every nerve ending is tellin me something' seriously off.
About our team. And Terra Verde.
What *isn't* Beast telling us?

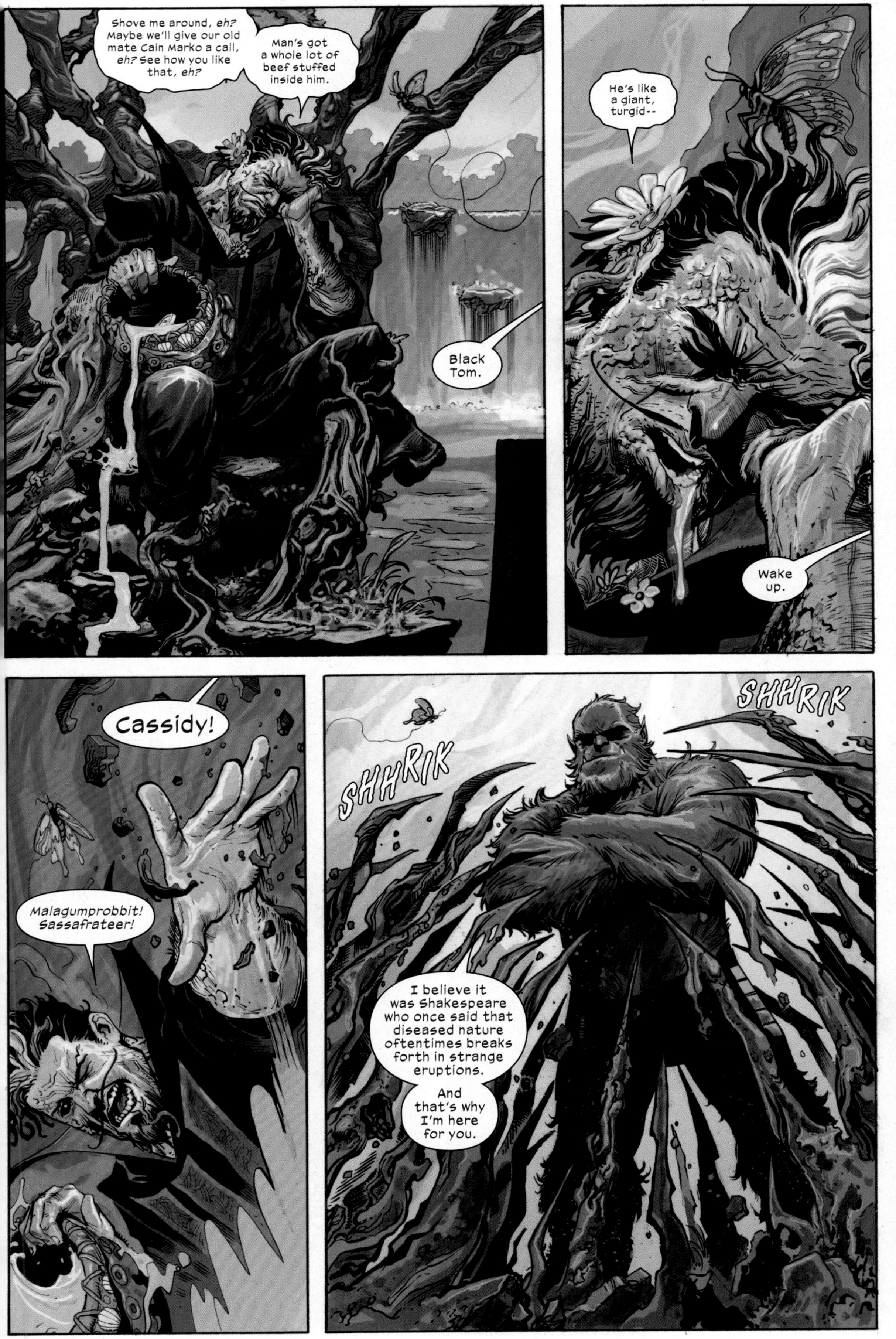

Shove me around, *eh?* Maybe we'll give our old mate Cain Marko a call, *eh?* See how you like that, *eh?*
Man's got a whole lot of beef stuffed inside him.
Black Tom.
He's like a giant, turgid--
Wake up.
Cassidy!
Malagumprobbit! Sassafrateer!
SHHRIK
SHHRIK
I believe it was Shakespeare who once said that diseased nature oftentimes breaks forth in strange eruptions.
And that's why I'm here for you.

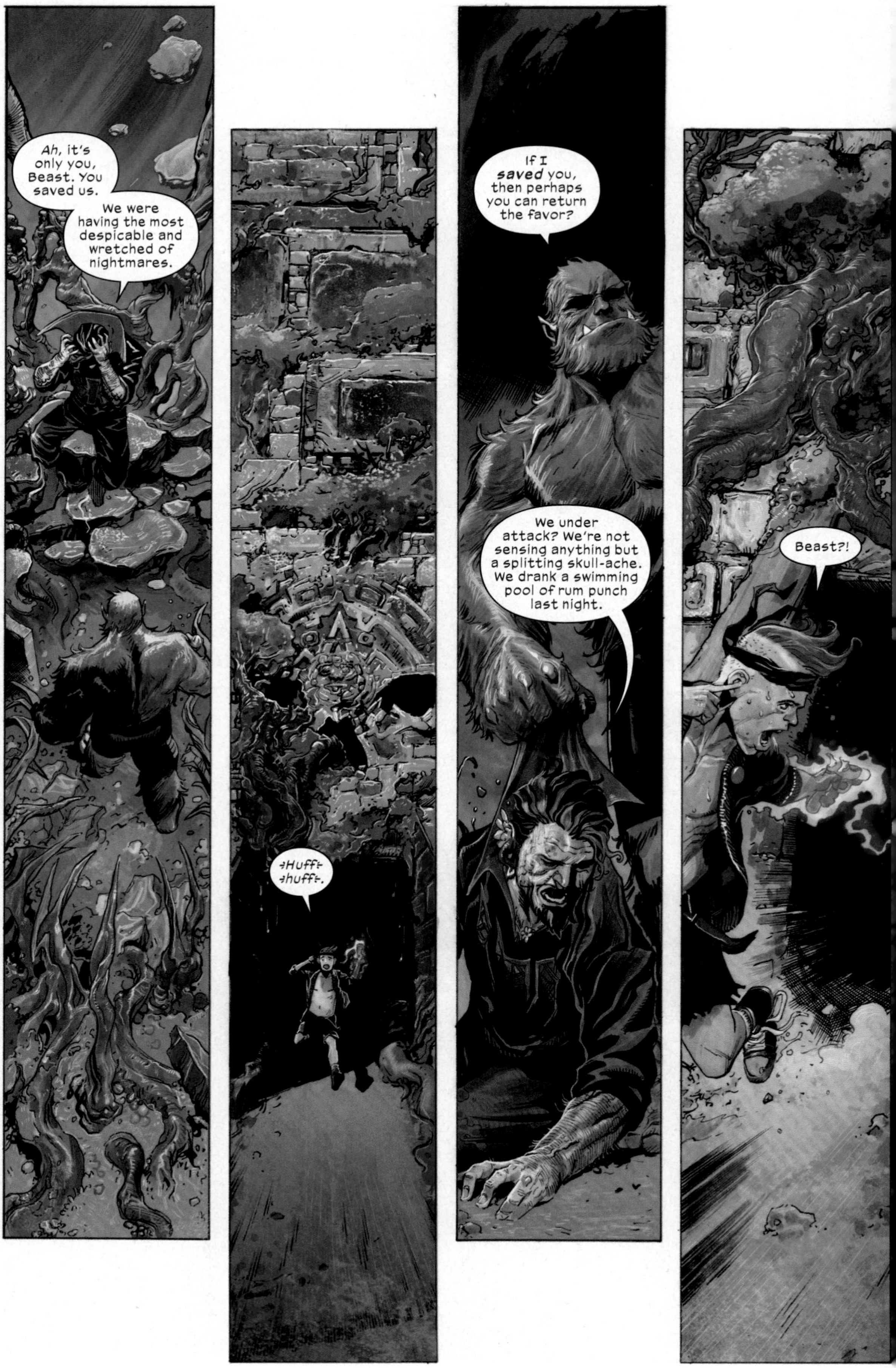
Ah, it's only you, Beast. You saved us.
We were having the most despicable and wretched of nightmares.
=Huff= =huff=.
If I saved you, then perhaps you can return the favor?
We under attack? We're not sensing anything but a splitting skull-ache. We drank a swimming pool of rum punch last night.
Beast?!

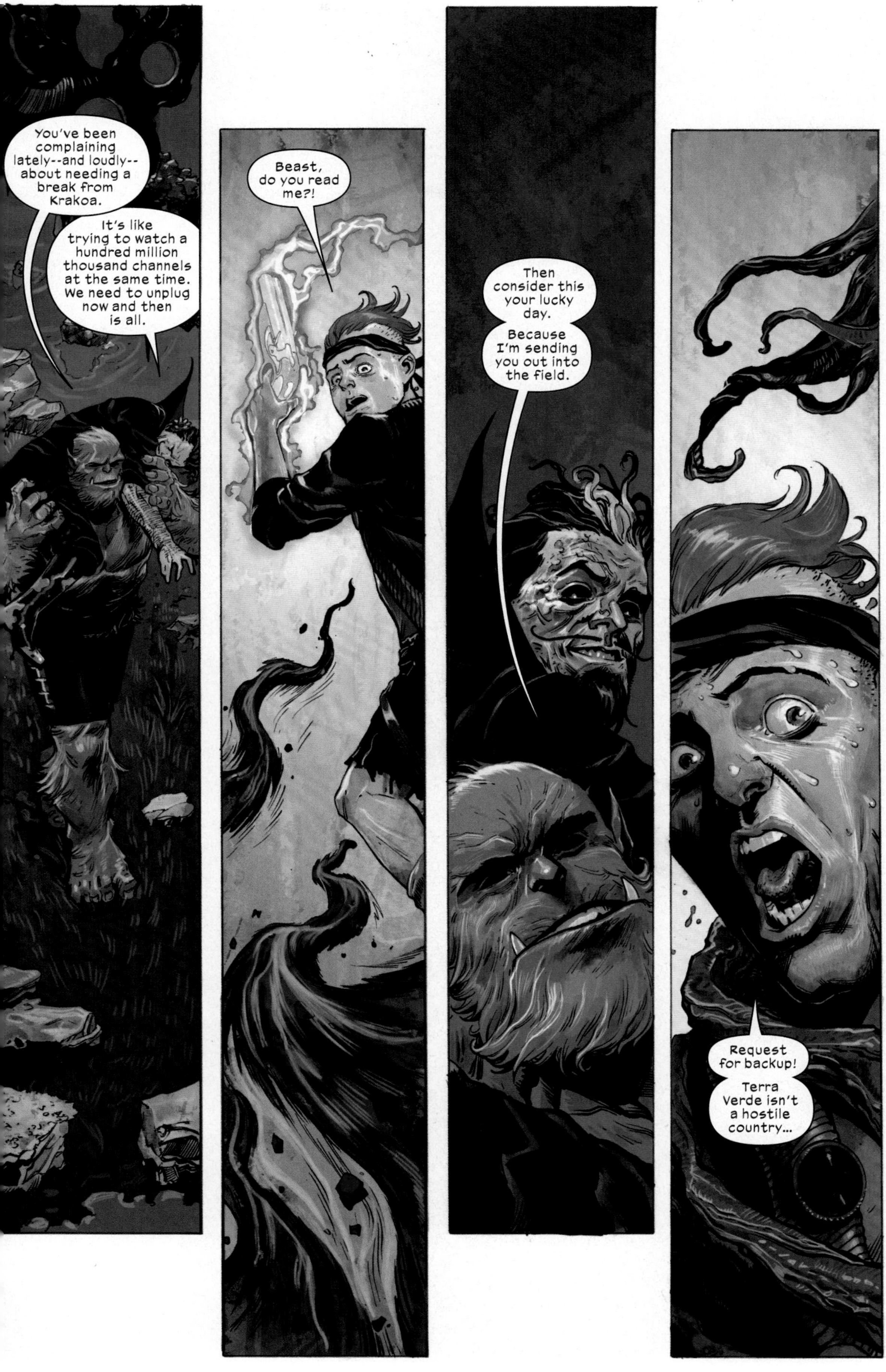
You've been complaining lately--and loudly--about needing a break from Krakoa.
It's like trying to watch a hundred million thousand channels at the same time. We need to unplug now and then is all.
Beast, do you read me?!
Then consider this your lucky day.
Because I'm sending you out into the field.
Request for backup!
Terra Verde isn't a hostile country...

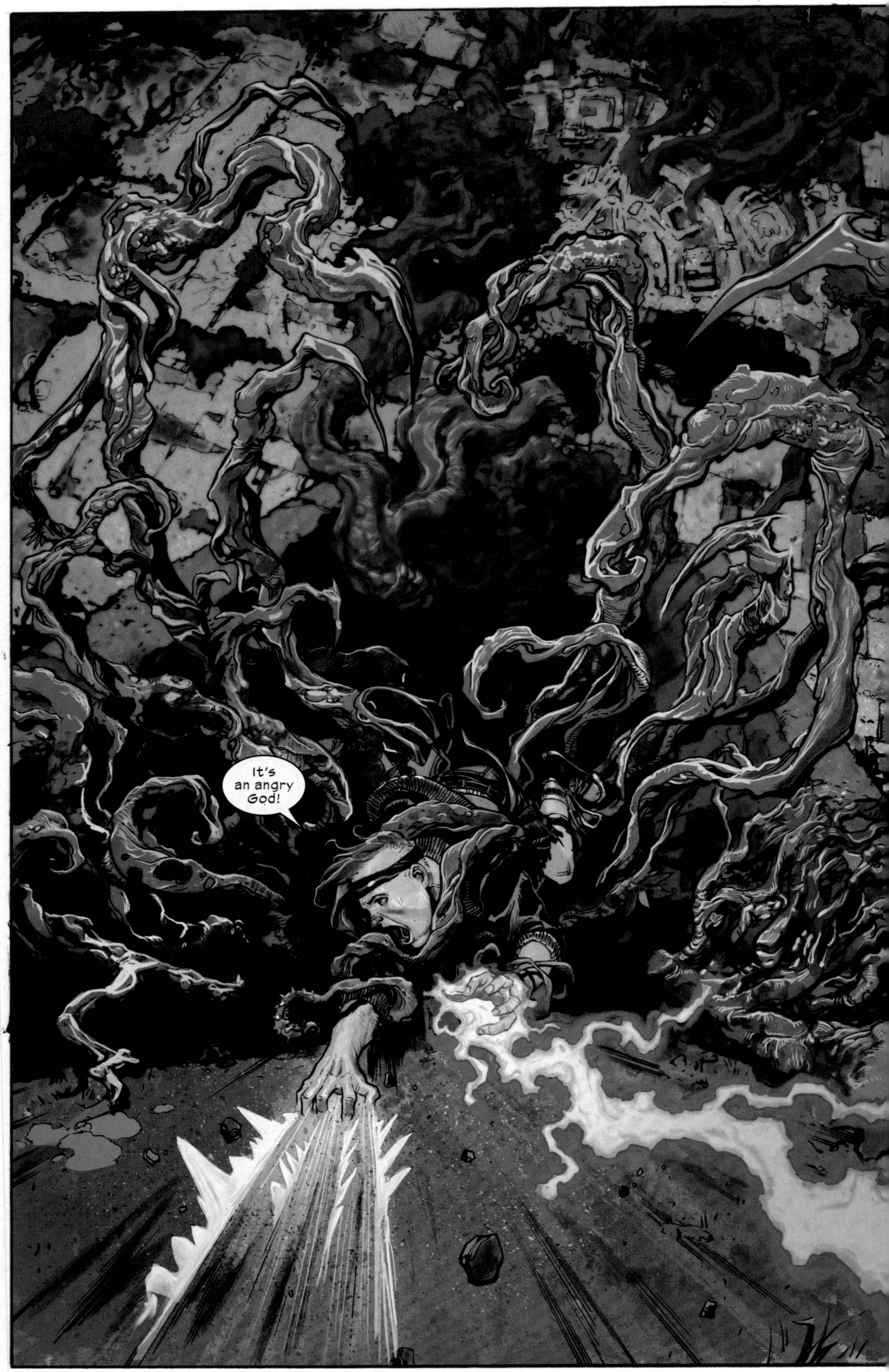
It's an angry God!

[dawn_of_x]

[kra_]
[koa_]

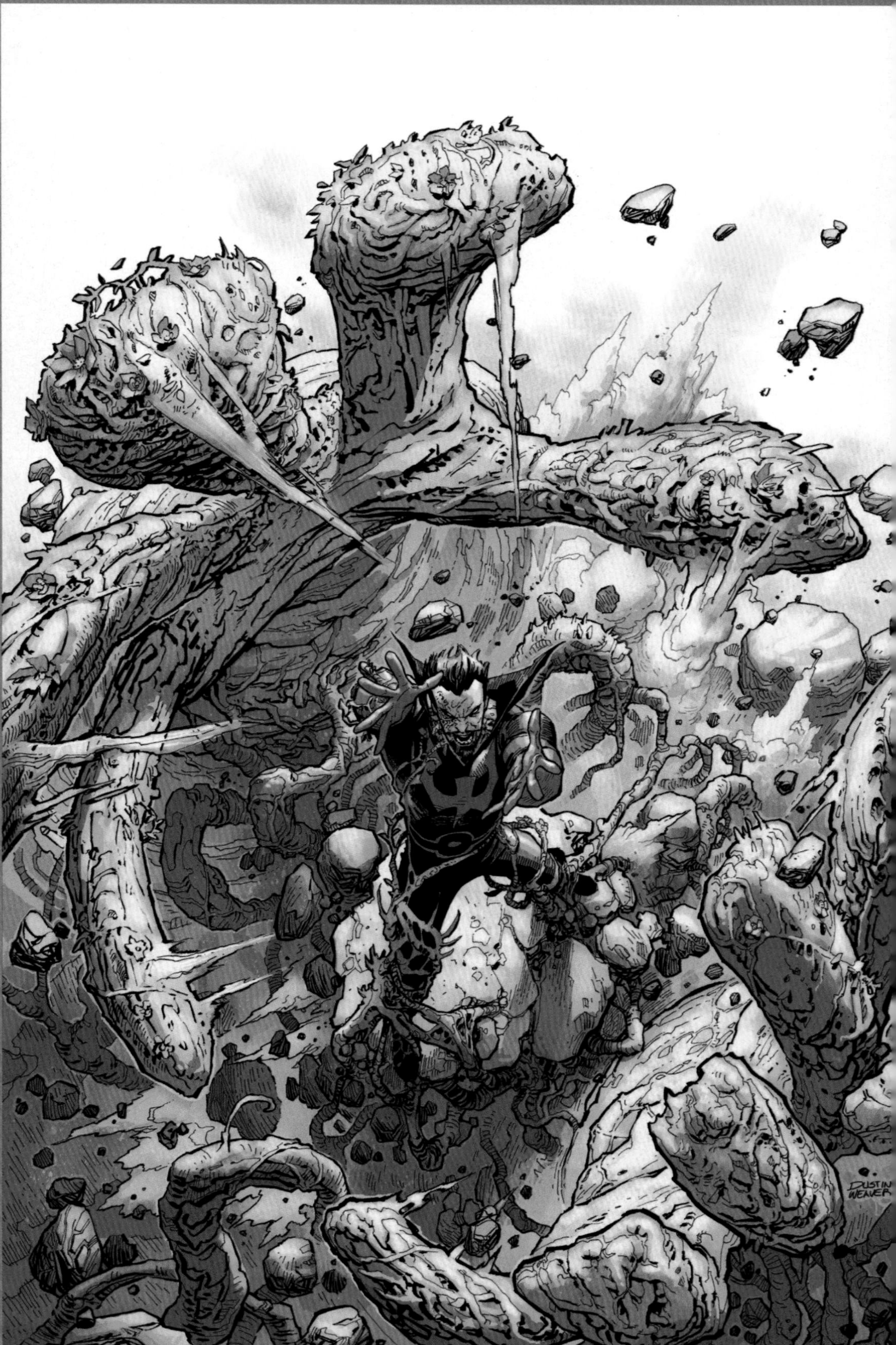
DUSTIN WEAVER

The Deadly Garden

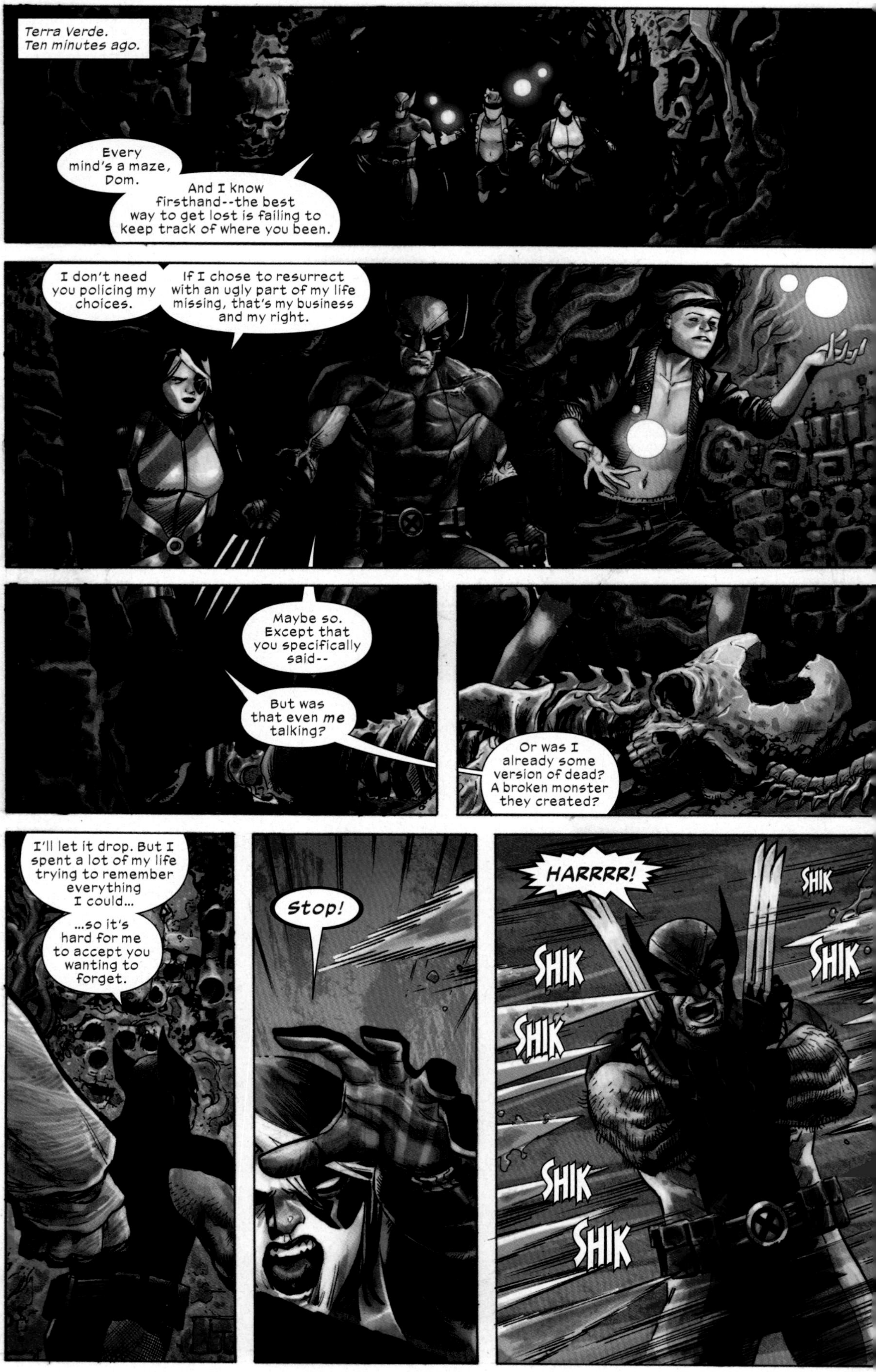
Terra Verde. Ten minutes ago.
Every mind's a maze, Dom.
And I know firsthand--the best way to get lost is failing to keep track of where you been.
I don't need you policing my choices.
If I chose to resurrect with an ugly part of my life missing, that's my business and my right.
Maybe so. Except that you specifically said--
But was that even *me* talking?
Or was I already some version of dead? A broken monster they created?
I'll let it drop. But I spent a lot of my life trying to remember everything I could...
...so it's hard for me to accept you wanting to forget.
Stop!
HARRRR!
SHIK
SHIK
SHIK
SHIK
SHIK
SHIK

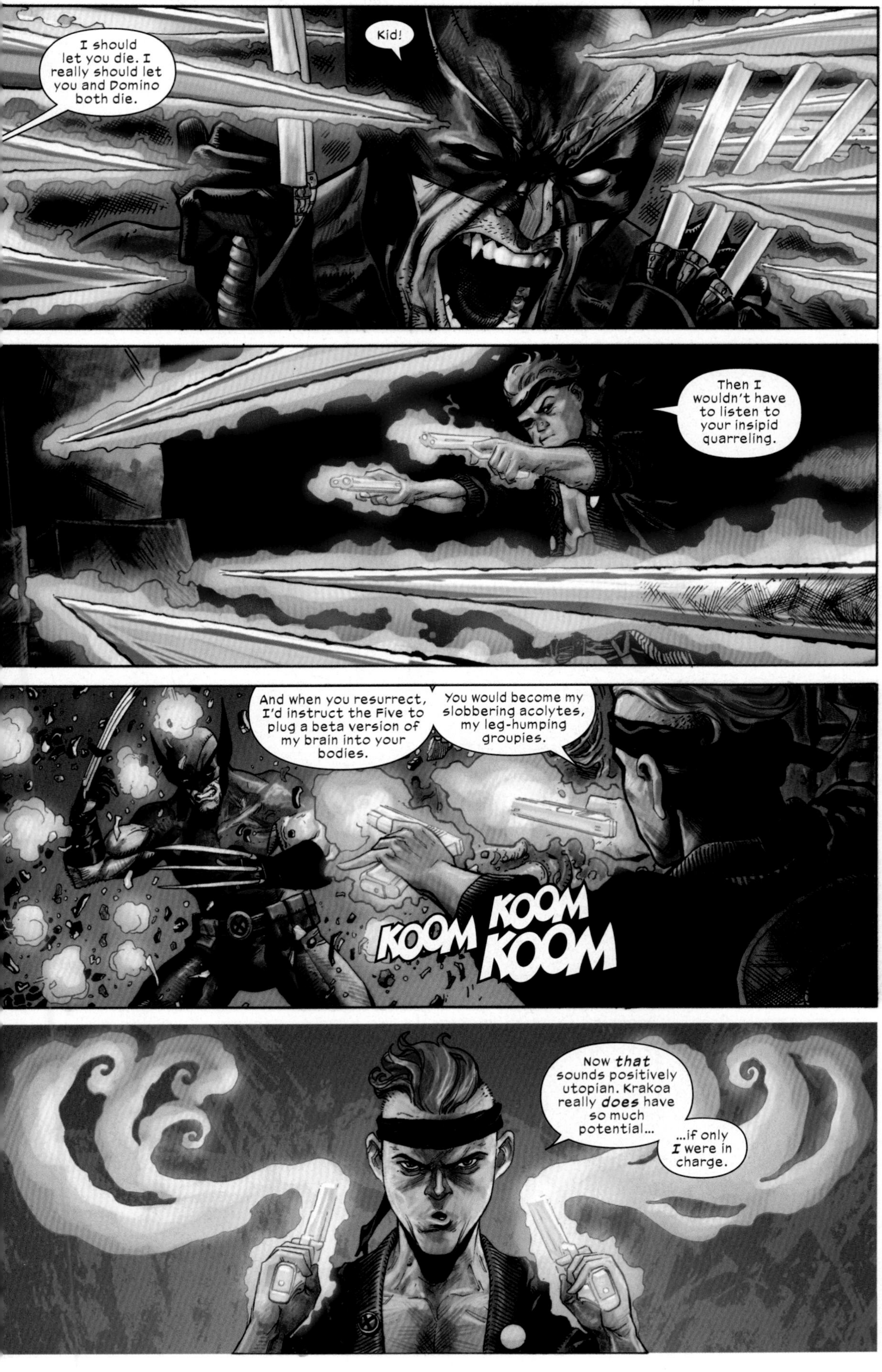
Kid!
I should let you die. I really should let you and Domino both die.
Then I wouldn't have to listen to your insipid quarreling.
And when you resurrect, I'd instruct the Five to plug a beta version of my brain into your bodies.
You would become my slobbering acolytes, my leg-humping groupies.
KOOM KOOM KOOM KOOM
Now *that* sounds positively utopian. Krakoa really *does* have so much potential...
...if only *I* were in charge.

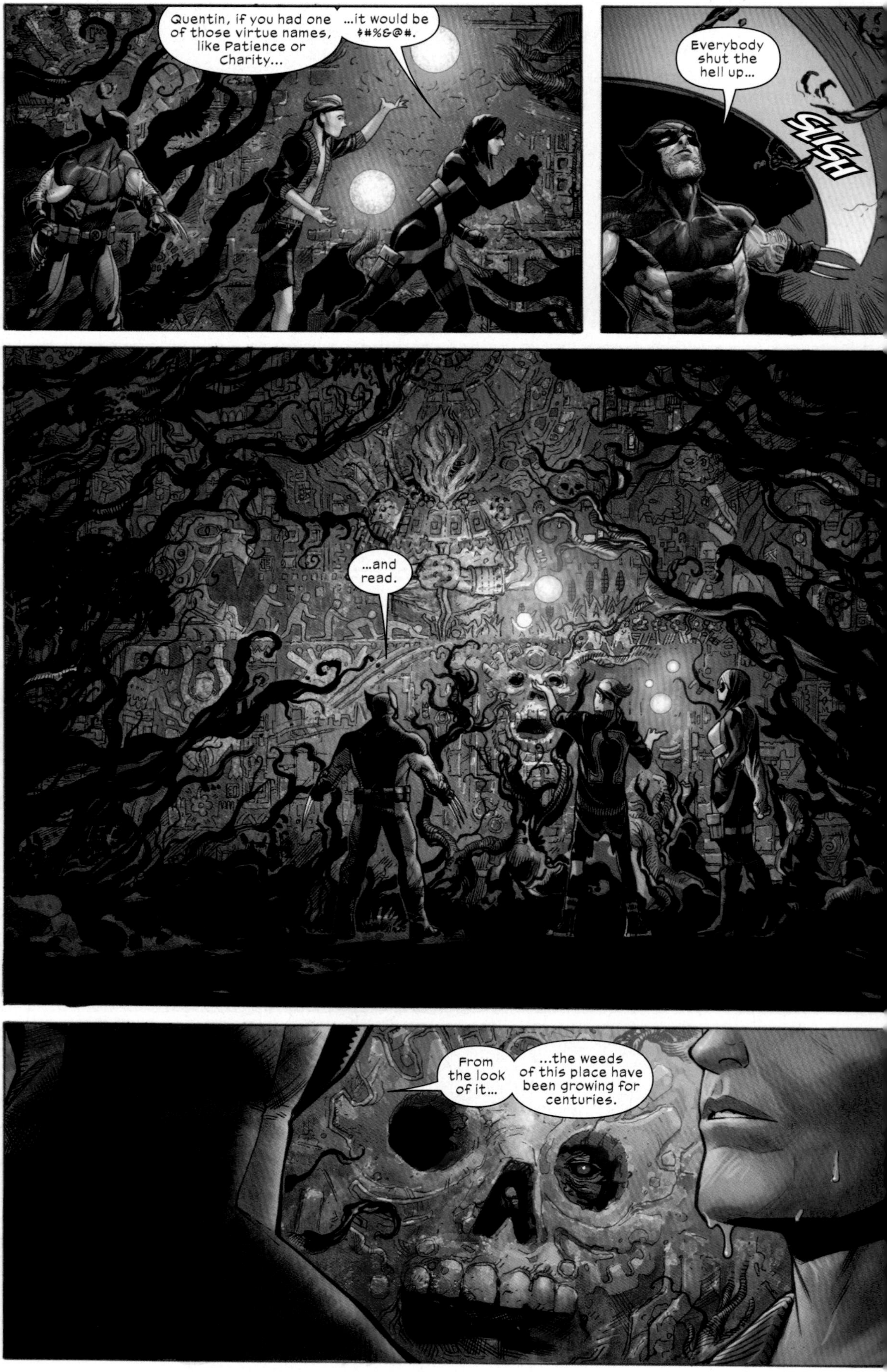

Quentin, if you had one of those virtue names, like Patience or Charity...
...it would be $#%&@#.
Everybody shut the hell up...
SLISH
...and read.
From the look of it...
...the weeds of this place have been growing for centuries.

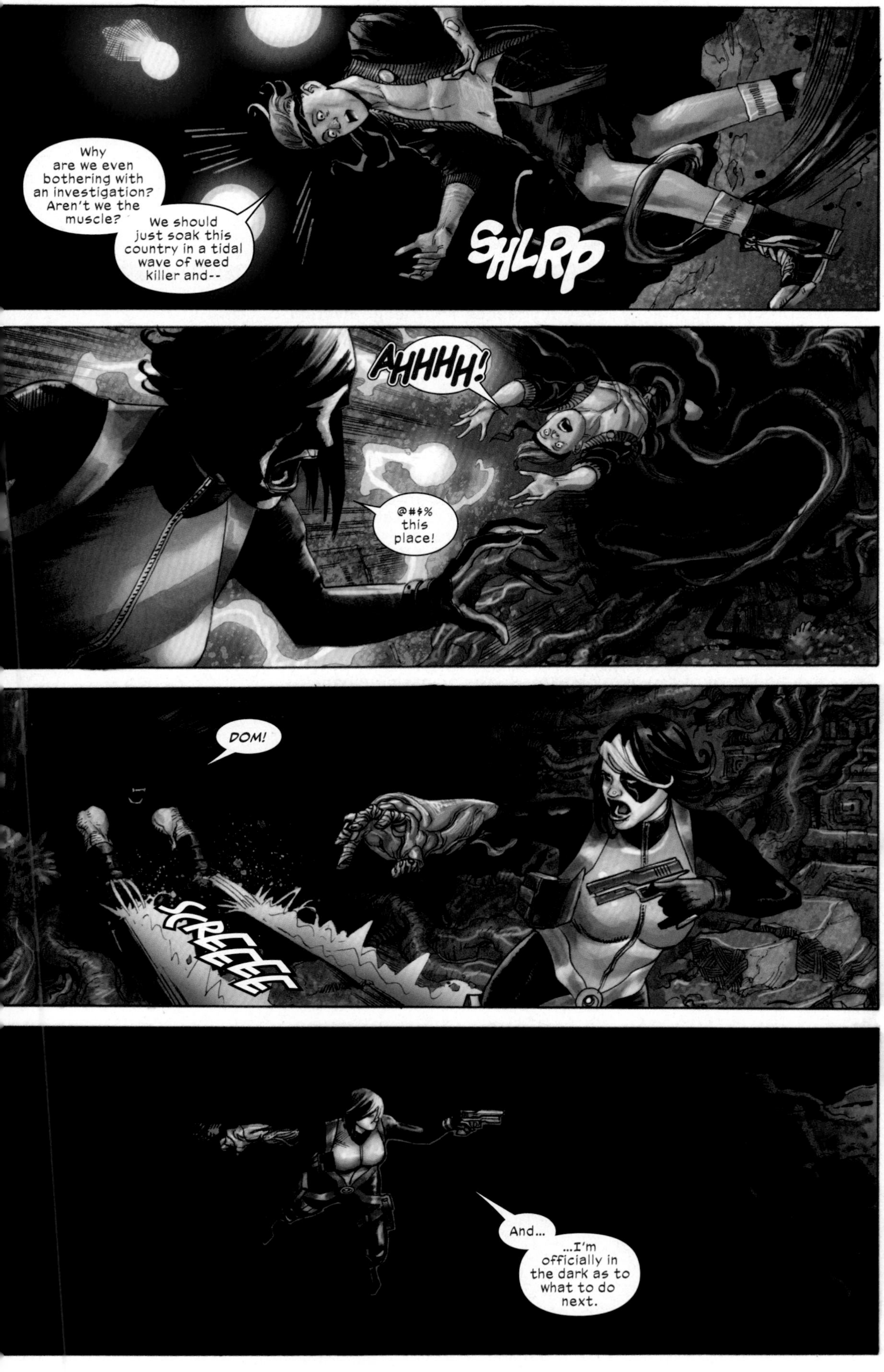
Why are we even bothering with an investigation? Aren't we the muscle?
We should just soak this country in a tidal wave of weed killer and--
SHLRP
AHHHH!
@#$% this place!
DOM!
SCREEEE
And...
...I'm officially in the dark as to what to do next.

BEAST'S LOGBOOK:
A MINOR MISCALCULATION

Telefloronic technology is an indigenous knowledge system bound up in thousands of years of Terra Verdean history (going back to the time of the Olmec).

Though one could say it is nothing new, its successful instrumentation has been lost as a result of both biological evolution, Roman Catholic acculturation, as well as pollution and modernization. For years it was dismissed by many as equivalent to alchemy or necromancy.

But even in recent years, when the country invested all of their resources into research that might bring telefloronics into the 21st century as a tool and as a weapon, they hadn't quite broken through the coding of the cellular data.

I did. Not intentionally. I studied the telefloronic source code and reprogrammed it to identify dendrites and axons as an infection. The plants would consume the host's mind. This was meant to put a terrorist out of commission. What I did not anticipate is that by disrupting the symbiotic give-and-take of the biotech...I made the plants dominant.

Terra Verde is now a fierce, collective intelligence. Not so dissimilar to Krakoa except as an enemy.

One could say that *Ak'* -- the punishing Olmec deity -- had been summoned.

I suppose this is a good thing, in that it will make us more aware and prepared -- as a nation ourselves -- as to how things could go wrong. Yes. Yes, it's absolutely a good thing. I might have made a minor miscalculation, but it will ultimately benefit us.

Krakoa. Now.

Go to Terra Verde, Beast says. Save the team, Beast says.

X-Force goes in for recon. Black Tom follows up with the rescue. Then the lot of us search and destroy.

Sounds like the craic, eh?

We've been feeling a bit... what's the word?... *smothered* lately.

Too much time with the veg will do that to a man.

Then why don't we just go? Just go. Just go!

Just march through the gate, raise some hell, swagger back a proper hero.

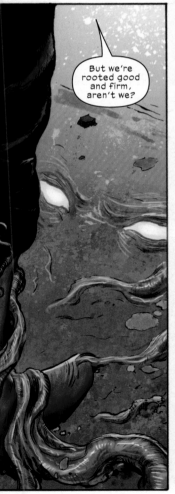

But we're rooted good and firm, aren't we?

How about this?

A pinch of the veg will bring us luck and reassurance.

Give us a kiss. *Mmff, mmff.*

We're packing the sweet groiny taste of Krakoa with us!

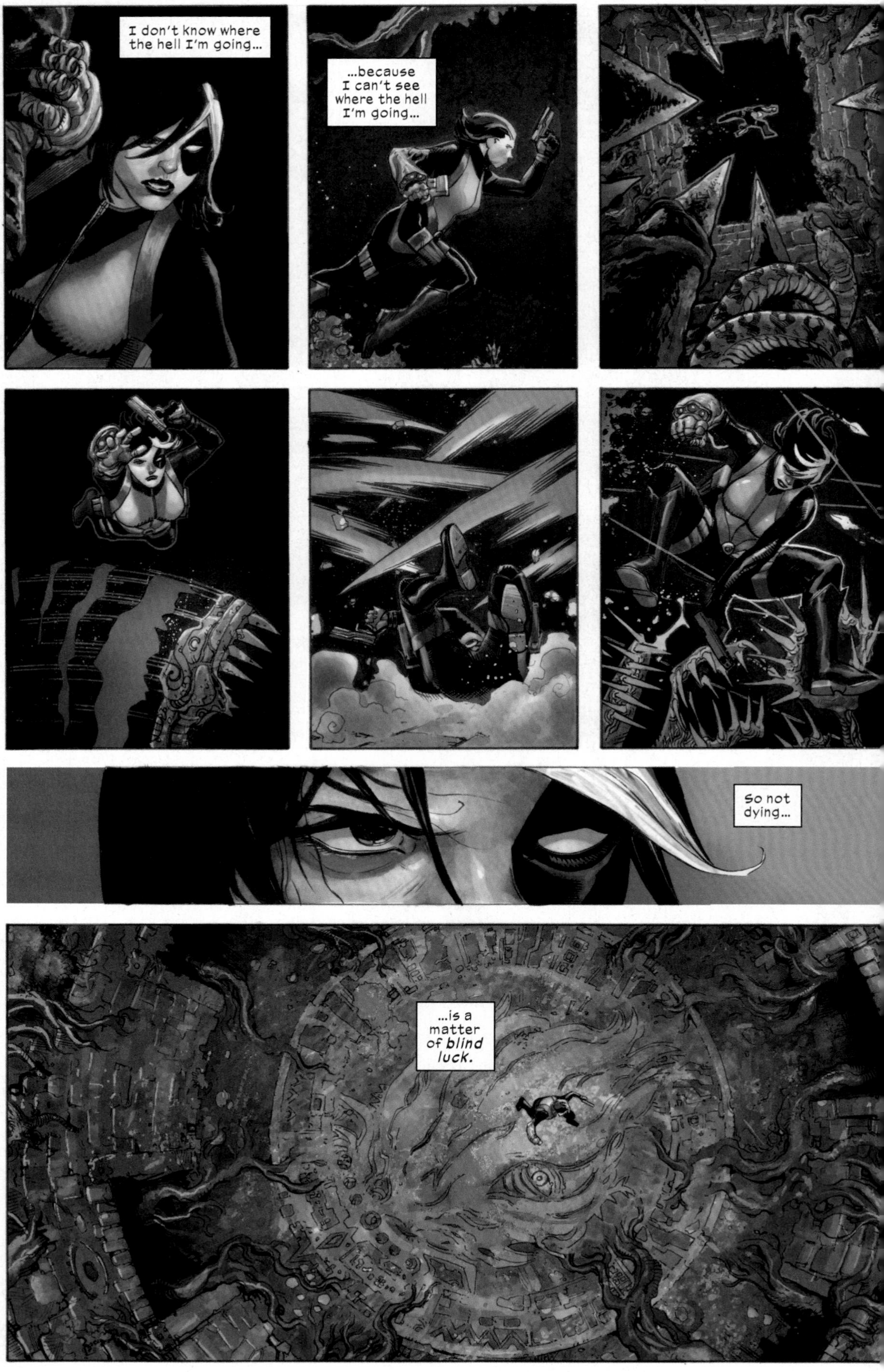

I don't know where the hell I'm going...
...because I can't see where the hell I'm going...
So not dying...
...is a matter of *blind luck.*

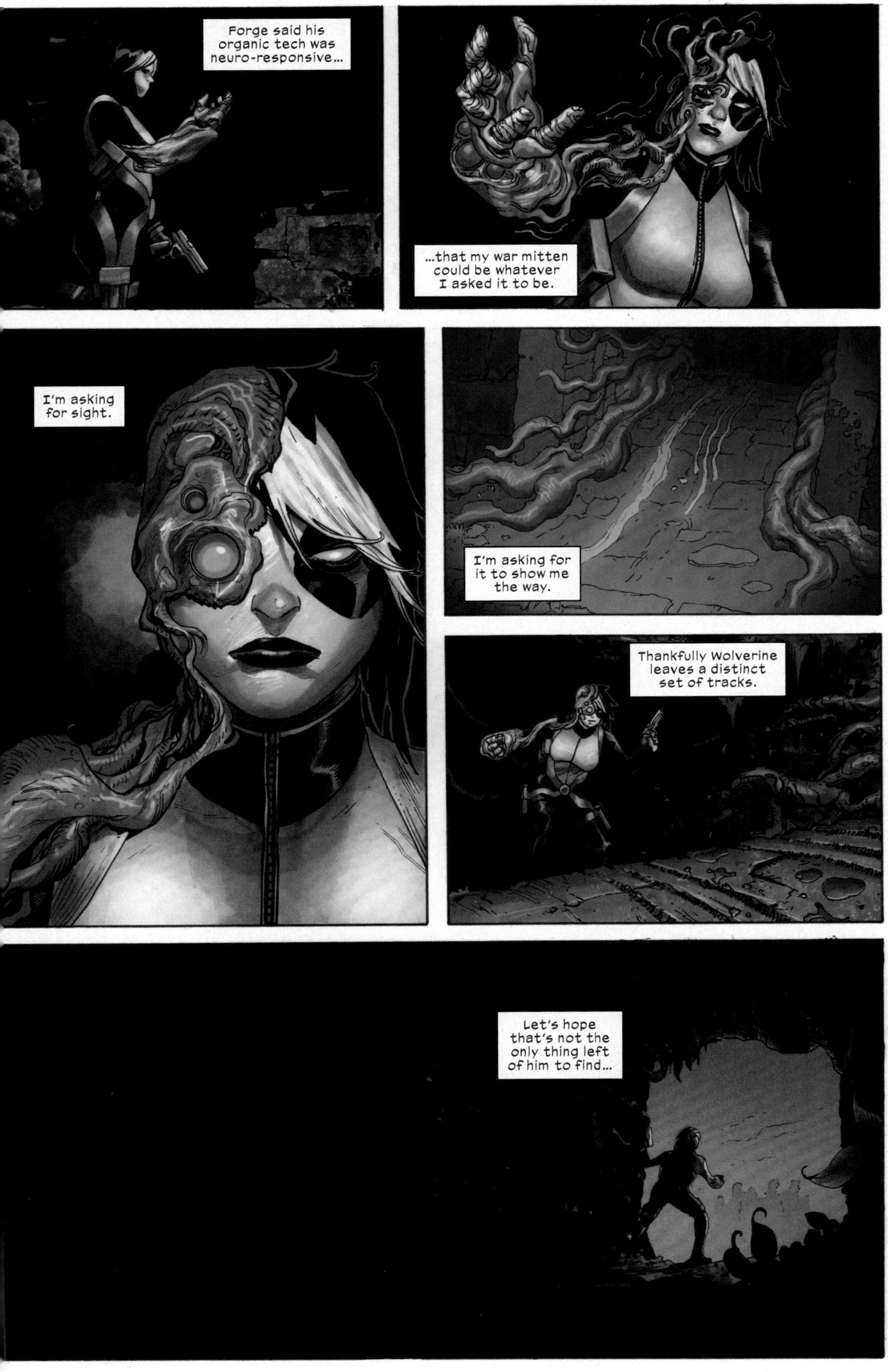
Forge said his organic tech was neuro-responsive...
...that my war mitten could be whatever I asked it to be.
I'm asking for sight.
I'm asking for it to show me the way.
Thankfully Wolverine leaves a distinct set of tracks.
Let's hope that's not the only thing left of him to find...

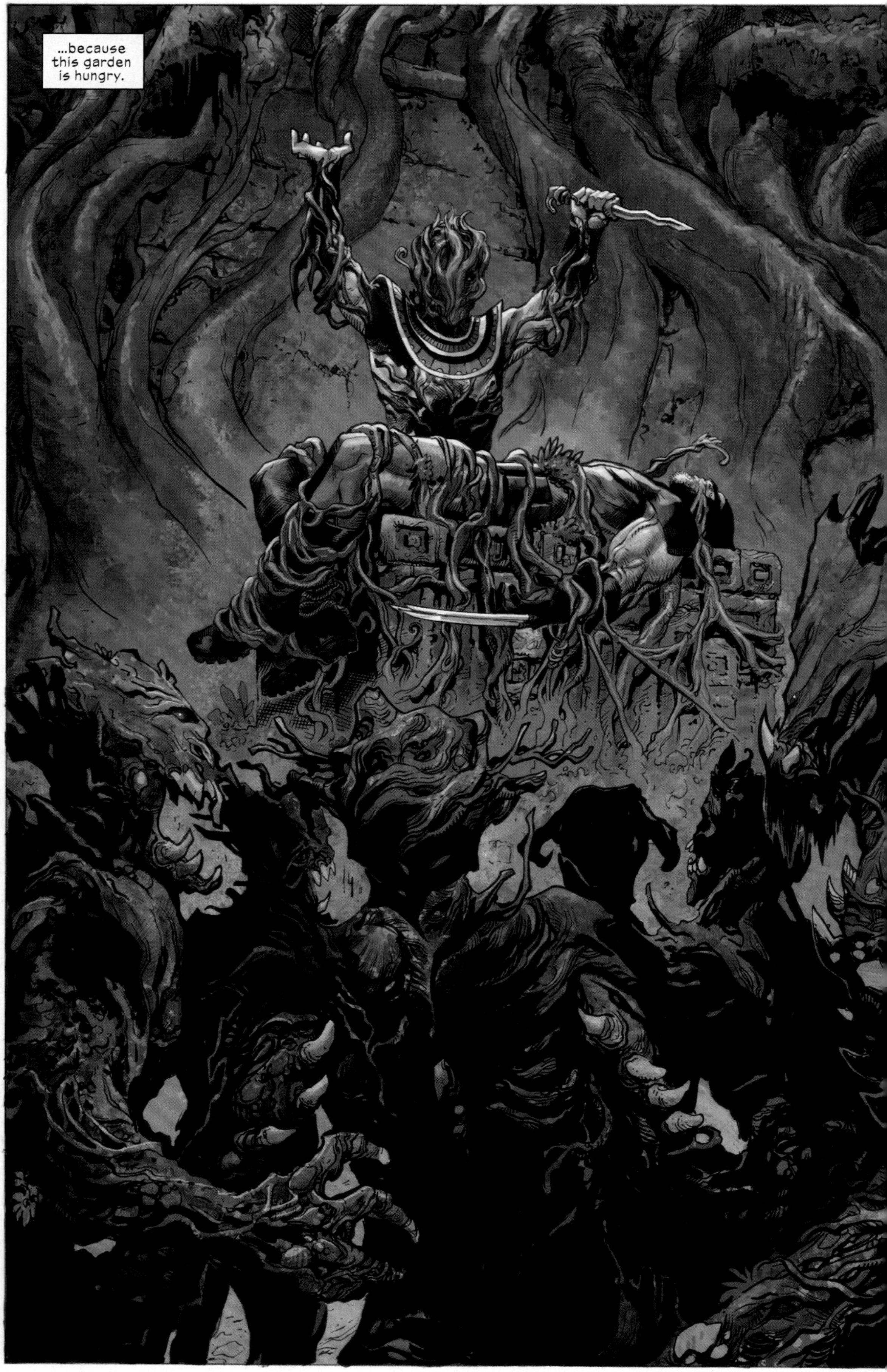
...because this garden is hungry.

You stick that thing in me...

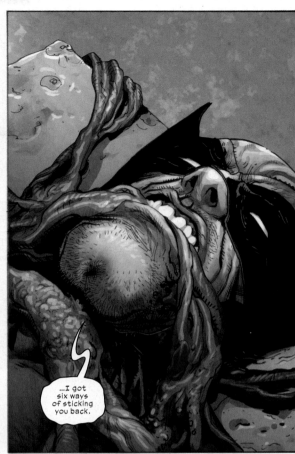

...I got six ways of sticking you back.

If they want a sacrifice...

SNARRR

...then they can go mulch themselves!

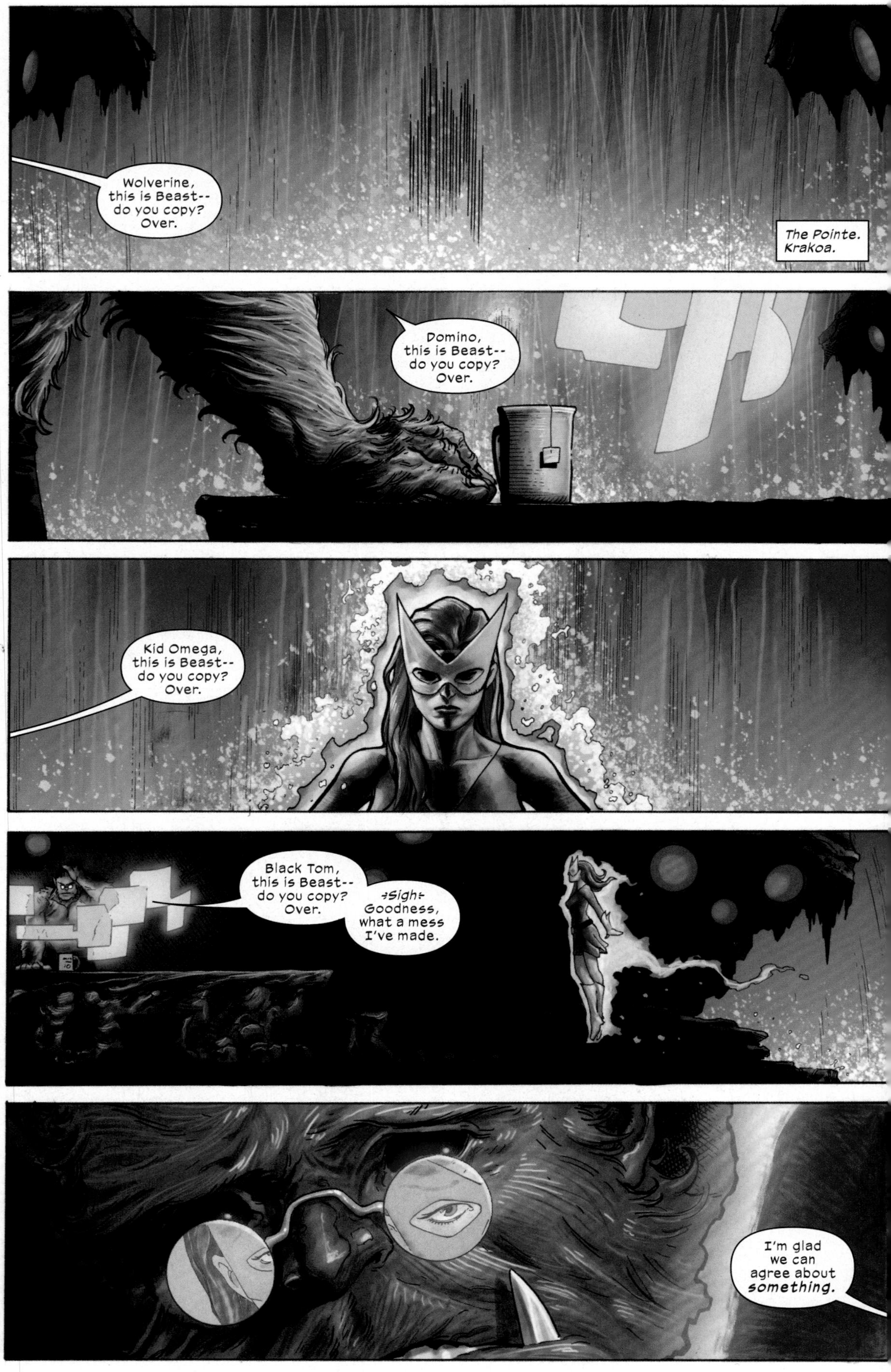
The Pointe. Krakoa.
Wolverine, this is Beast-- do you copy? Over.
Domino, this is Beast-- do you copy? Over.
Kid Omega, this is Beast-- do you copy? Over.
Black Tom, this is Beast-- do you copy? Over.
Sigh Goodness, what a mess I've made.
I'm glad we can agree about *something.*

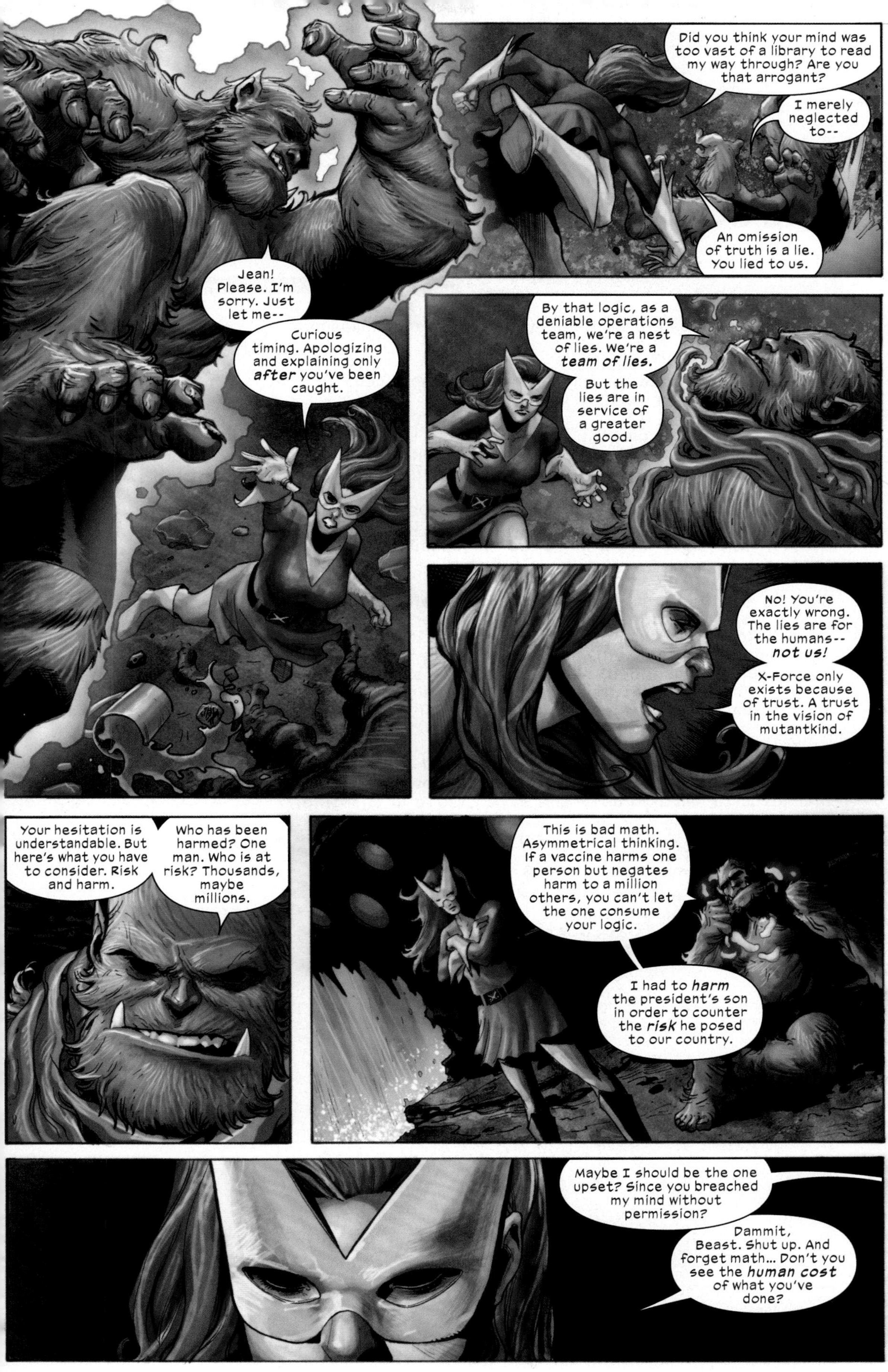

Did you think your mind was too vast of a library to read my way through? Are you that arrogant?
I merely neglected to--
An omission of truth is a lie. You lied to us.
Jean! Please. I'm sorry. Just let me--
Curious timing. Apologizing and explaining only *after* you've been caught.
By that logic, as a deniable operations team, we're a nest of lies. We're a *team of lies.*
But the lies are in service of a greater good.
No! You're exactly wrong. The lies are for the humans-- *not us!*
X-Force only exists because of trust. A trust in the vision of mutantkind.
Your hesitation is understandable. But here's what you have to consider. Risk and harm.
Who has been harmed? One man. Who is at risk? Thousands, maybe millions.
This is bad math. Asymmetrical thinking. If a vaccine harms one person but negates harm to a million others, you can't let the one consume your logic.
I had to *harm* the president's son in order to counter the *risk* he posed to our country.
Maybe I should be the one upset? Since you breached my mind without permission?
Dammit, Beast. Shut up. And forget math... Don't you see the *human cost* of what you've done?

THE CONSCIENCE OF WARFARE

Jean does not need to tell Beast anything. So she makes him **feel** it instead.

There isn't simply one person who has been sacrificed. There is a whole country's worth of them.

Beast has created a clear and present danger to mutantkind by weaponizing a hostile nation with a botanical armament far more dangerous to Krakoa than any nuclear warhead.

And in doing so he very well might be responsible for the "death" of a nation, the genocide of the Terra Verdean people, who have been inhabited or consumed by the telefloronic force.

Before, when the mutants lost Xavier and Cerebro, they all saw a possible end. If resurrection was no longer possible, they had lost their major advantage. But what if all of Krakoa was destroyed (or hacked)? The loss would be even greater. They would be disarmed, neutered, homeless. That is the threat telefloronics, in aggregate, pose in their more robust second generation -- as a conduit for surveillance and arms.

Before Jean abandons Beast -- before she blasts out of this shadowy lair and through the waterfall and into the green music of the day, before she rushes toward the gate that leads to Terra Verde -- she says, "We're in charge of the secrets. Us. We've been trusted with them by Xavier. We can't keep things from each other. We can't have secrets beneath secrets. Or how can we hold each other accountable?"

And though no one was there to see for sure, Beast might have let a single tear track down his muzzle before roughing it away with the back of his hand.

летописец

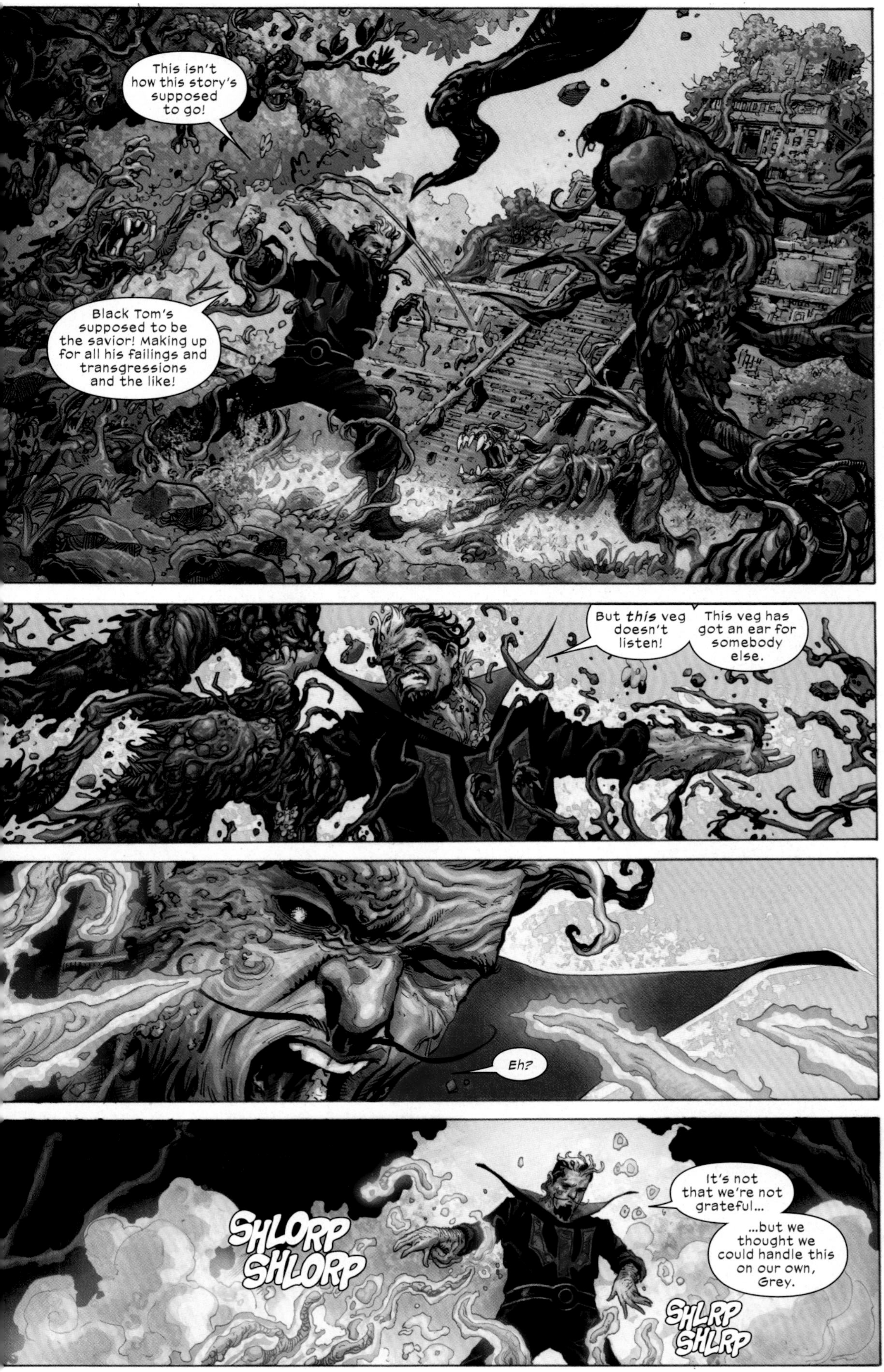
This isn't how this story's supposed to go!
Black Tom's supposed to be the savior! Making up for all his failings and transgressions and the like!
But *this* veg doesn't listen!
This veg has got an ear for somebody else.
Eh?
SHLORP SHLORP
It's not that we're not grateful...
...but we thought we could handle this on our own, Grey.
SHLRP SHLRP

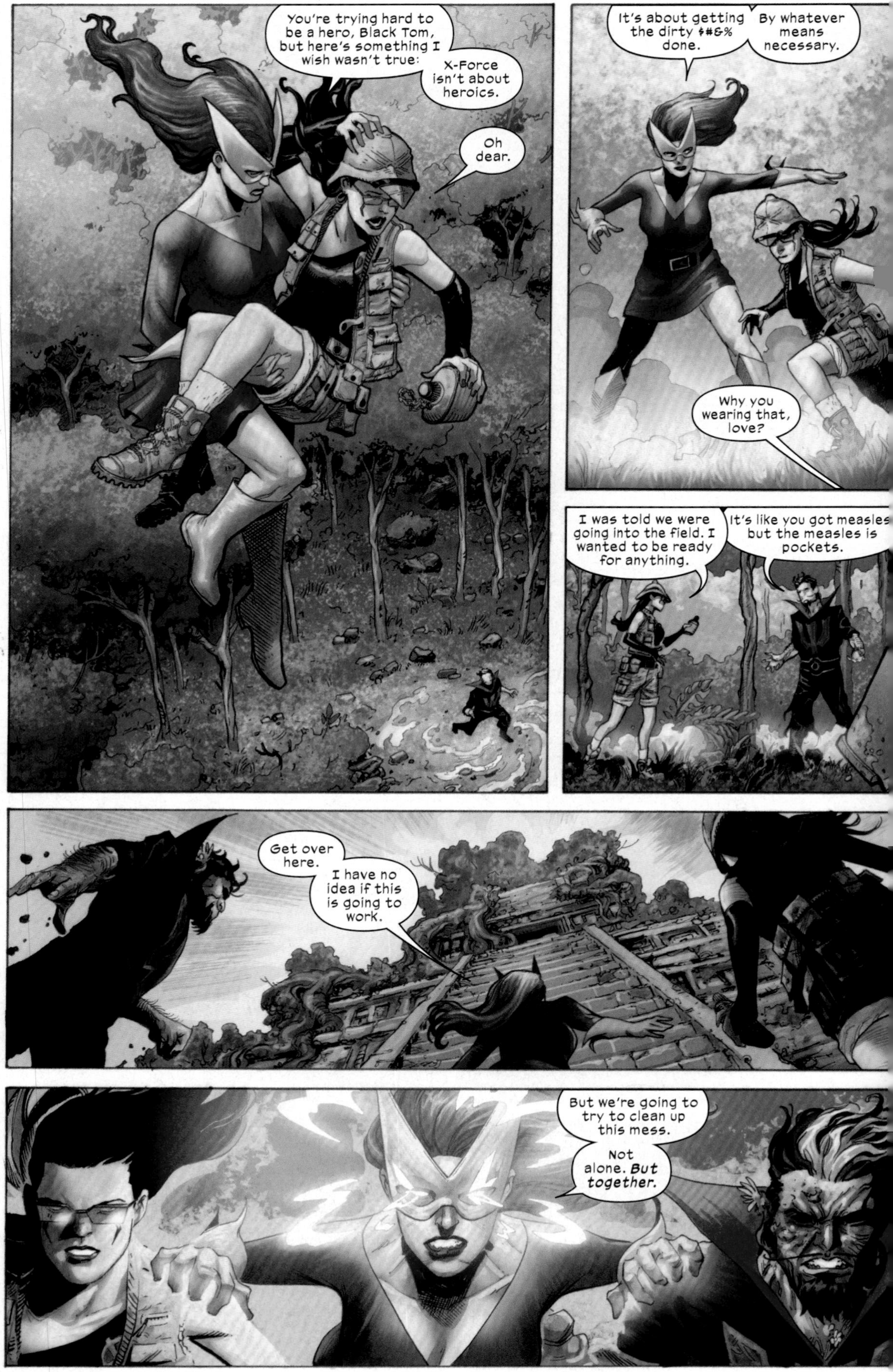
You're trying hard to be a hero, Black Tom, but here's something I wish wasn't true:
X-Force isn't about heroics.
Oh dear.
It's about getting the dirty $#&% done.
By whatever means necessary.
Why you wearing that, love?
I was told we were going into the field. I wanted to be ready for anything.
It's like you got measles but the measles is pockets.
Get over here.
I have no idea if this is going to work.
But we're going to try to clean up this mess.
Not alone. *But together.*

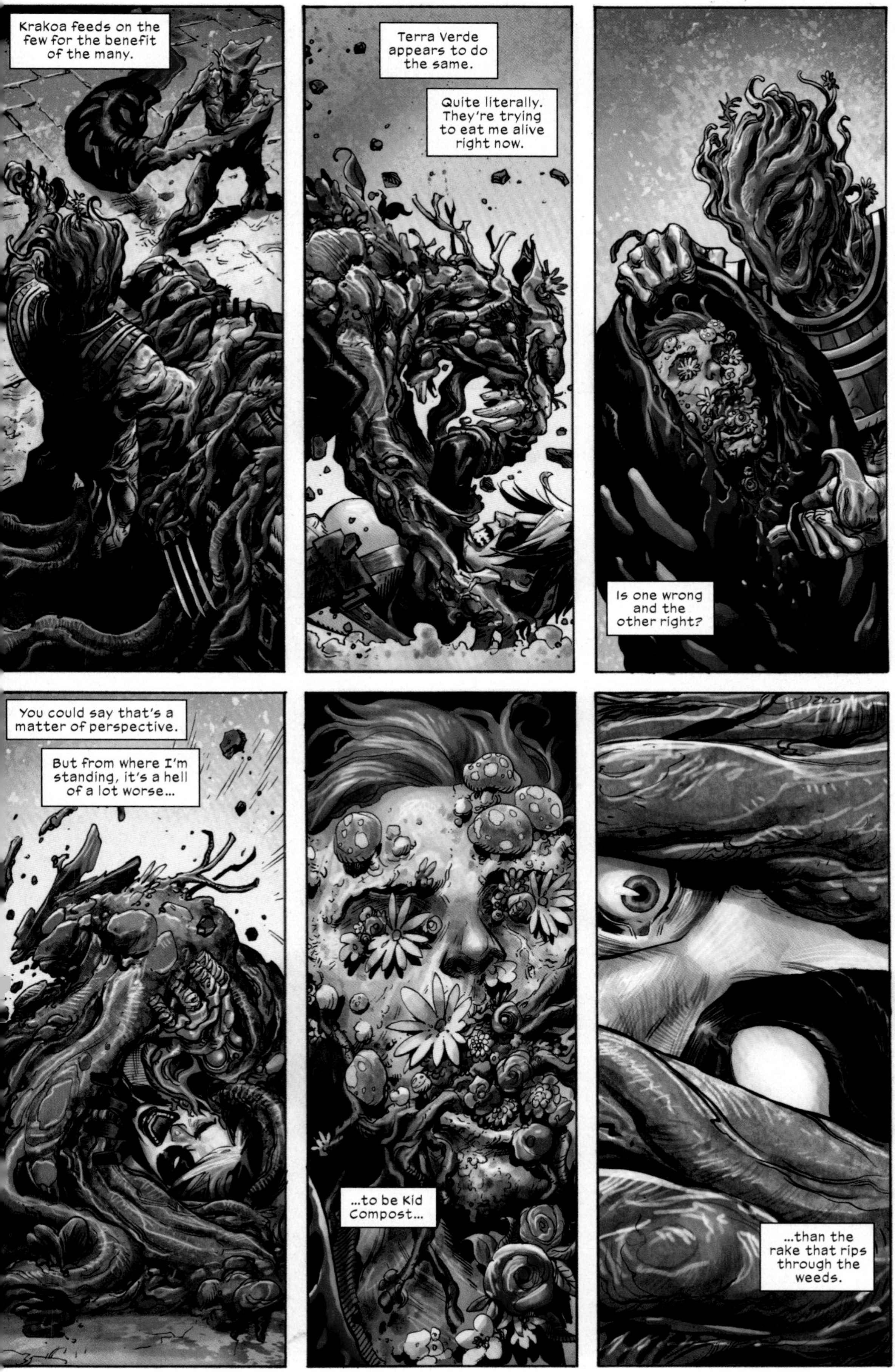
Krakoa feeds on the few for the benefit of the many.
Terra Verde appears to do the same.
Quite literally. They're trying to eat me alive right now.
Is one wrong and the other right?
You could say that's a matter of perspective.
But from where I'm standing, it's a hell of a lot worse...
...to be Kid Compost...
...than the rake that rips through the weeds.

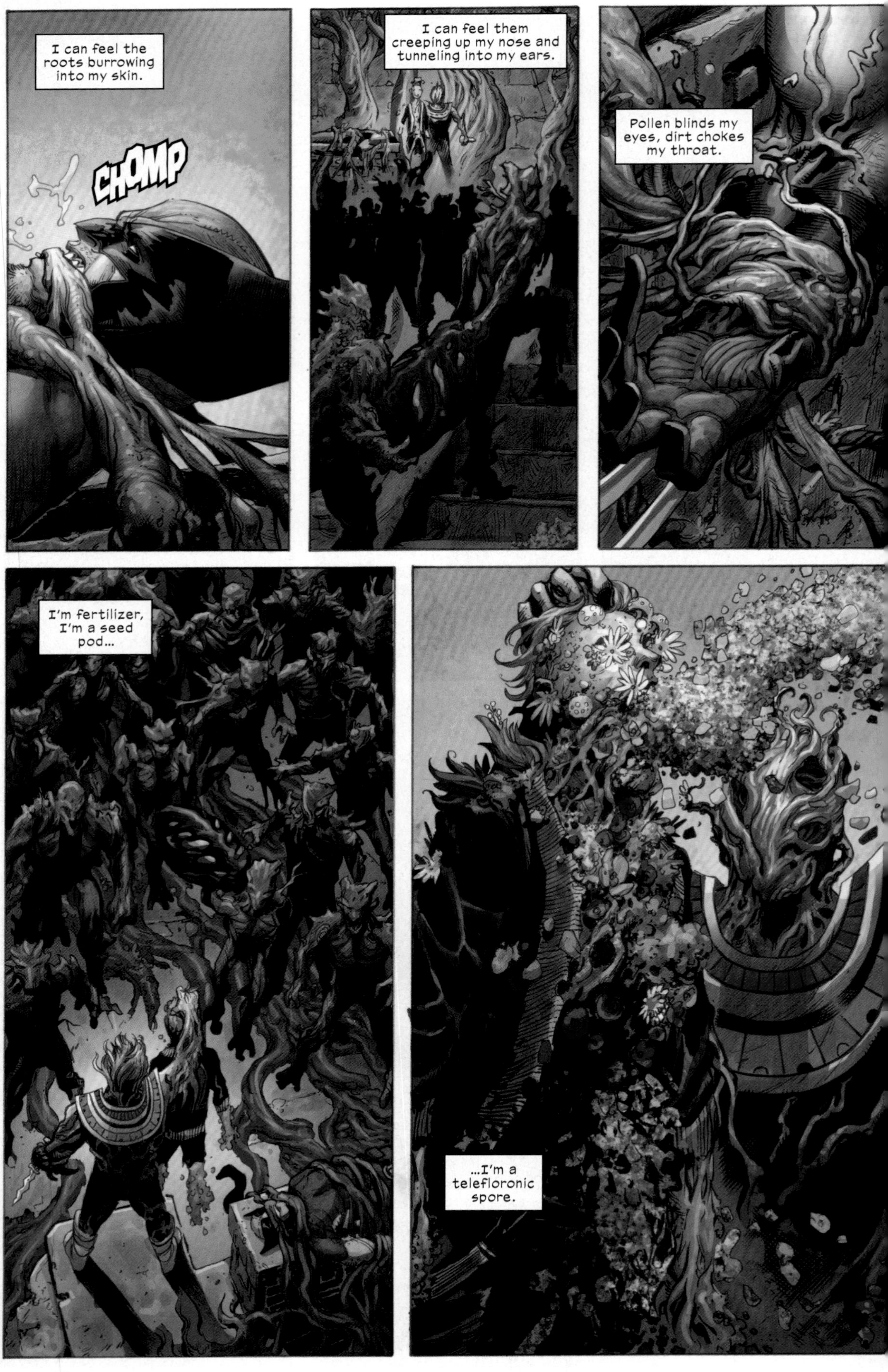
I can feel the roots burrowing into my skin.
CHOMP
I can feel them creeping up my nose and tunneling into my ears.
Pollen blinds my eyes, dirt chokes my throat.
I'm fertilizer, I'm a seed pod...
...I'm a telefloronic spore.

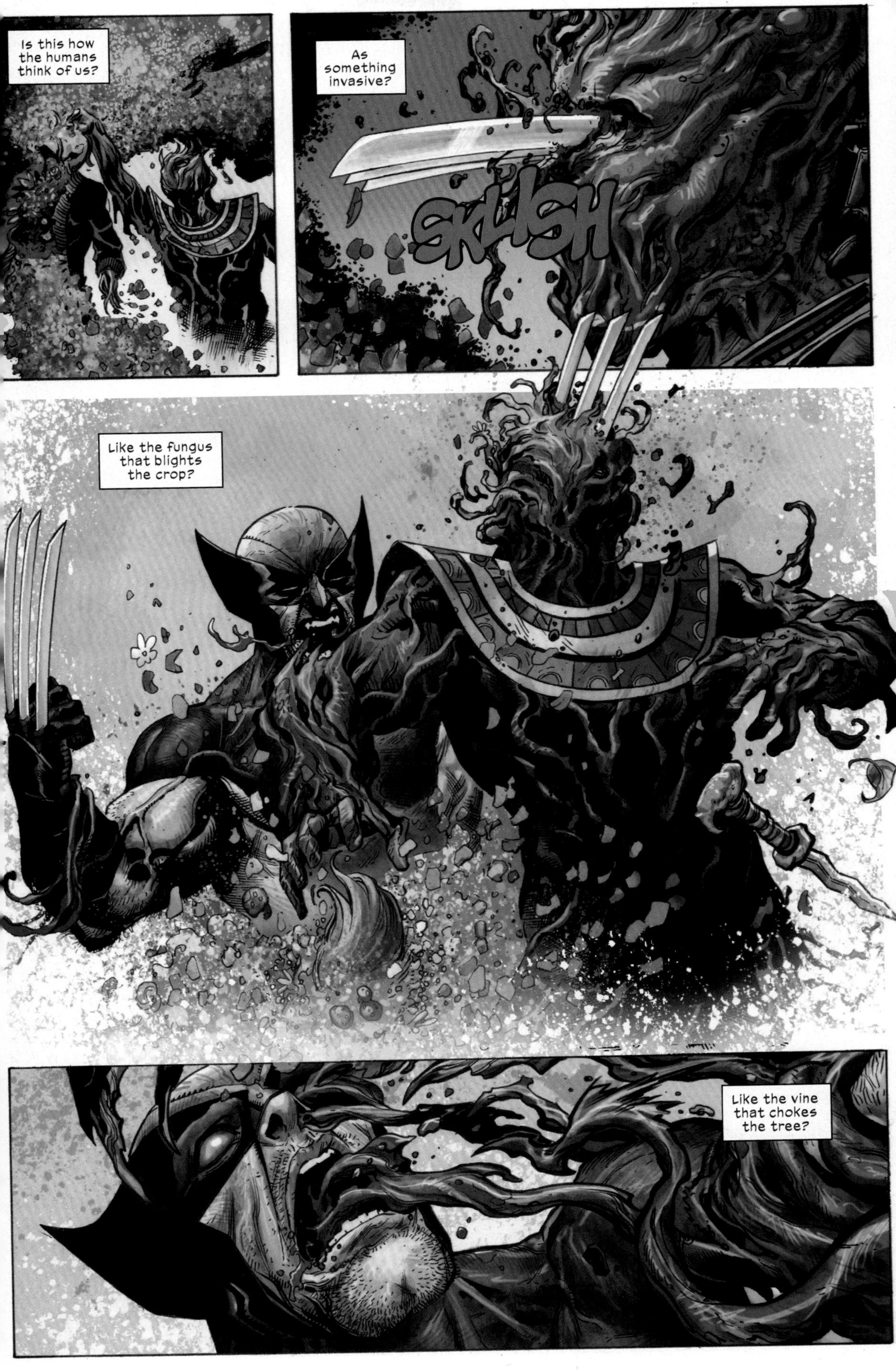
Is this how the humans think of us?
As something invasive?
SKLISH
Like the fungus that blights the crop?
Like the vine that chokes the tree?

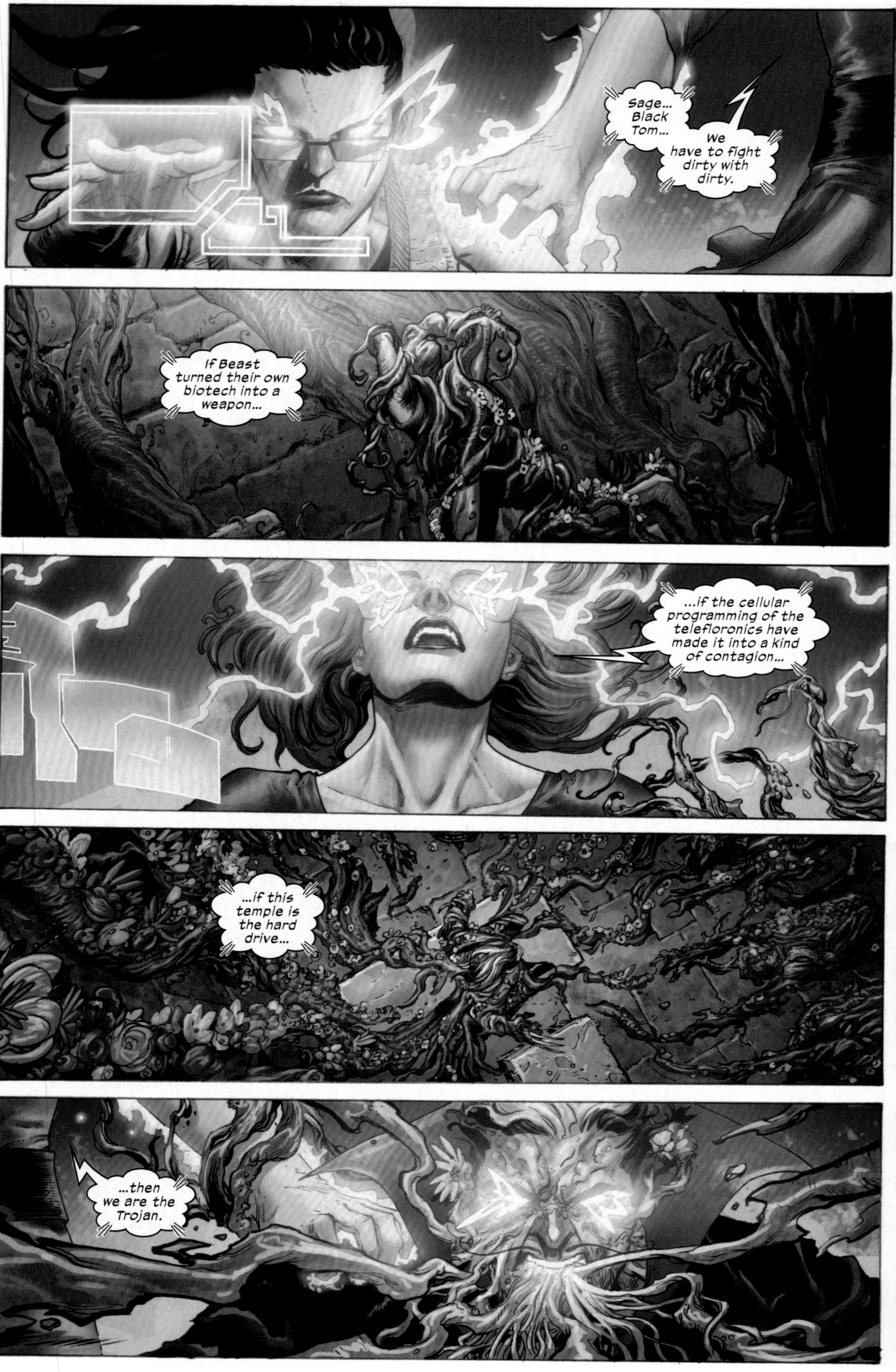
Sage... Black Tom...
We have to fight dirty with dirty.
If Beast turned their own biotech into a weapon...
...if the cellular programming of the telefloronics have made it into a kind of contagion...
...if this temple is the hard drive...
...then we are the Trojan.

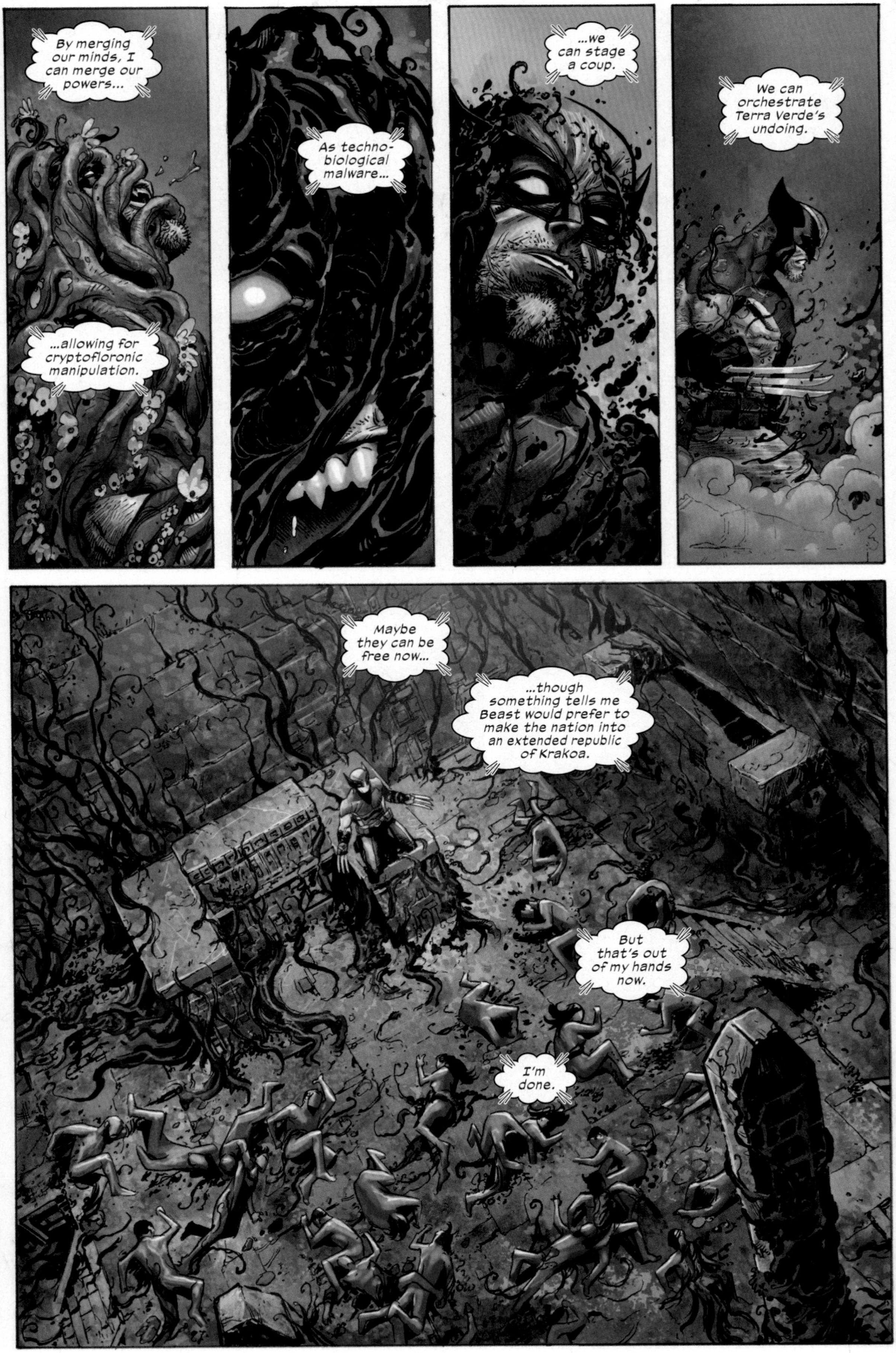
By merging our minds, I can merge our powers...
...allowing for cryptofloronic manipulation.
As techno-biological malware...
...we can stage a coup.
We can orchestrate Terra Verde's undoing.
Maybe they can be free now...
...though something tells me Beast would prefer to make the nation into an extended republic of Krakoa.
But that's out of my hands now.
I'm done.

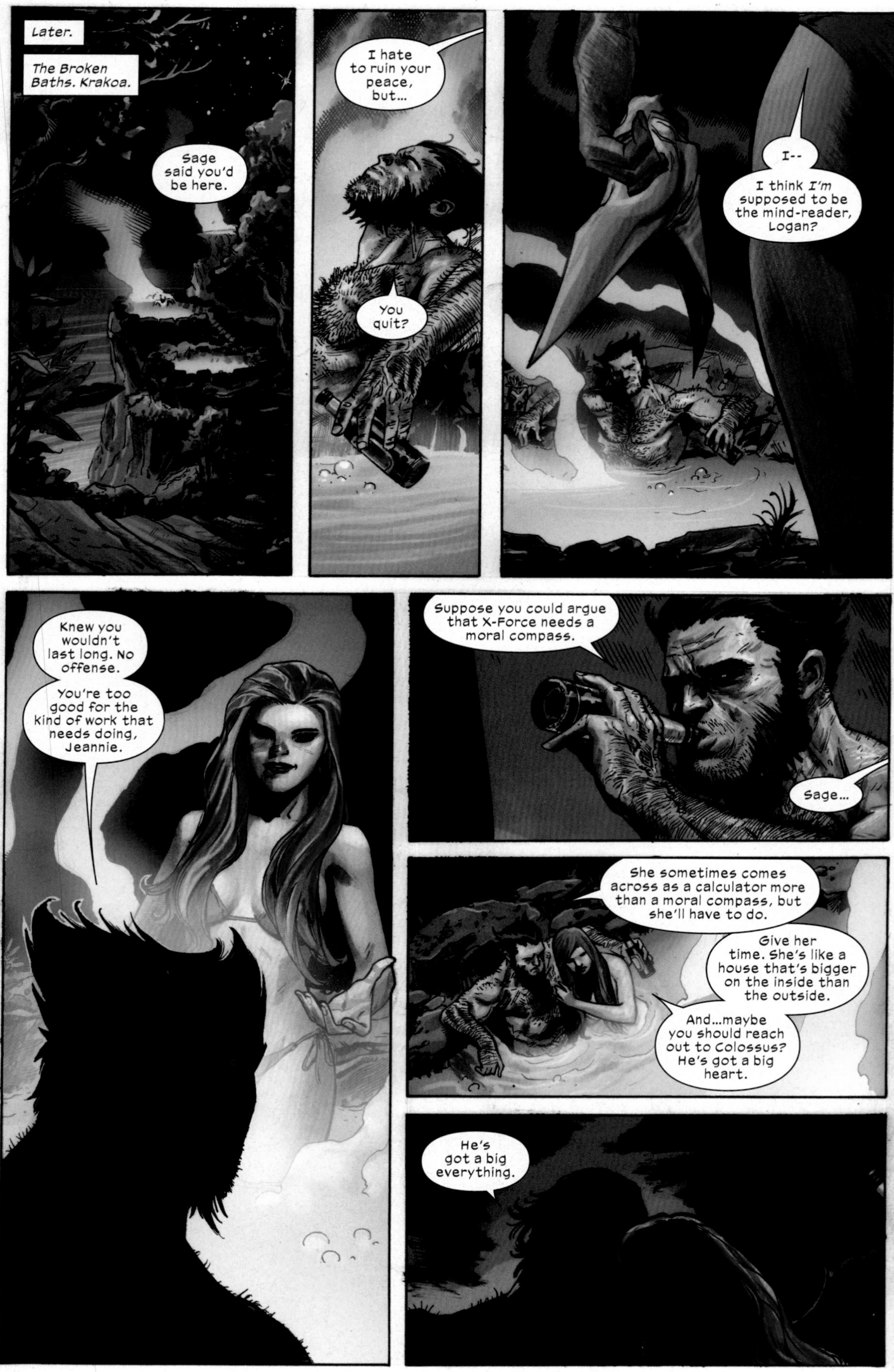
Later.
The Broken Baths. Krakoa.
Sage said you'd be here.
I hate to ruin your peace, but...
You quit?
I--
I think *I'm* supposed to be the mind-reader, Logan?
Knew you wouldn't last long. No offense.
You're too good for the kind of work that needs doing, Jeannie.
Suppose you could argue that X-Force needs a moral compass.
Sage...
She sometimes comes across as a calculator more than a moral compass, but she'll have to do.
Give her time. She's like a house that's bigger on the inside than the outside.
And...maybe you should reach out to Colossus? He's got a big heart.
He's got a big everything.

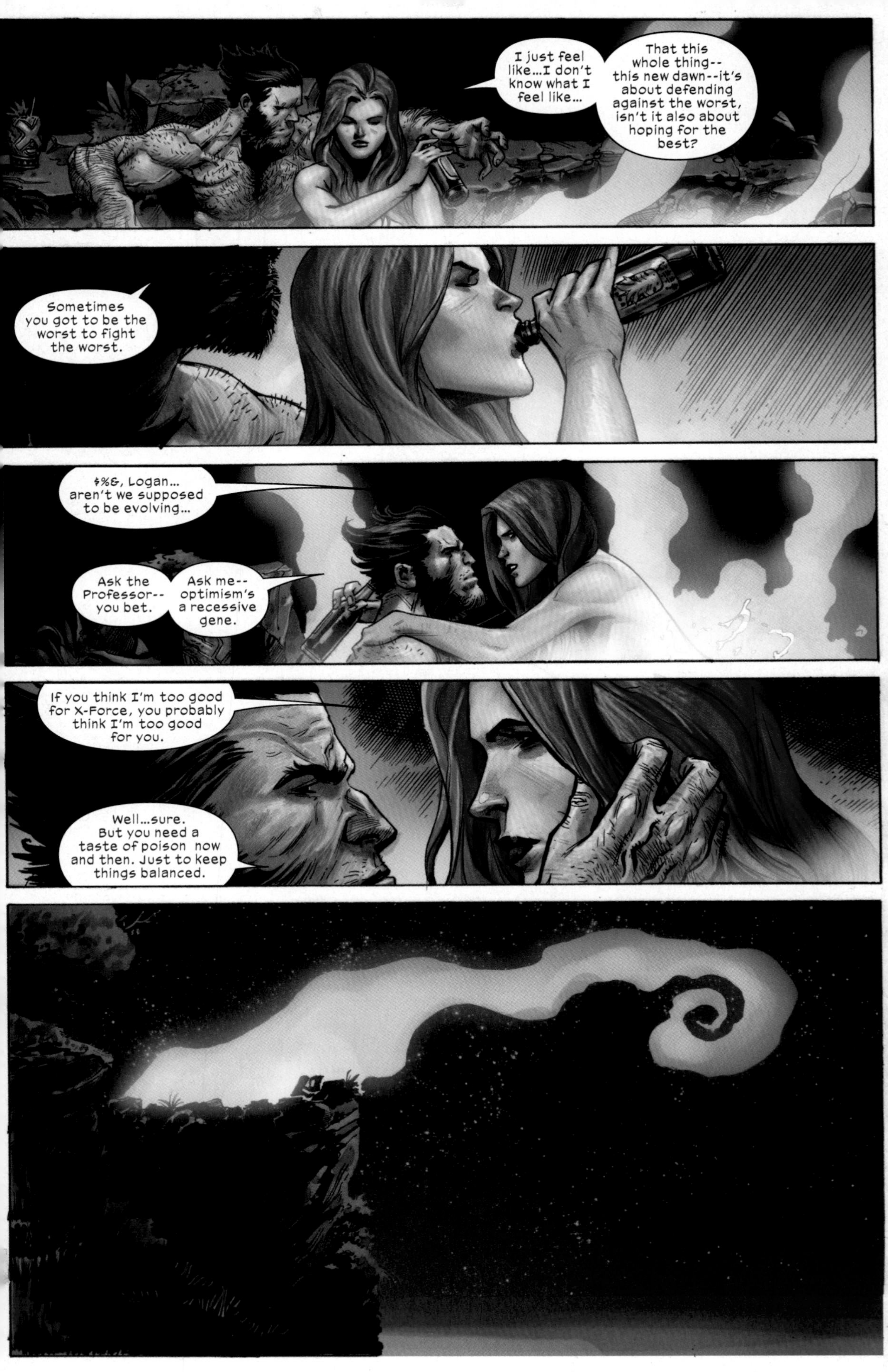
I just feel like...I don't know what I feel like...
That this whole thing--this new dawn--it's about defending against the worst, isn't it also about hoping for the best?
Sometimes you got to be the worst to fight the worst.
$%&, Logan... aren't we supposed to be evolving...
Ask the Professor--you bet.
Ask me--optimism's a recessive gene.
If you think I'm too good for X-Force, you probably think I'm too good for you.
Well...sure. But you need a taste of poison now and then. Just to keep things balanced.

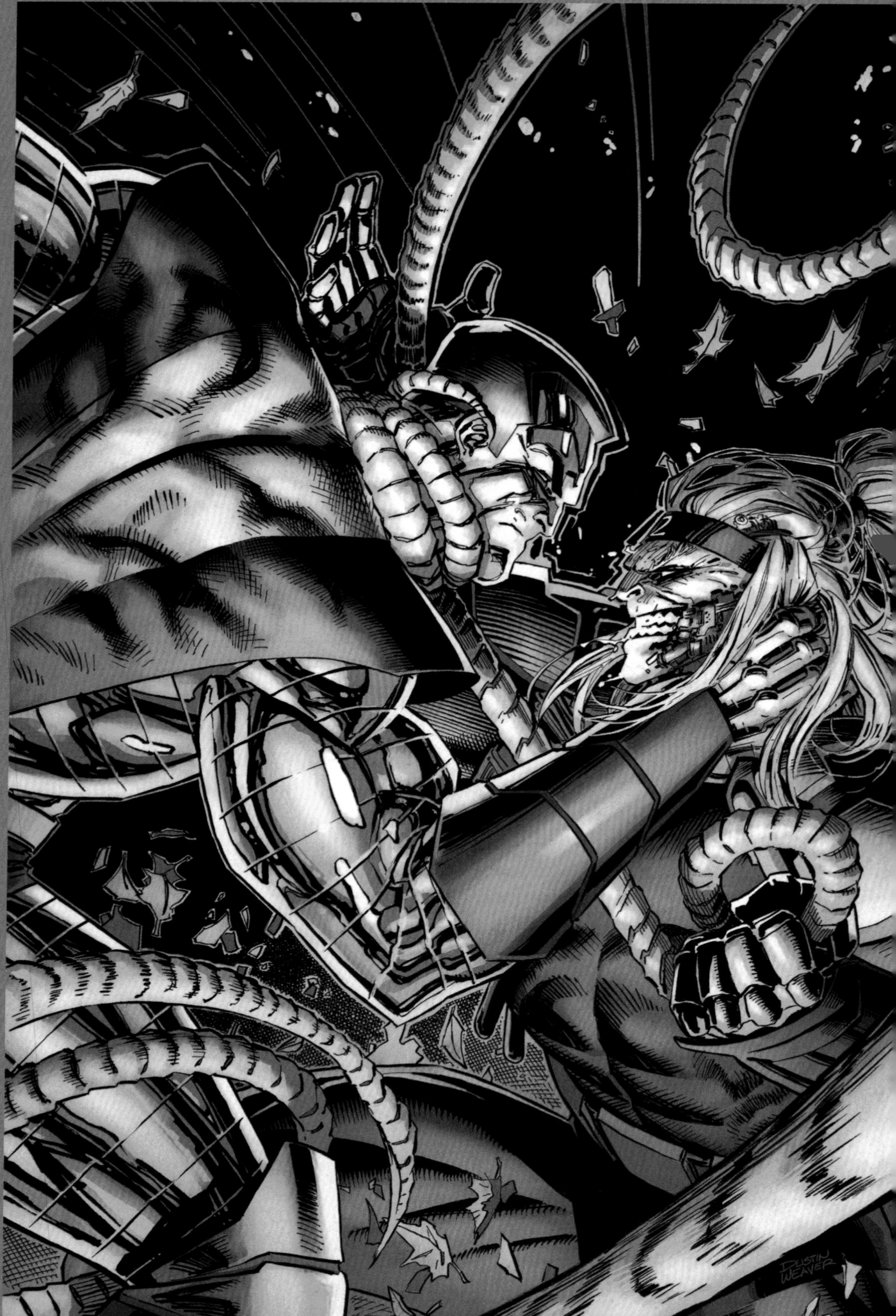
DUSTIN
WEAVER

Red Dawn

11

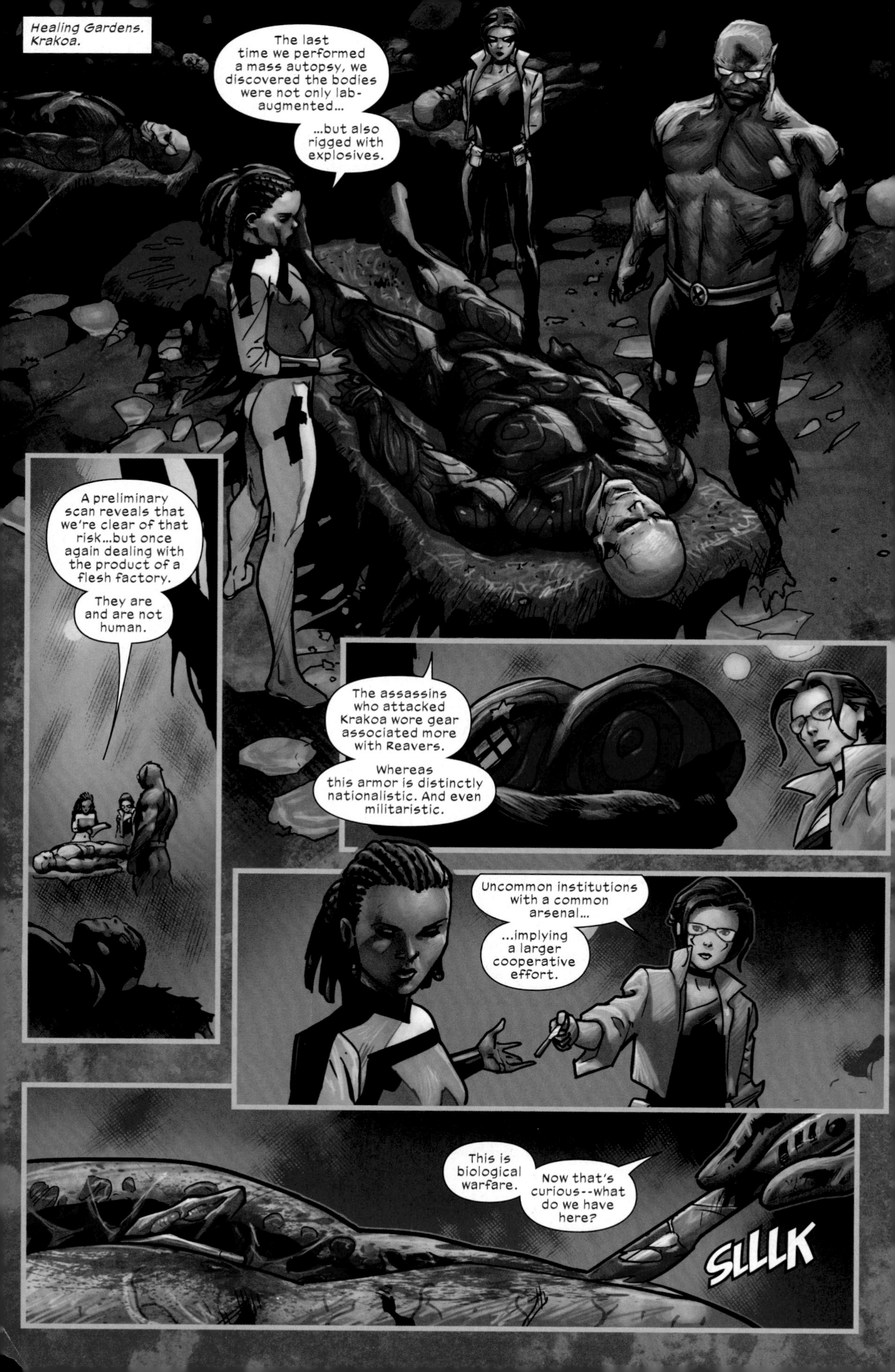
Healing Gardens. Krakoa.
The last time we performed a mass autopsy, we discovered the bodies were not only lab-augmented...
...but also rigged with explosives.
A preliminary scan reveals that we're clear of that risk...but once again dealing with the product of a flesh factory.
They are and are not human.
The assassins who attacked Krakoa wore gear associated more with Reavers.
Whereas this armor is distinctly nationalistic. And even militaristic.
Uncommon institutions with a common arsenal...
...implying a larger cooperative effort.
This is biological warfare.
Now that's curious--what do we have here?
SLLLK

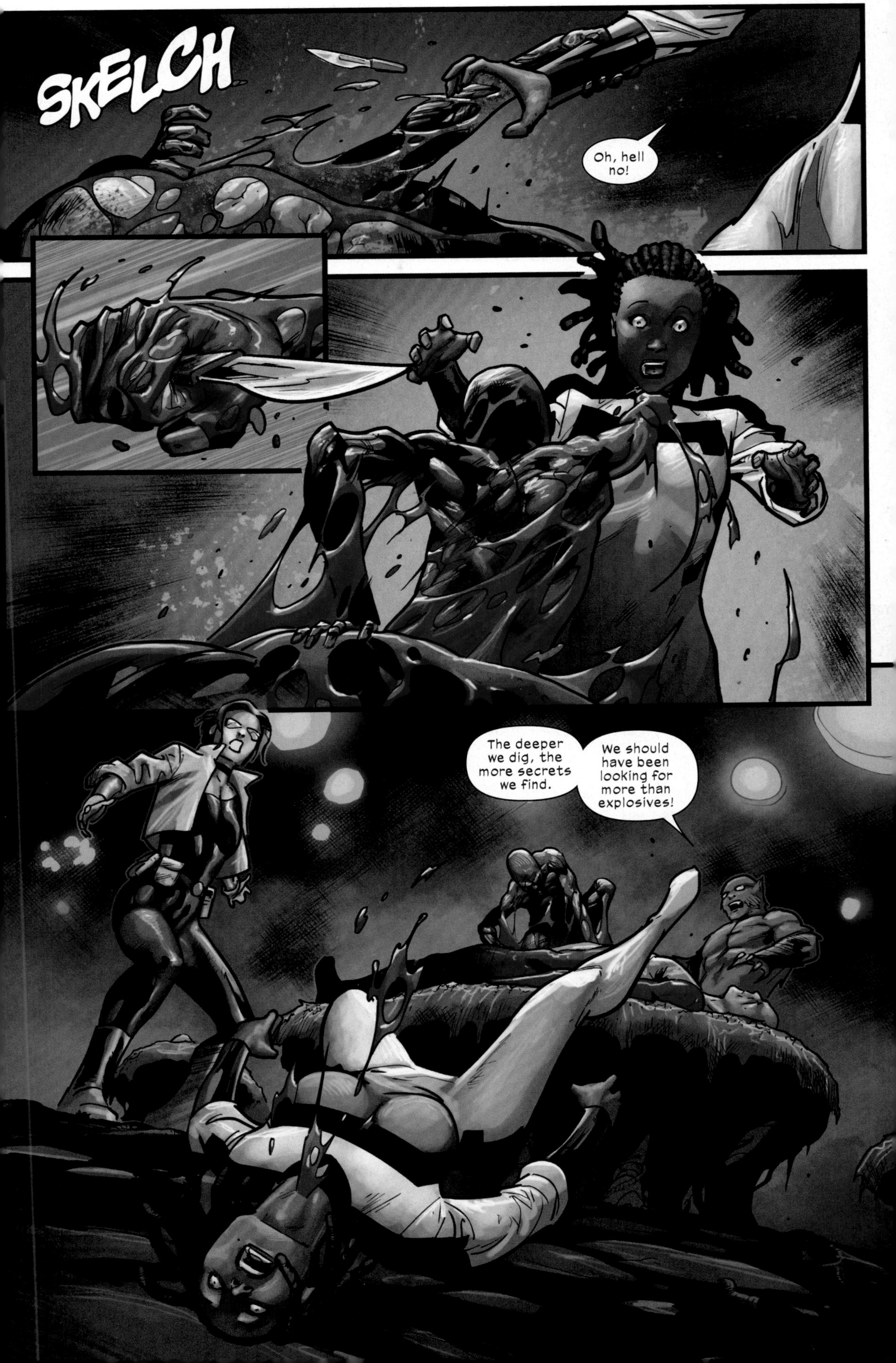
SKELCH
Oh, hell no!
The deeper we dig, the more secrets we find.
We should have been looking for more than explosives!

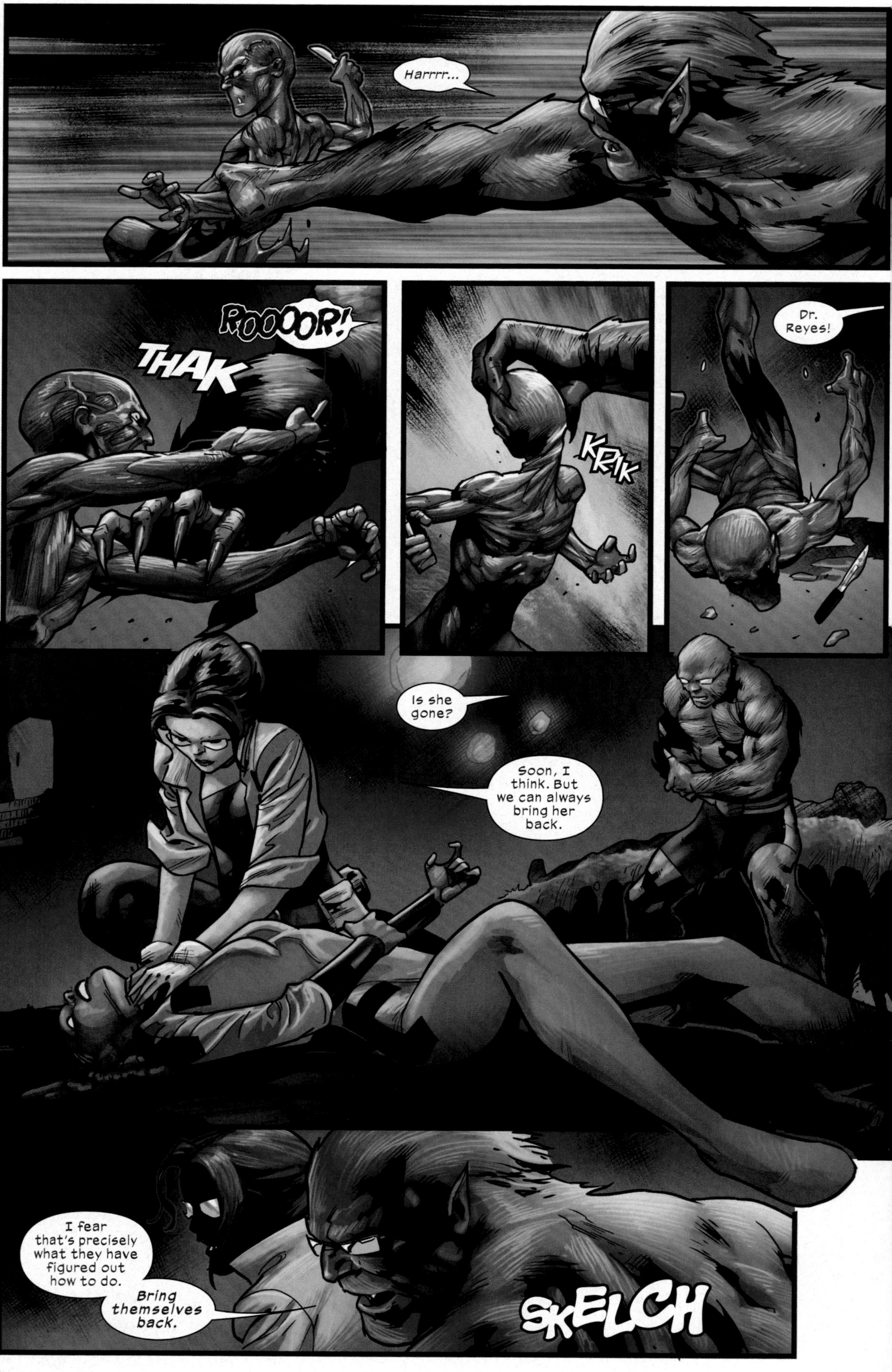
Harrrr...
ROOOOR!
THAK
KRIK
Dr. Reyes!
Is she gone?
Soon, I think. But we can always bring her back.
I fear that's precisely what they have figured out how to do.
Bring themselves back.
SKELCH

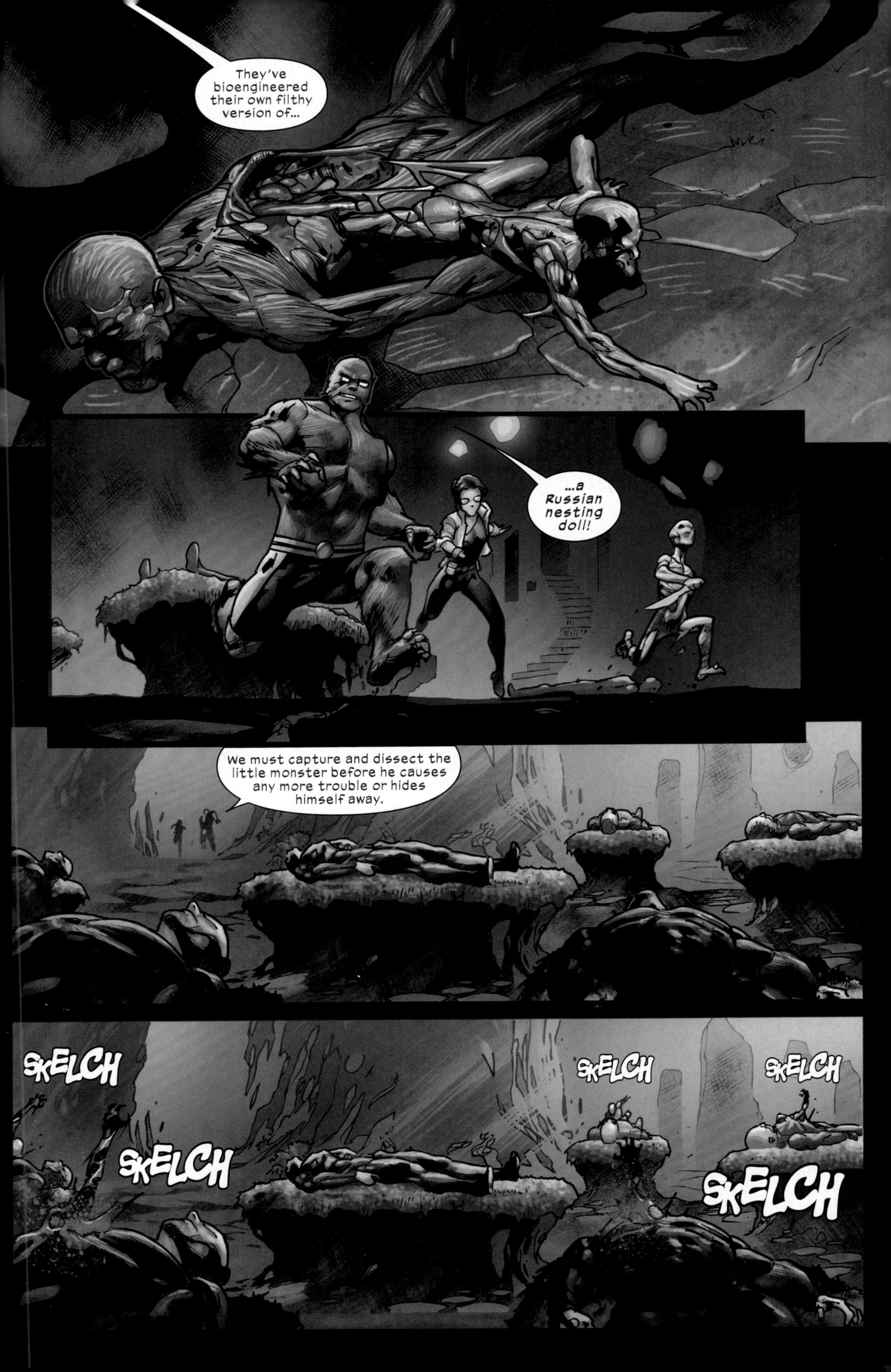
They've bioengineered their own filthy version of...
...a Russian nesting doll!
We must capture and dissect the little monster before he causes any more trouble or hides himself away.
SKELCH
SKELCH
SKELCH
SKELCH
SKELCH

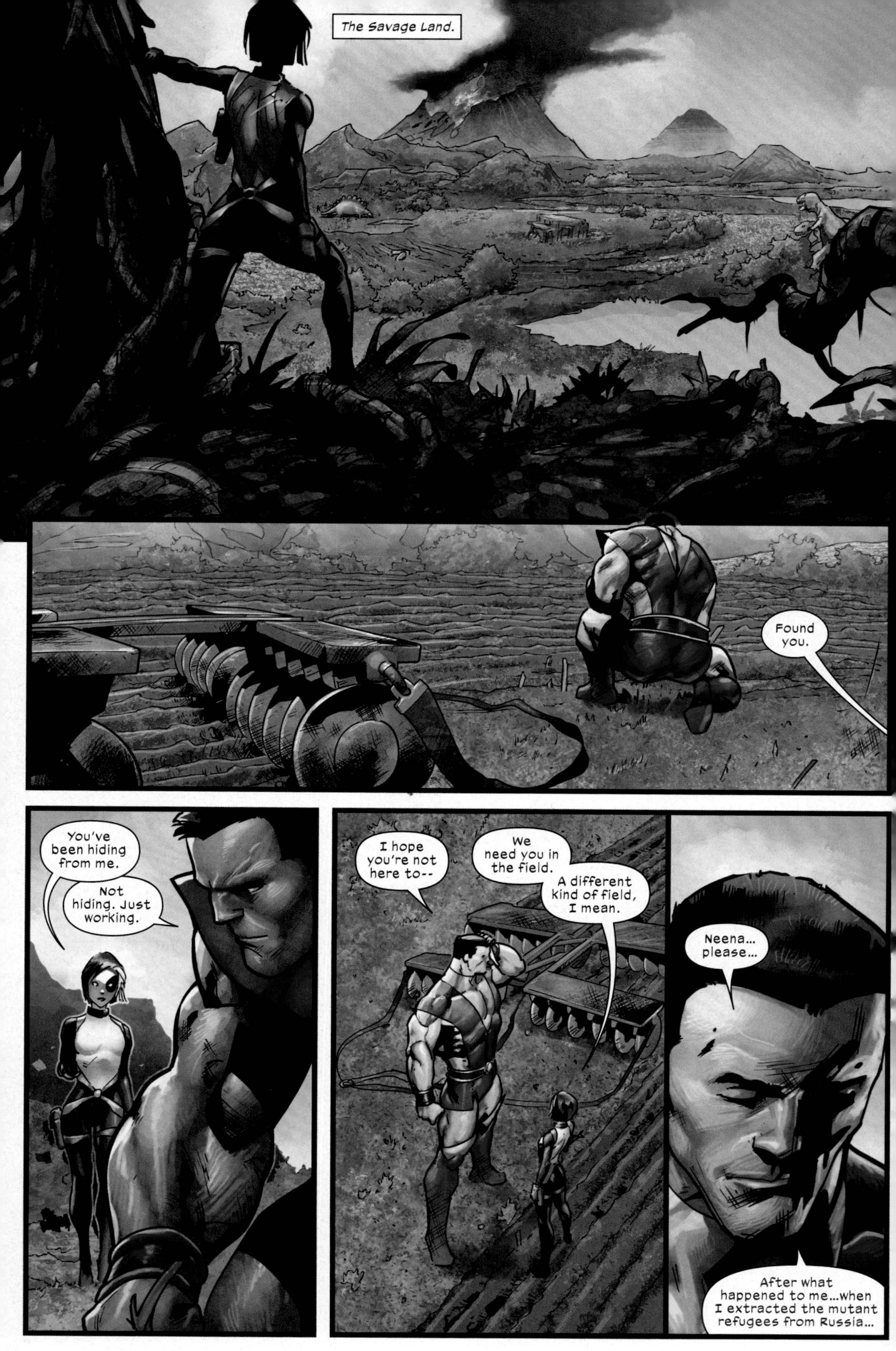
The Savage Land.
Found you.
You've been hiding from me.
Not hiding. Just working.
I hope you're not here to--
We need you in the field.
A different kind of field, I mean.
Neena... please...
After what happened to me...when I extracted the mutant refugees from Russia...

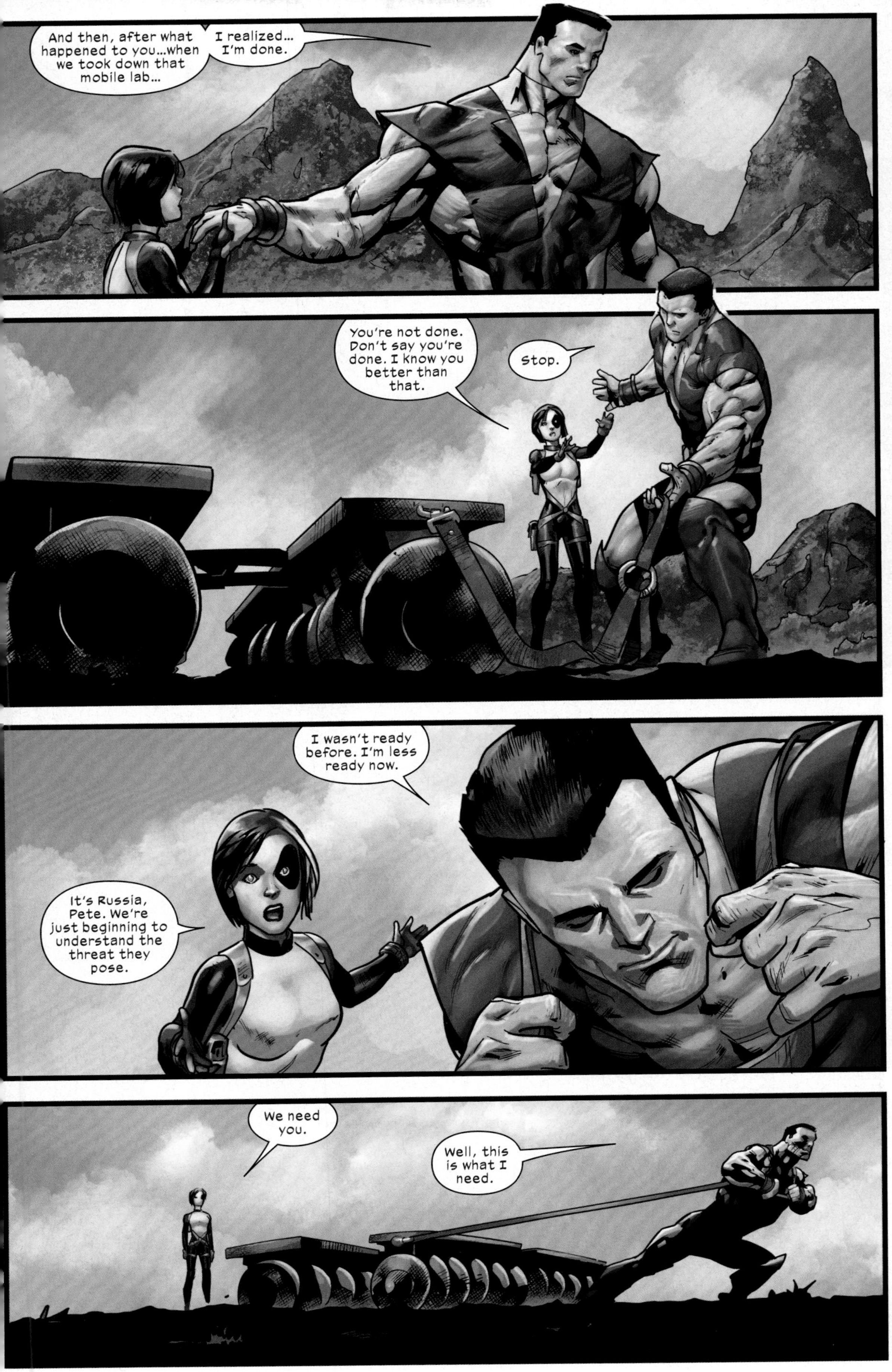
And then, after what happened to you...when we took down that mobile lab...
I realized... I'm done.
You're not done. Don't say you're done. I know you better than that.
Stop.
I wasn't ready before. I'm less ready now.
It's Russia, Pete. We're just beginning to understand the threat they pose.
We need you.
Well, this is what I need.

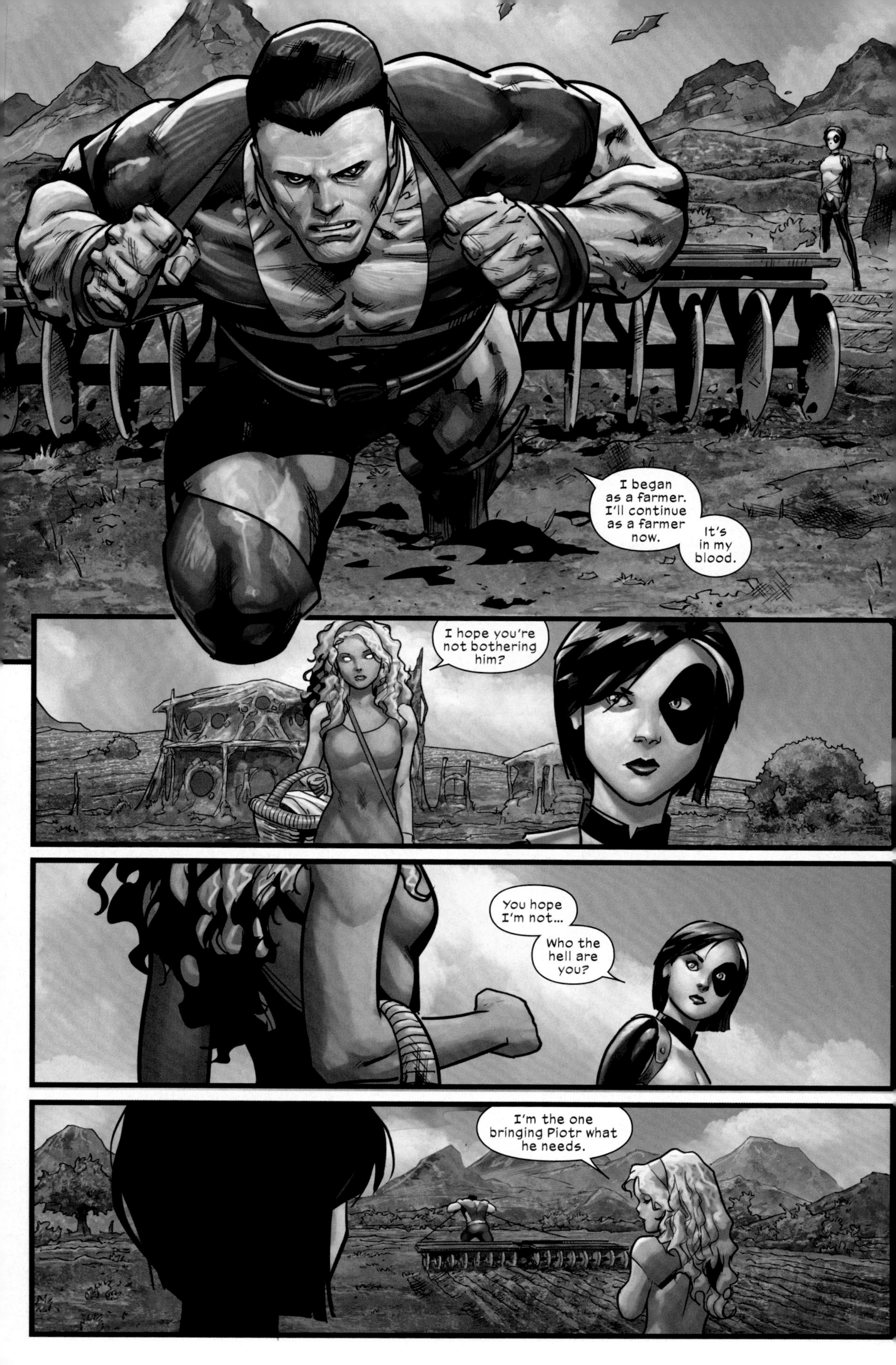
I began as a farmer. I'll continue as a farmer now.
It's in my blood.
I hope you're not bothering him?
You hope I'm not...
Who the hell are you?
I'm the one bringing Piotr what he needs.

CHAPTER 1

Drink is a writer's affliction. The need for it. The belief that it can lubricate the imagination or help an overactive mind finally find sleep. I suppose alcoholism is the only occupational hazard of my trade besides bleary eyes, a bad back, the occasional paper cut. Madness does tend to find us.

When I started making money off my writing, I didn't really know what to do with it. I don't care for luxurious clothes or expensive cars or international travel. I only wish to be home with my work. I've bought a few paintings, some first-edition novels, but wine is my investment of choice.

My cellar is rather elaborate and a point of guilty pride. Among its many treasures are: a 1945 Château Mouton Rothschild, with its hints of coffee and chocolate and black currants. The powerfully complex and nuanced 1921 Château d'Yquem. And a 1982 Pichon Longueville Comtesse de Lalande, a Bourdeaux that offers an unmatched velvety sweetness.

And it was here, in the cellar, that he found me.

Mutton was on the menu for dinner, and I went hunting for a leathery pinot noir to pair with it. The scrape of his boot startled me. He filled the doorway so that only a little light filtered through. His hair was more like the coarse, dark fur of the bear that he resembled. He wore a costume of armor. When he spoke, his voice was subterranean in its bass.

To be continued...

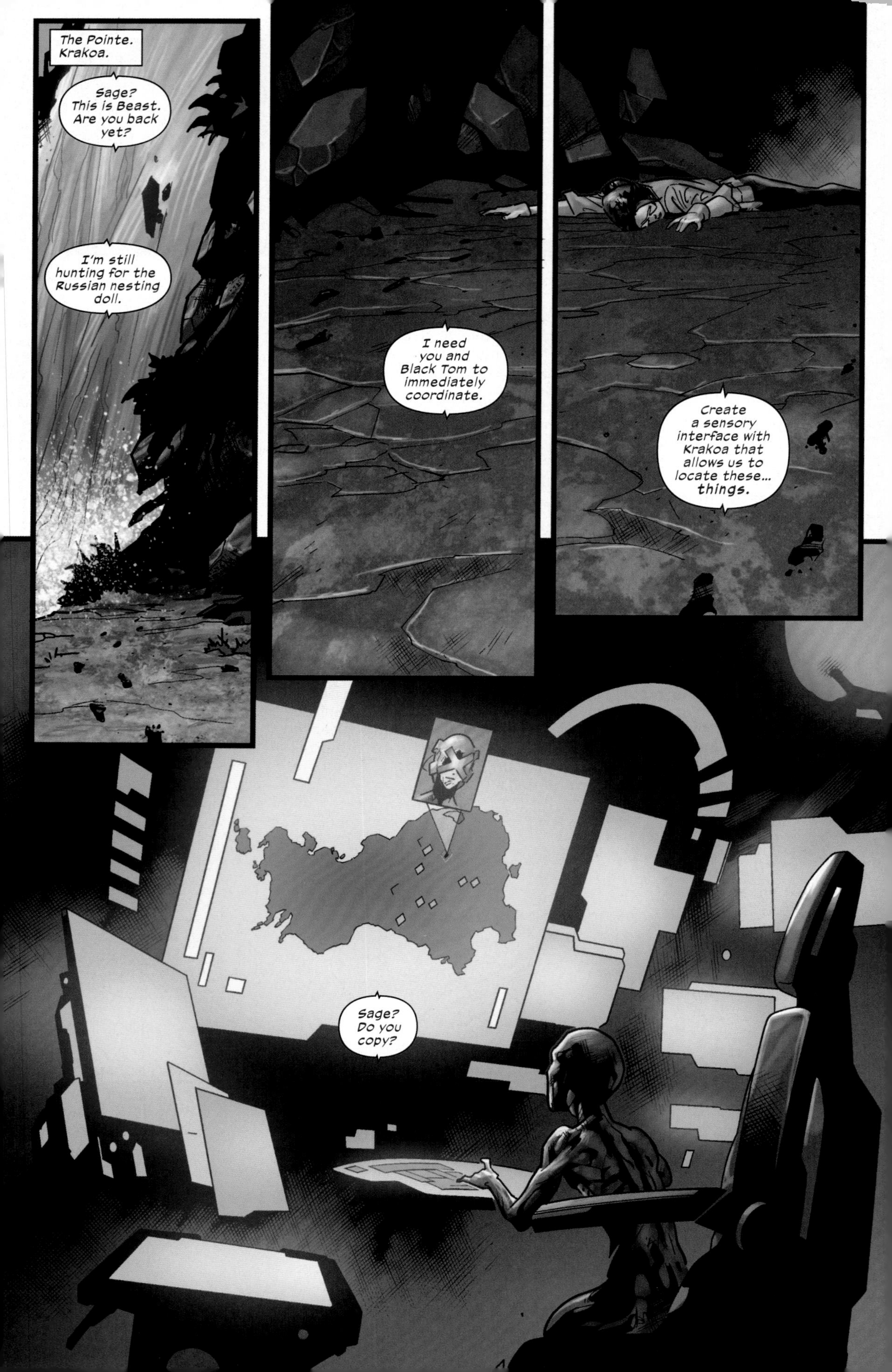
The Pointe. Krakoa.
Sage? This is Beast. Are you back yet?
I'm still hunting for the Russian nesting doll.
I need you and Black Tom to immediately coordinate.
Create a sensory interface with Krakoa that allows us to locate these... **things.**
Sage? Do you copy?

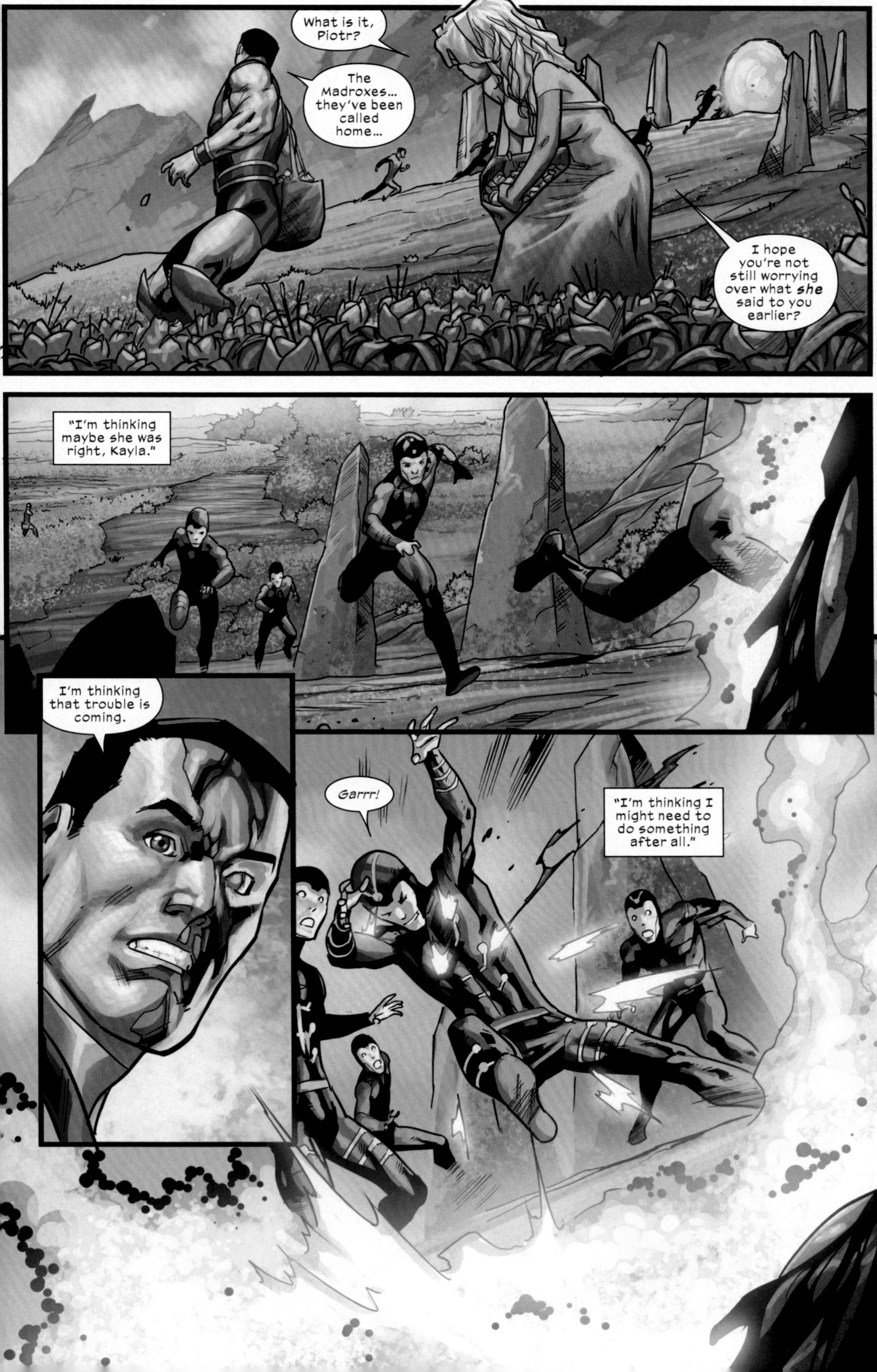

What is it, Piotr?
The Madroxes... they've been called home...
I hope you're not still worrying over what *she* said to you earlier?
"I'm thinking maybe she was right, Kayla."
I'm thinking that trouble is coming.
Garrr!
"I'm thinking I might need to do something after all."

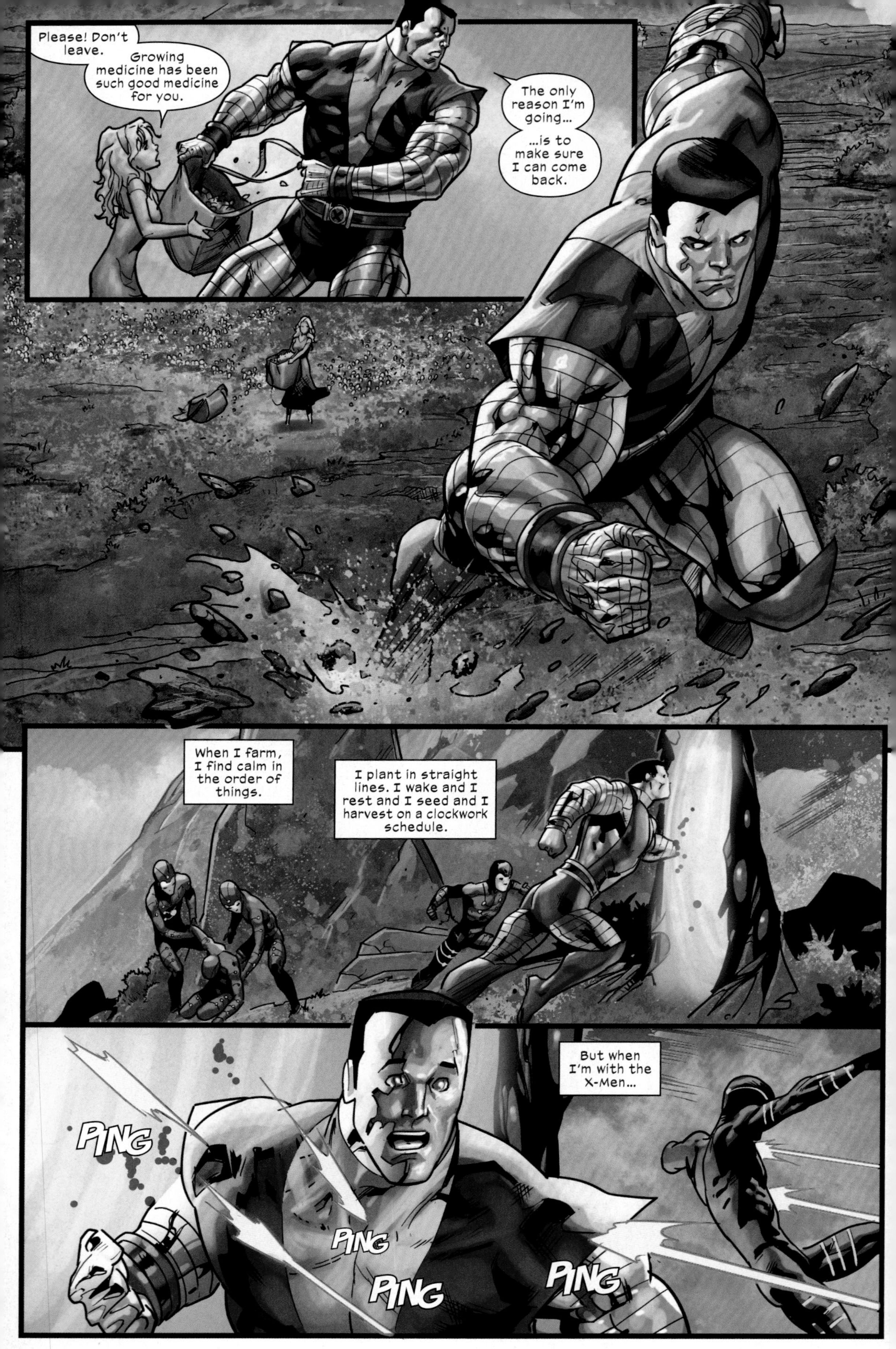
Please! Don't leave.
Growing medicine has been such good medicine for you.
The only reason I'm going...
...is to make sure I can come back.
When I farm, I find calm in the order of things.
I plant in straight lines. I wake and I rest and I seed and I harvest on a clockwork schedule.
But when I'm with the X-Men...
PING
PING
PING
PING

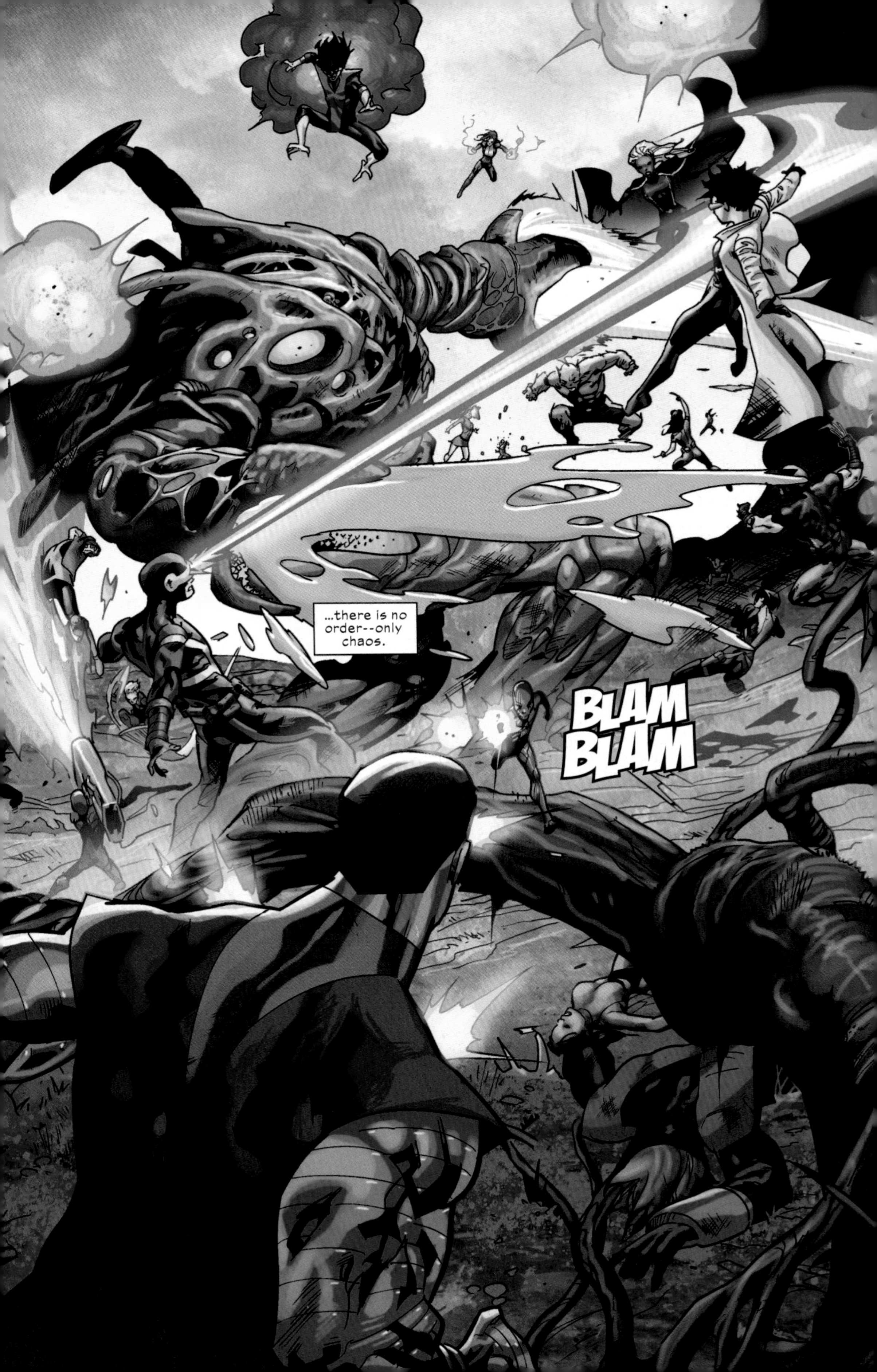
...there is no order--only chaos.
BLAM BLAM

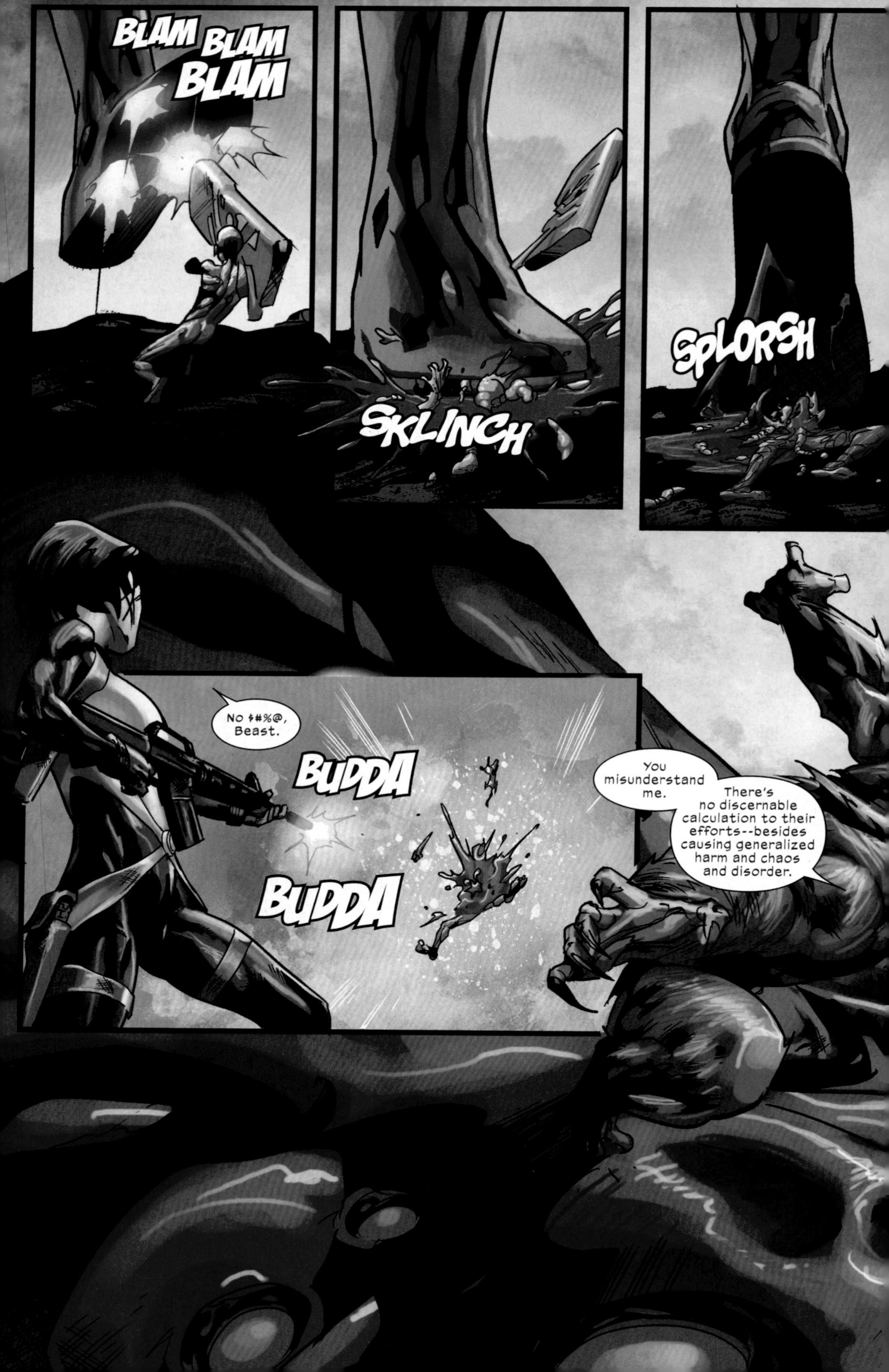
BLAM BLAM
BLAM
SKLINCH
SPLORSH
No $#%@, Beast.
BUDDA
BUDDA
You misunderstand me.
There's no discernable calculation to their efforts--besides causing generalized harm and chaos and disorder.

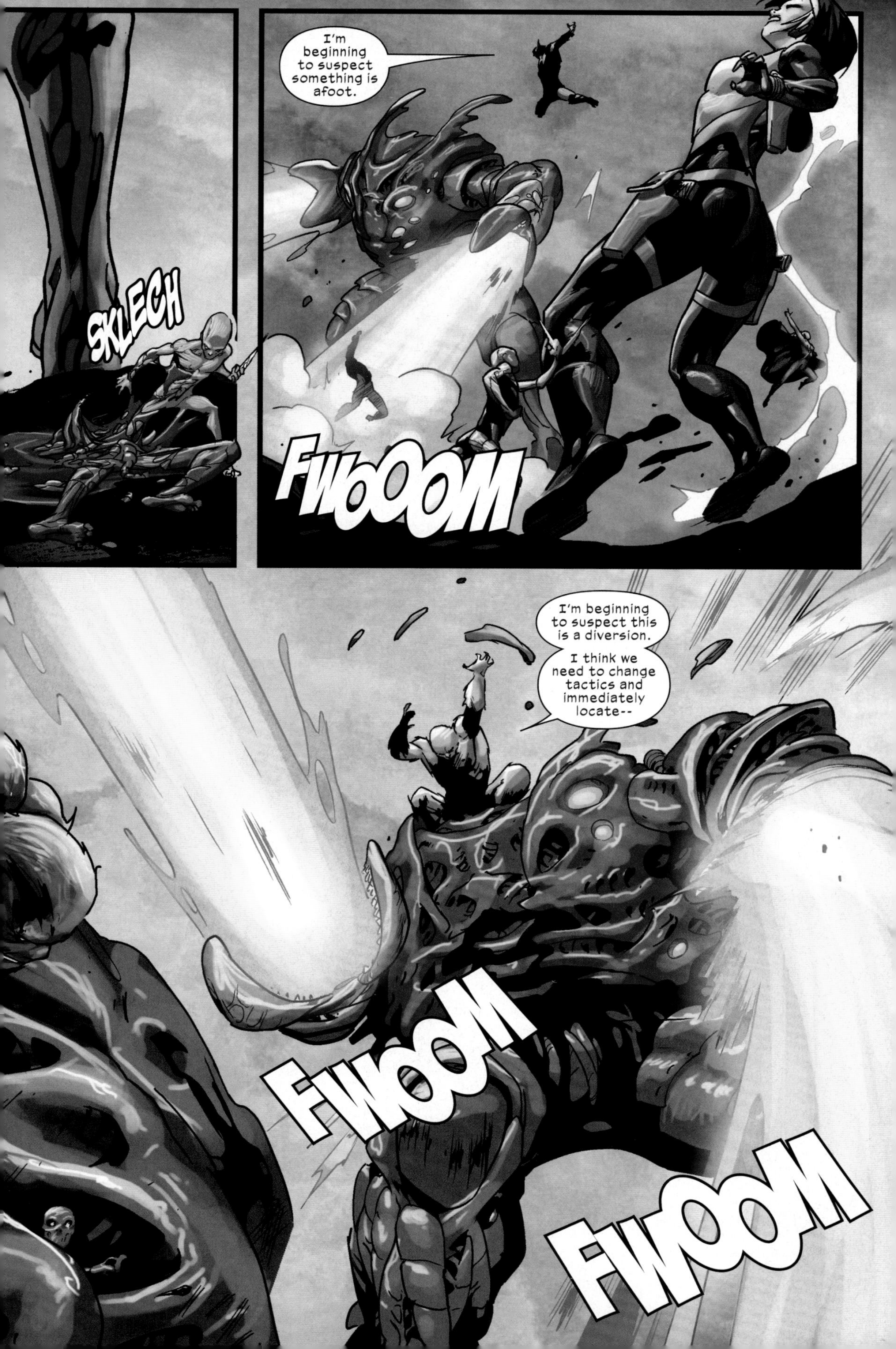
SKLECH
I'm beginning to suspect something is afoot.
FWOOOM
I'm beginning to suspect this is a diversion.
I think we need to change tactics and immediately locate--
FWOOM
FWOOM

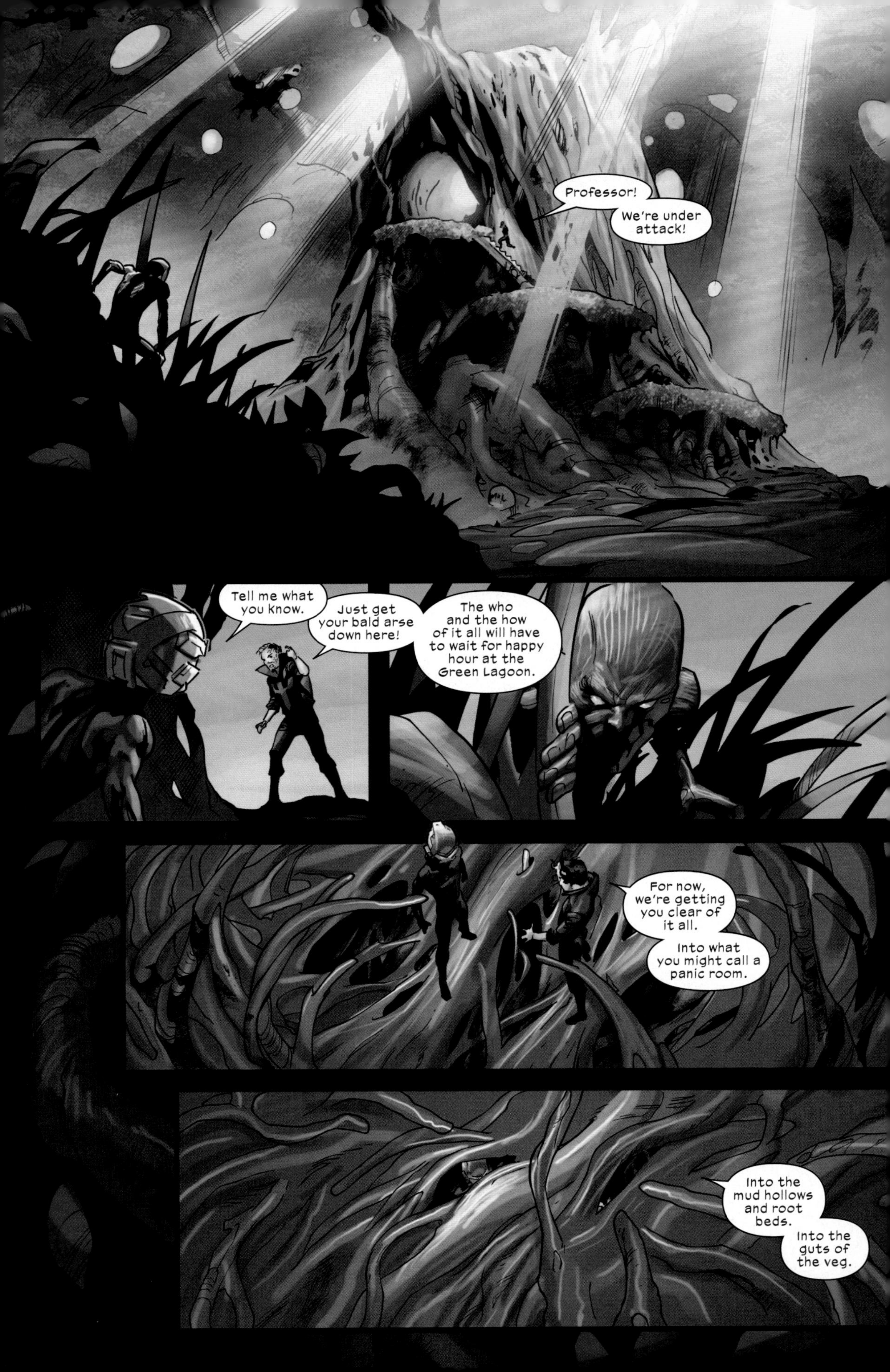

Professor!
We're under attack!
Tell me what you know.
Just get your bald arse down here!
The who and the how of it all will have to wait for happy hour at the Green Lagoon.
For now, we're getting you clear of it all.
Into what you might call a panic room.
Into the mud hollows and root beds.
Into the guts of the veg.

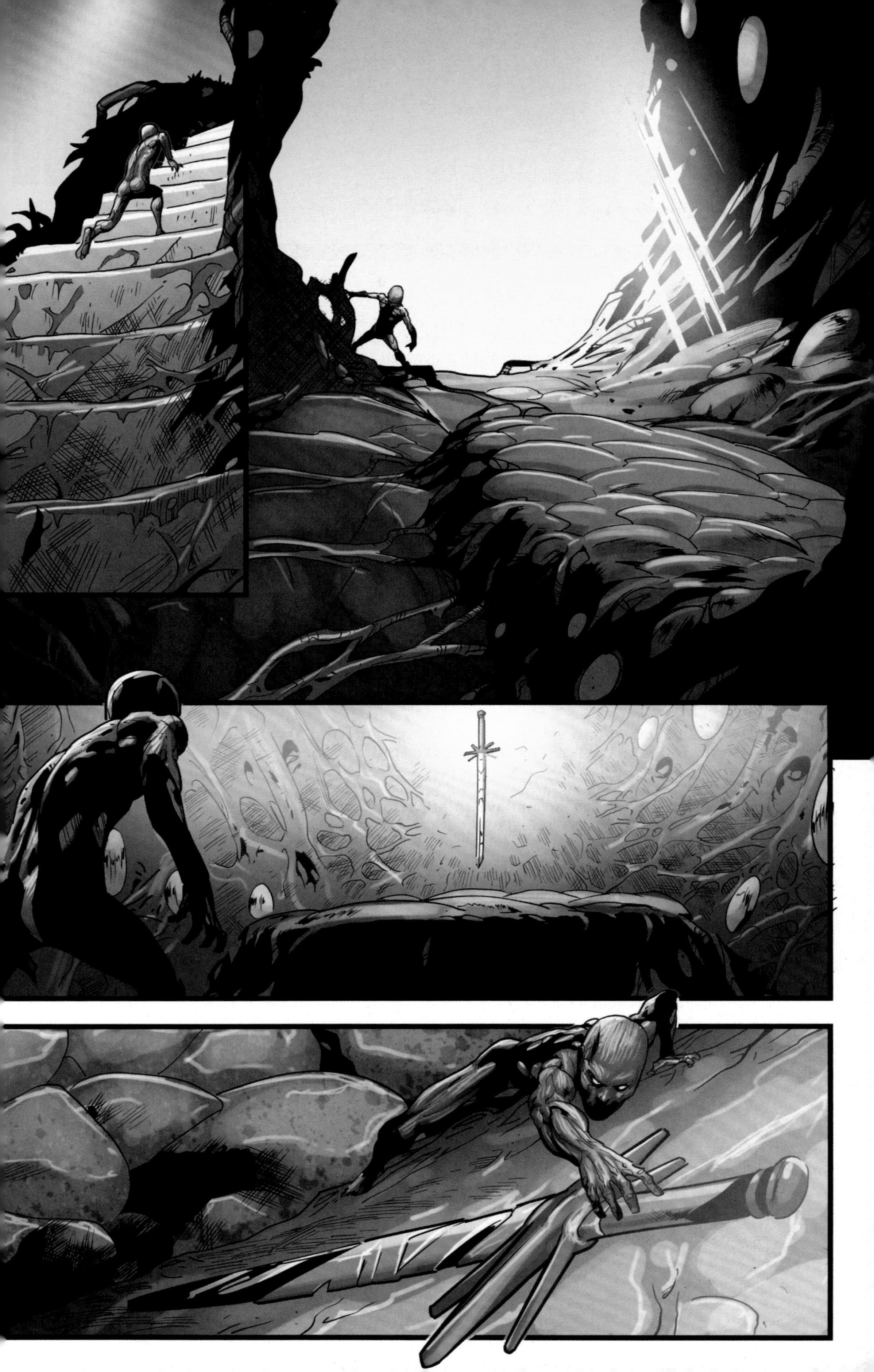

CHAPTER 2

He said that he admired my writing very much. Russia has had many greats, he said. Dostoevsky. Tolstoy. Turgenev. Chekov. "But you," he said. "You are the most *powerful*."

But what had I done with that power? Won some prizes? Made a few people weep in their armchairs? Animate some dinnertime conversations? "You are capable of so much more."

But I don't want for much, I told him. I only want a quiet life. I only want to do my best to illuminate the human condition.

"You must recognize your superiority and use it to celebrate the superiority of your country."

"I am not," I said, stammering some, as he approached. "We are *not* superior."

He swung out an arm then, and I flinched. Though it was clear he did not mean to strike me, something came rolling off him, like a big block of energy. The air thrummed. And I heard a great rustling tear. By the time I had recovered my senses, I saw that every wine bottle was suddenly bare.

"No," I said. "No!" And I fell to my knees, hurrying through the shed labels, trying desperately to match them with their bottles.

"You see," he said. "You do believe in superiority after all." He held out his giant hand to me. "Now come."

летописец

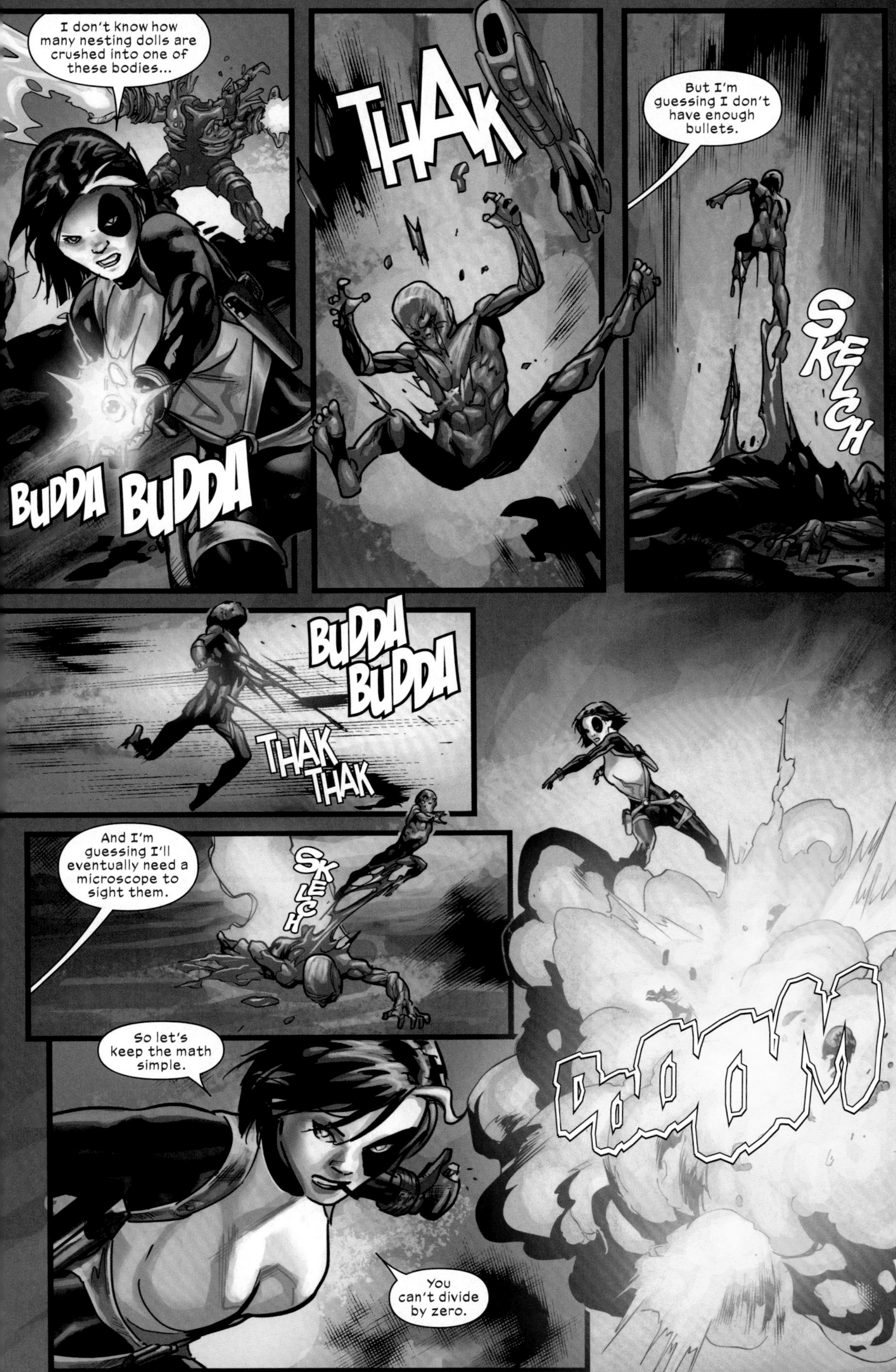
I don't know how many nesting dolls are crushed into one of these bodies...
BUDDA BUDDA
THAK
But I'm guessing I don't have enough bullets.
SKELCH
BUDDA BUDDA
THAK THAK
And I'm guessing I'll eventually need a microscope to sight them.
SKELCH
So let's keep the math simple.
You can't divide by zero.
DOOOM

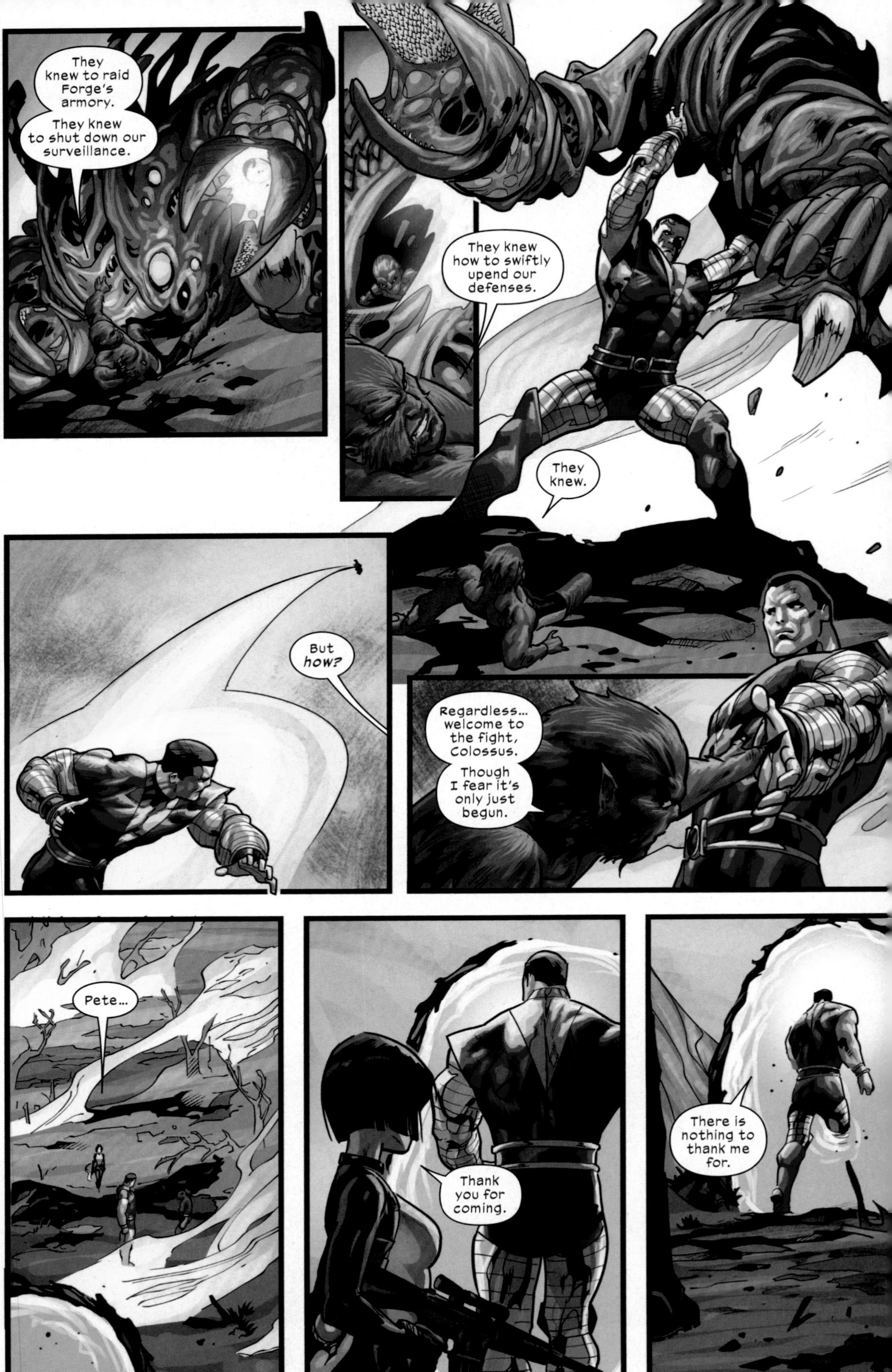
They knew to raid Forge's armory.
They knew to shut down our surveillance.
They knew how to swiftly upend our defenses.
They knew.
But *how?*
Regardless... welcome to the fight, Colossus.
Though I fear it's only just begun.
Pete...
Thank you for coming.
There is nothing to thank me for.

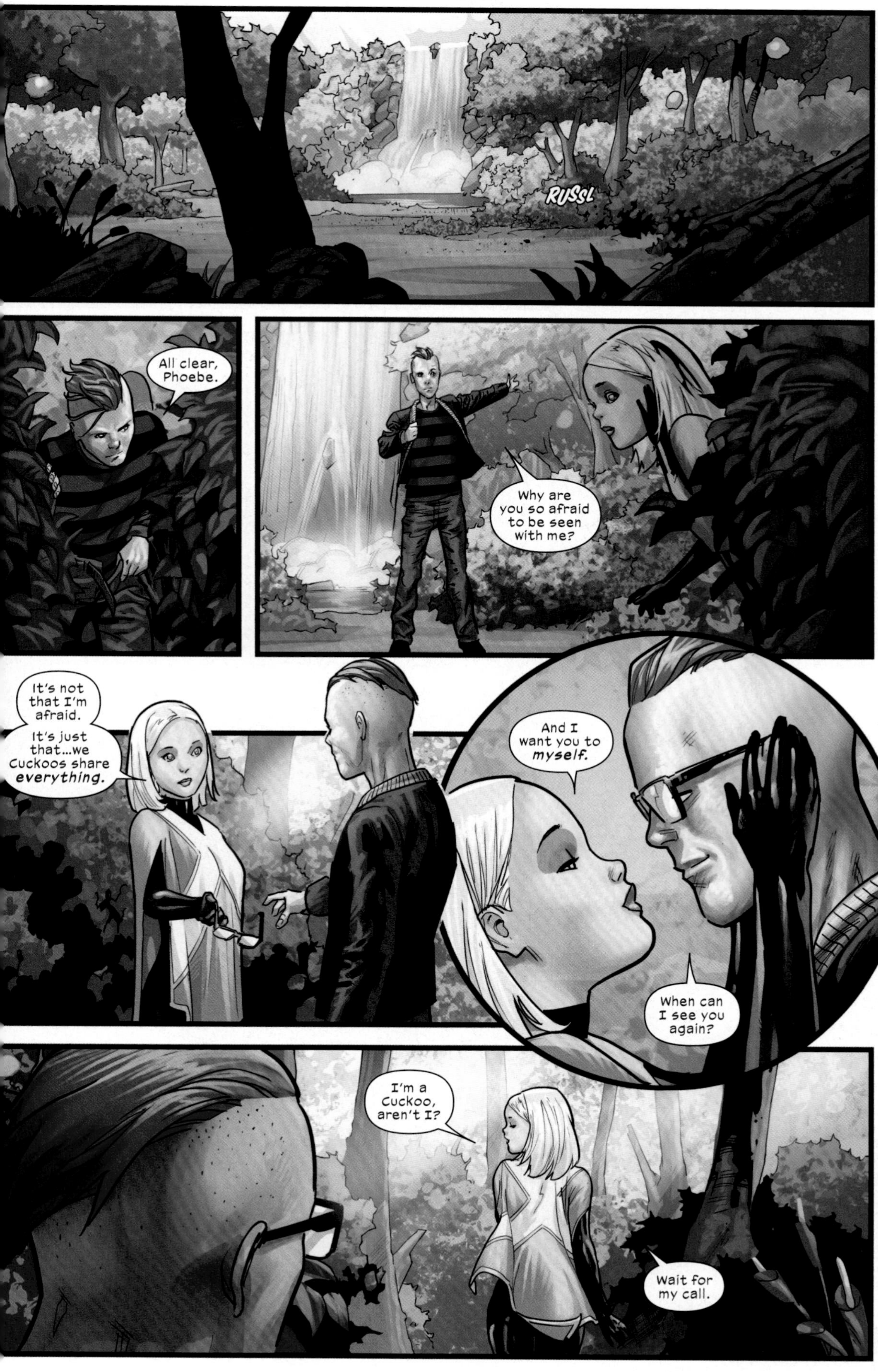
RUSSL
All clear, Phoebe.
Why are you so afraid to be seen with me?
It's not that I'm afraid.
It's just that...we Cuckoos share *everything.*
And I want you to *myself.*
When can I see you again?
I'm a Cuckoo, aren't I?
Wait for my call.

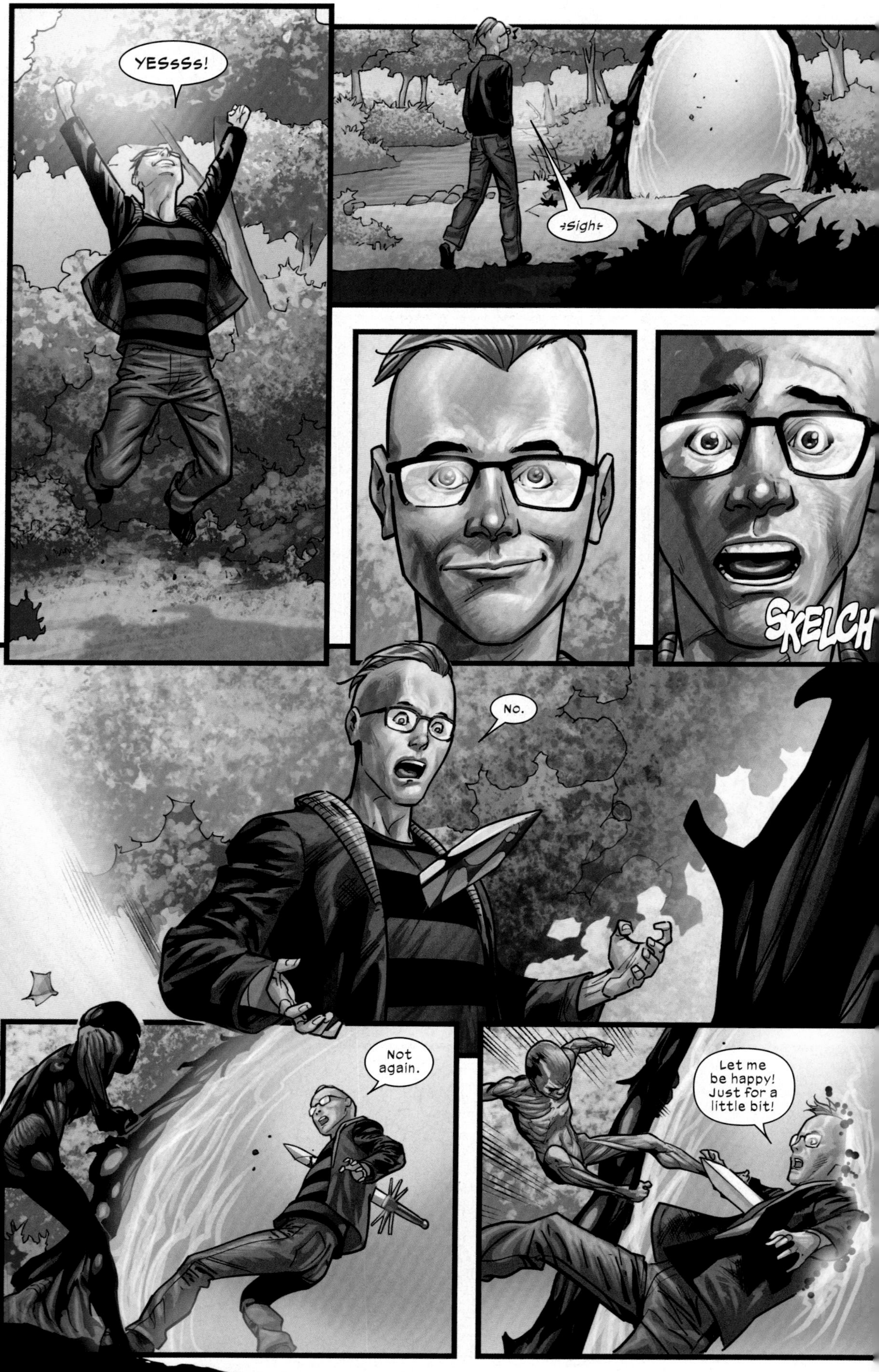
YESSSs!
-sigh-
SKELCH
No.
Not again.
Let me be happy! Just for a little bit!

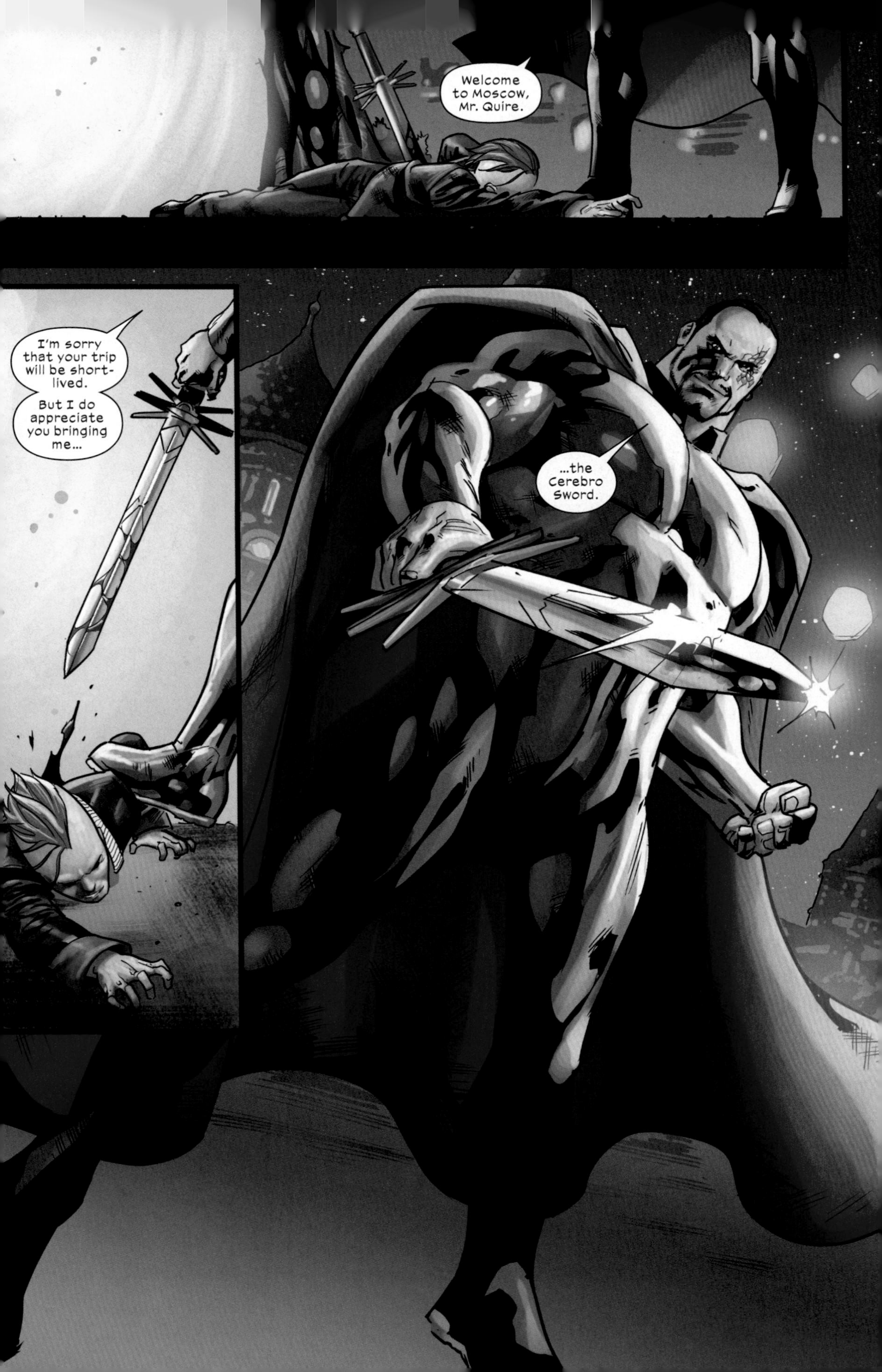
Welcome to Moscow, Mr. Quire.
I'm sorry that your trip will be short-lived.
But I do appreciate you bringing me...
...the Cerebro Sword.

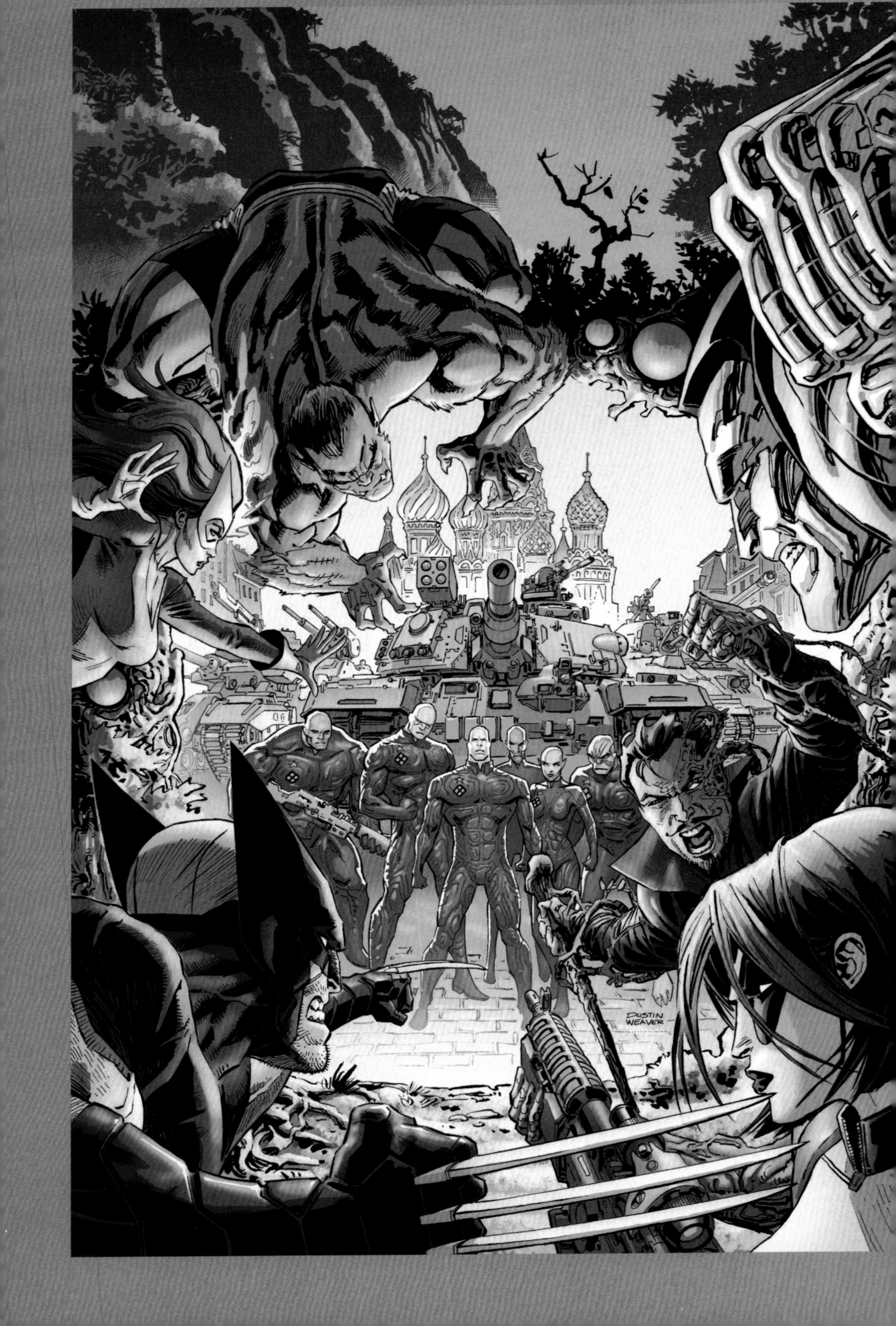
DUSTIN
WEAVER

The Cerebro Sword

12

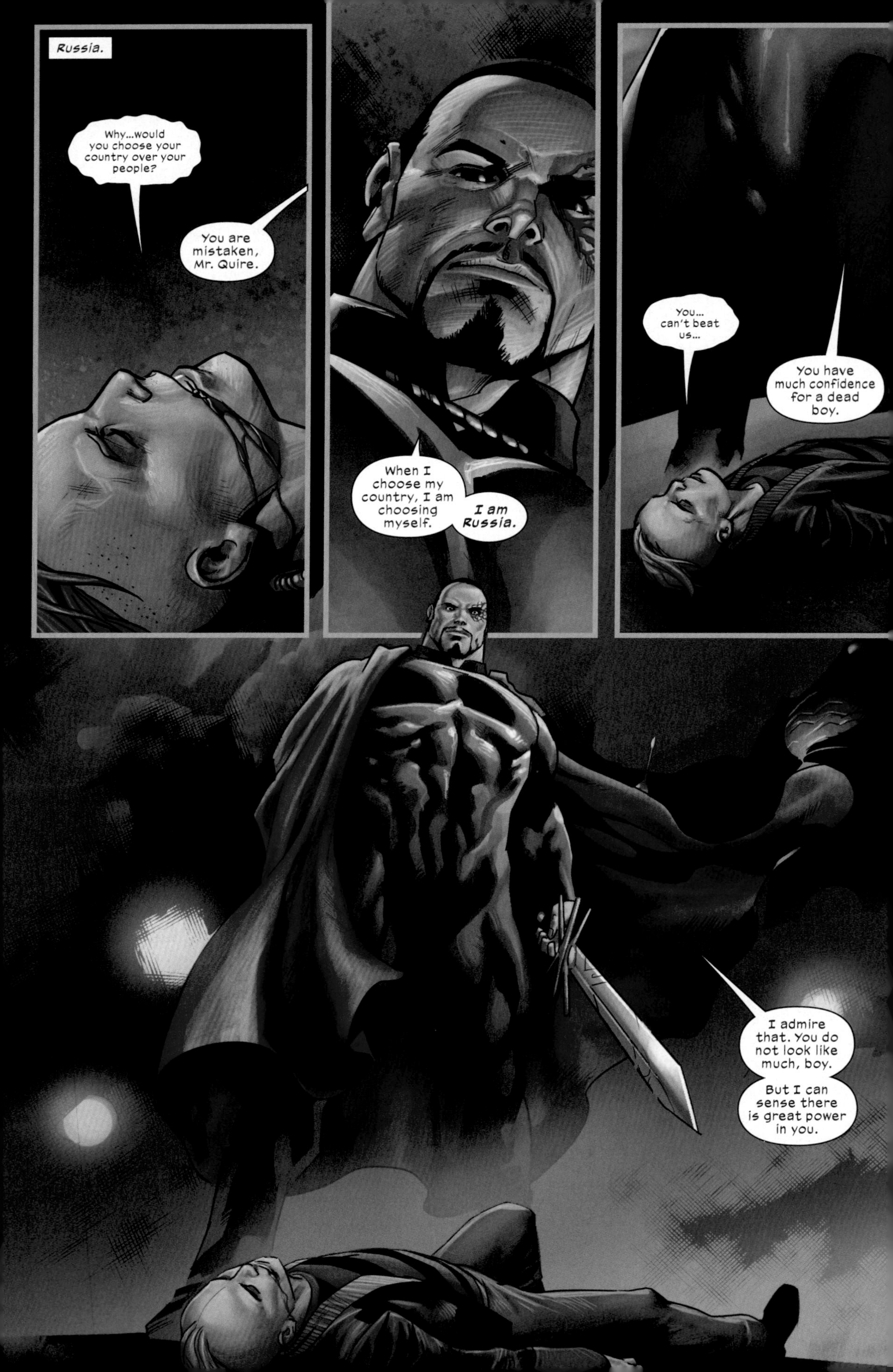
Russia.
Why...would you choose your country over your people?
You are mistaken, Mr. Quire.
When I choose my country, I am choosing myself.
I am Russia.
You... can't beat us...
You have much confidence for a dead boy.
I admire that. You do not look like much, boy.
But I can sense there is great power in you.

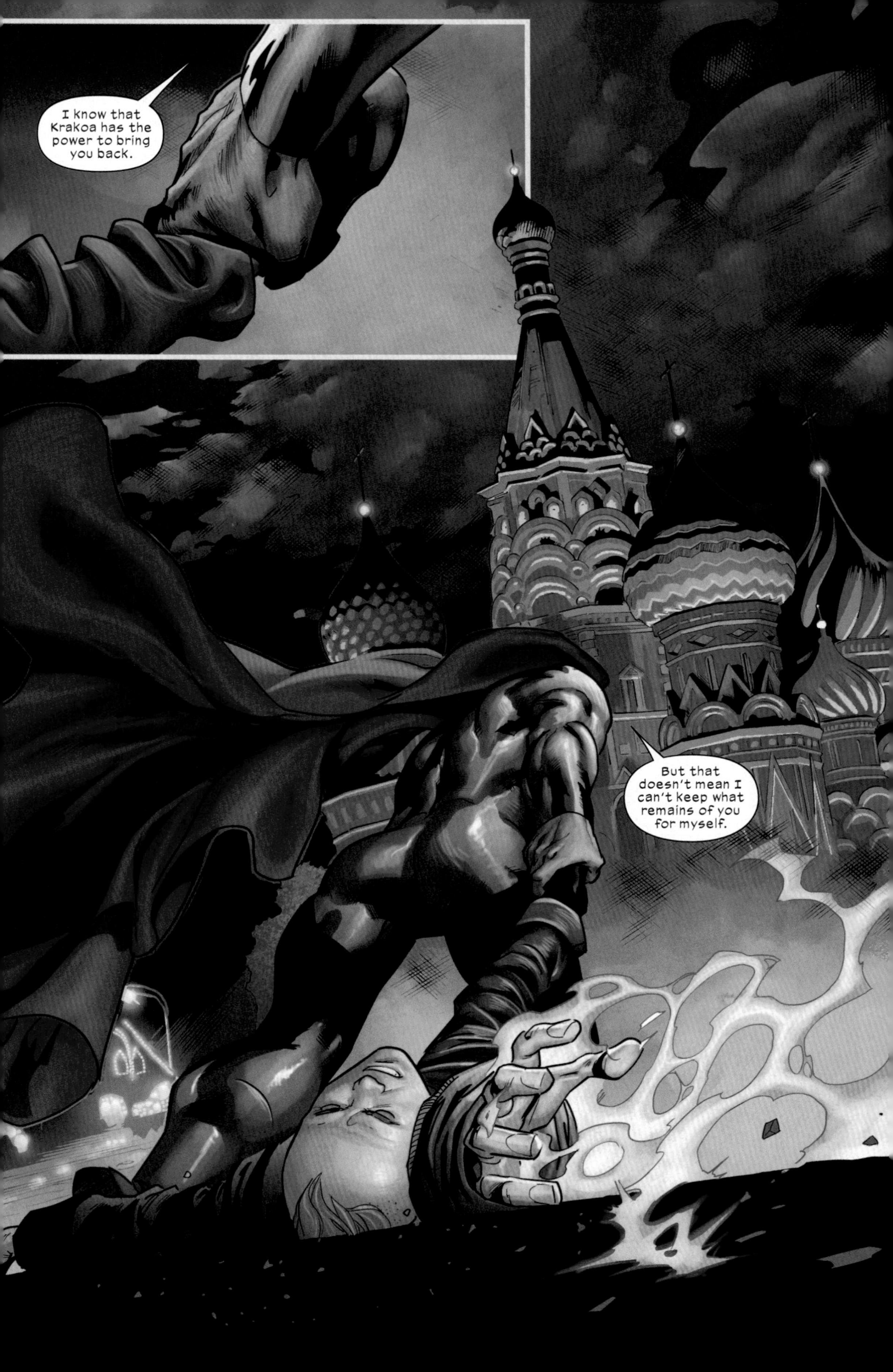
I know that Krakoa has the power to bring you back.
But that doesn't mean I can't keep what remains of you for myself.

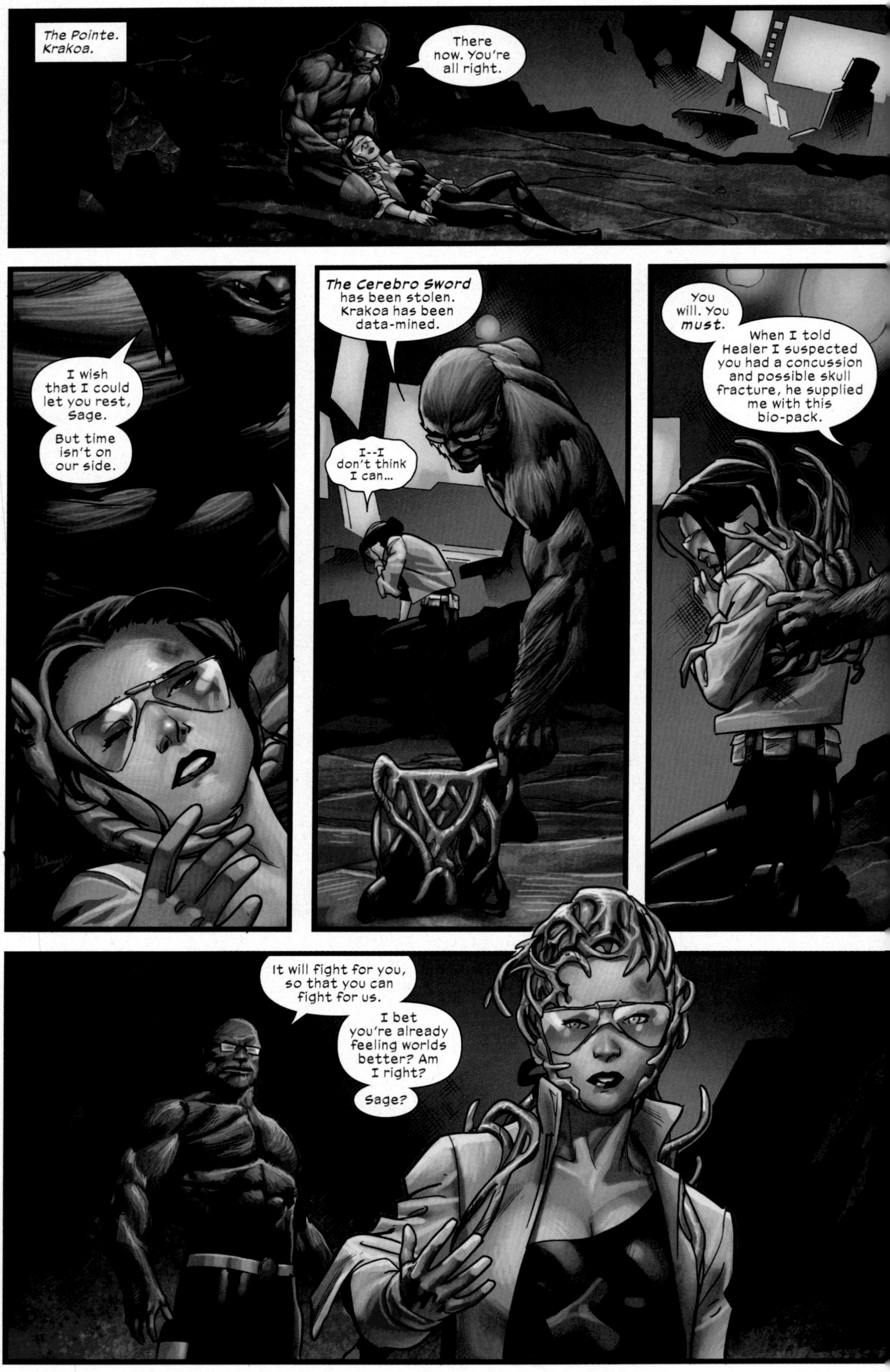
The Pointe.
Krakoa.
There now. You're all right.
I wish that I could let you rest, Sage.
But time isn't on our side.
The Cerebro Sword has been stolen. Krakoa has been data-mined.
I--I don't think I can...
You will. You must.
When I told Healer I suspected you had a concussion and possible skull fracture, he supplied me with this bio-pack.
It will fight for you, so that you can fight for us.
I bet you're already feeling worlds better? Am I right?
Sage?

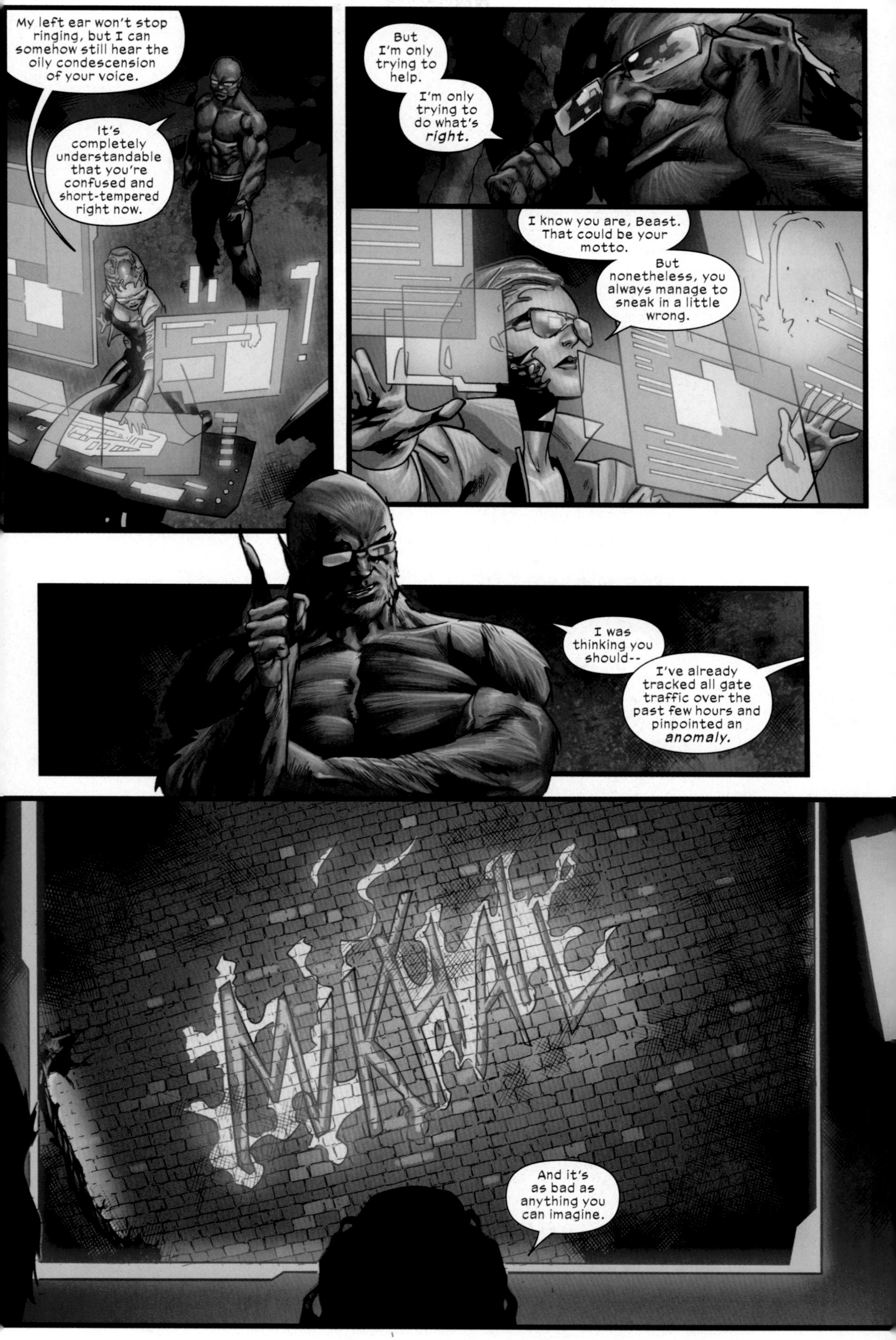
My left ear won't stop ringing, but I can somehow still hear the oily condescension of your voice.
It's completely understandable that you're confused and short-tempered right now.
But I'm only trying to help.
I'm only trying to do what's *right.*
I know you are, Beast. That could be your motto.
But nonetheless, you always manage to sneak in a little wrong.
I was thinking you should--
I've already tracked all gate traffic over the past few hours and pinpointed an *anomaly.*
MIKHAIL
And it's as bad as anything you can imagine.

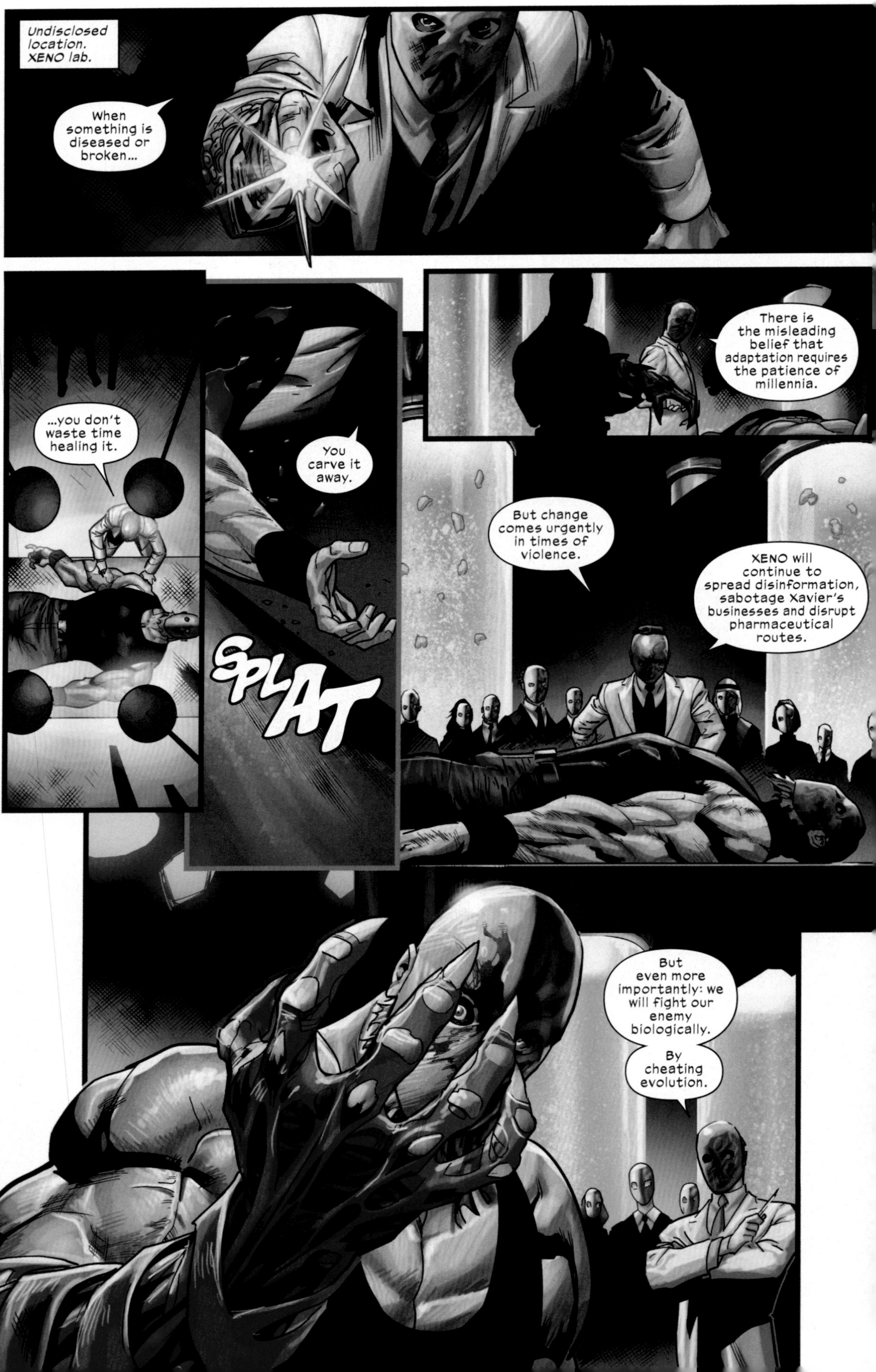
Undisclosed location. XENO lab.
When something is diseased or broken...
...you don't waste time healing it.
You carve it away.
SPLAT
There is the misleading belief that adaptation requires the patience of millennia.
But change comes urgently in times of violence.
XENO will continue to spread disinformation, sabotage Xavier's businesses and disrupt pharmaceutical routes.
But even more importantly: we will fight our enemy biologically.
By cheating evolution.

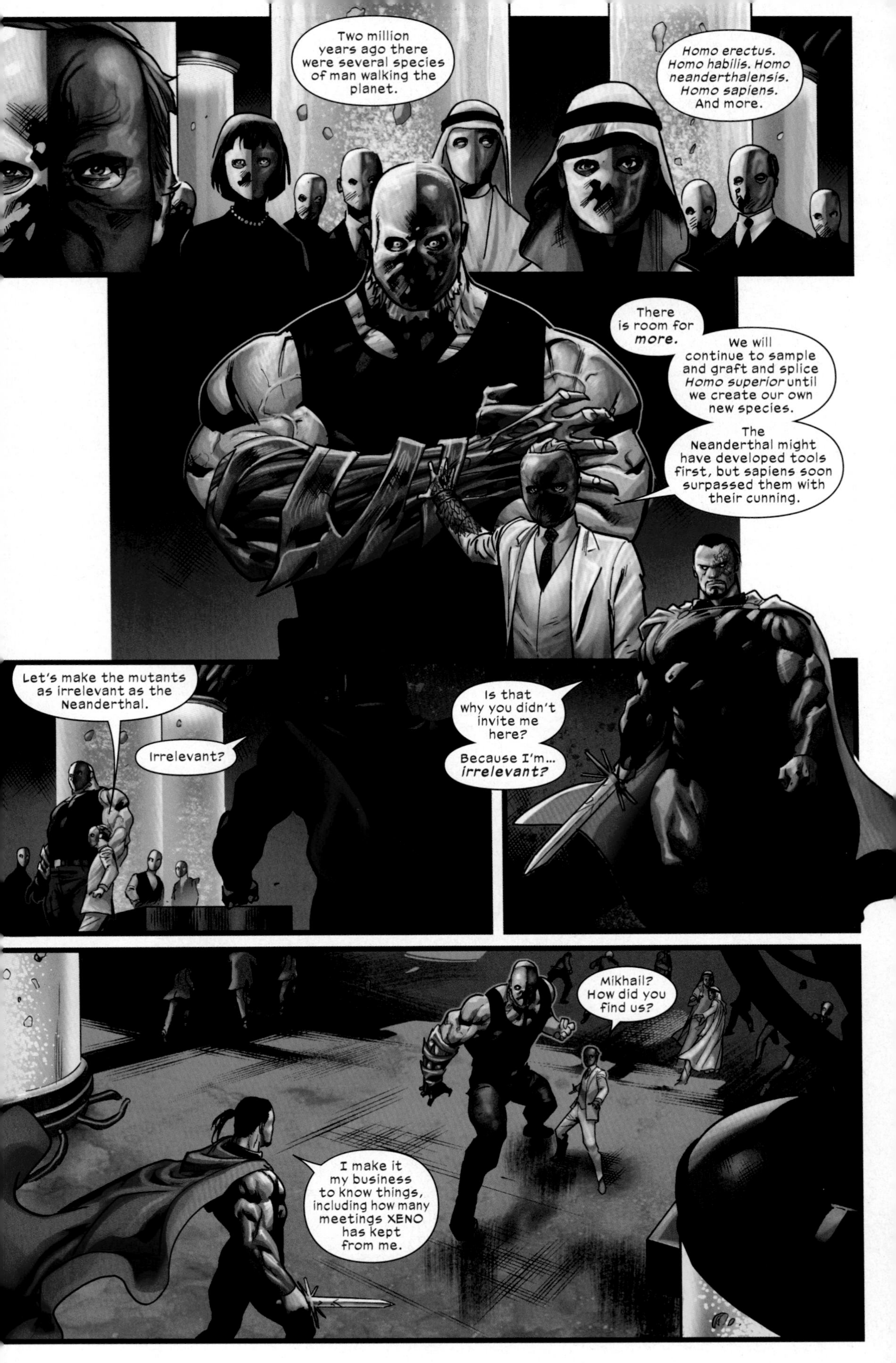
Two million years ago there were several species of man walking the planet.
Homo erectus. Homo habilis. Homo neanderthalensis. Homo sapiens. And more.
There is room for *more.*
We will continue to sample and graft and splice *Homo superior* until we create our own new species.
The Neanderthal might have developed tools first, but sapiens soon surpassed them with their cunning.
Let's make the mutants as irrelevant as the Neanderthal.
Irrelevant?
Is that why you didn't invite me here?
Because I'm... *irrelevant?*
Mikhail? How did you find us?
I make it my business to know things, including how many meetings XENO has kept from me.

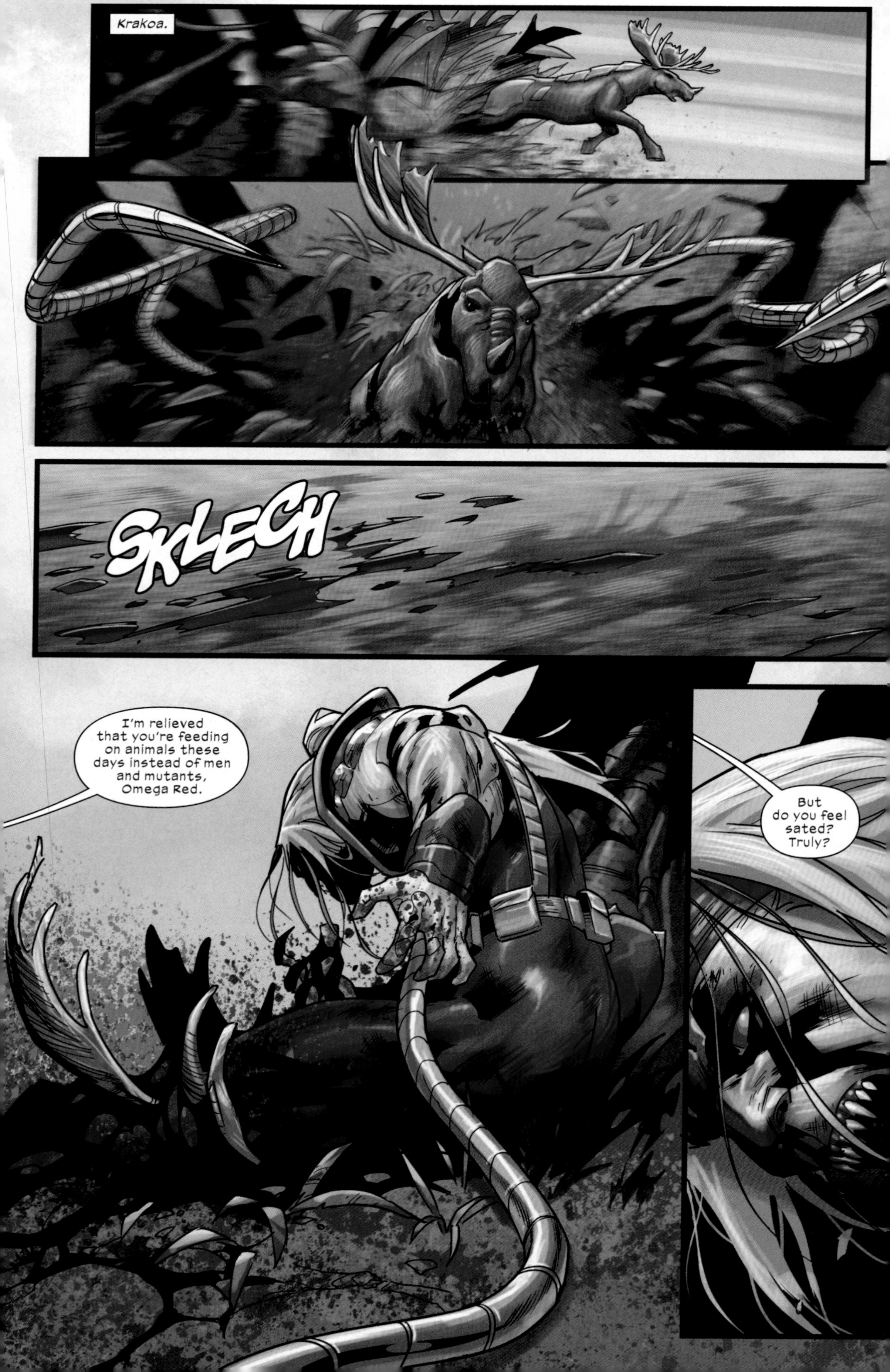
Krakoa.
SKLECH
I'm relieved that you're feeding on animals these days instead of men and mutants, Omega Red.
But do you feel sated? Truly?

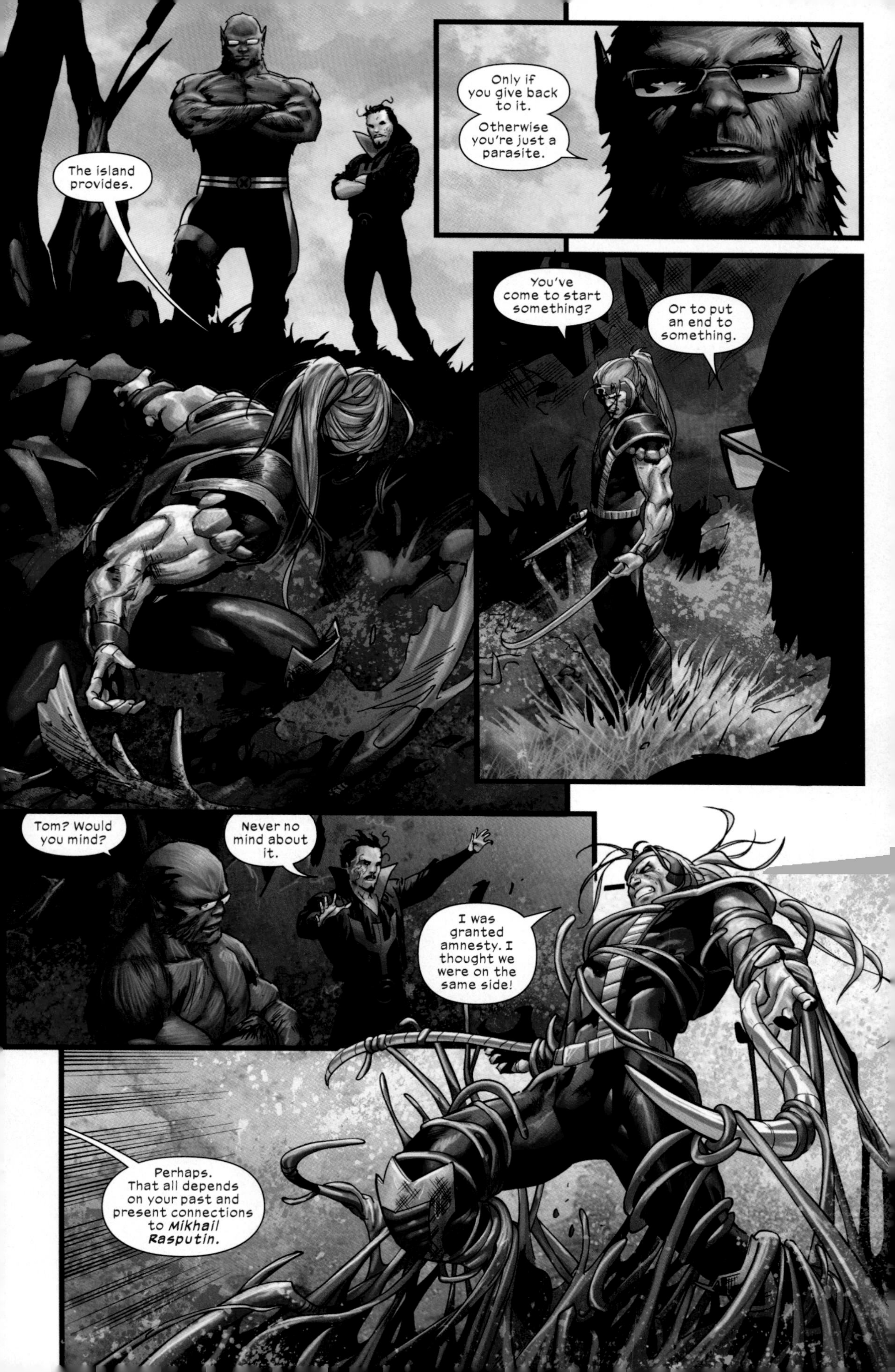
The island provides.
Only if you give back to it.
Otherwise you're just a parasite.
You've come to start something?
Or to put an end to something.
Tom? Would you mind?
Never no mind about it.
I was granted amnesty. I thought we were on the same side!
Perhaps. That all depends on your past and present connections to *Mikhail Rasputin*.

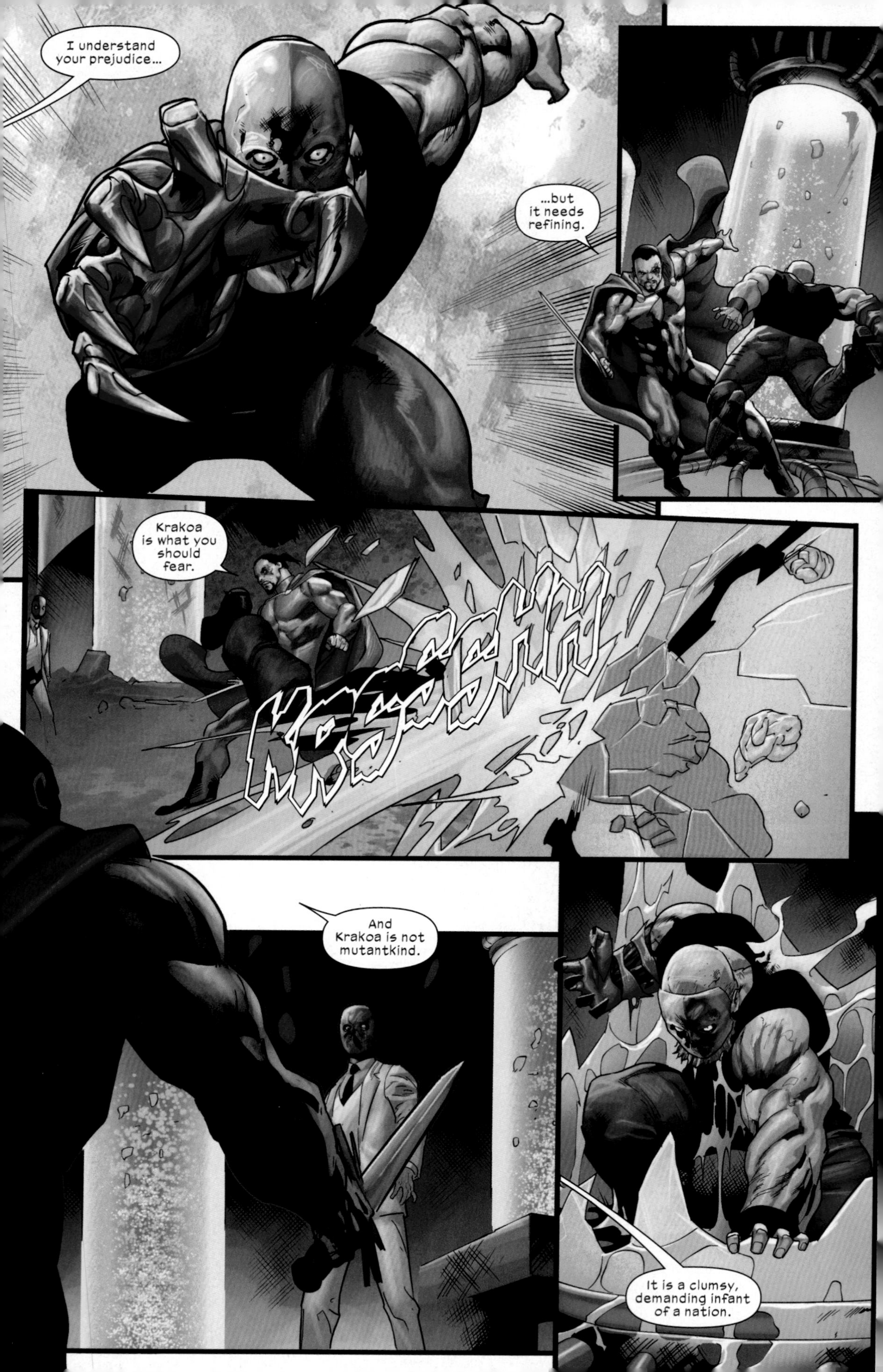
I understand your prejudice...
...but it needs refining.
Krakoa is what you should fear.
KRSSSHH
And Krakoa is not mutantkind.
It is a clumsy, demanding infant of a nation.

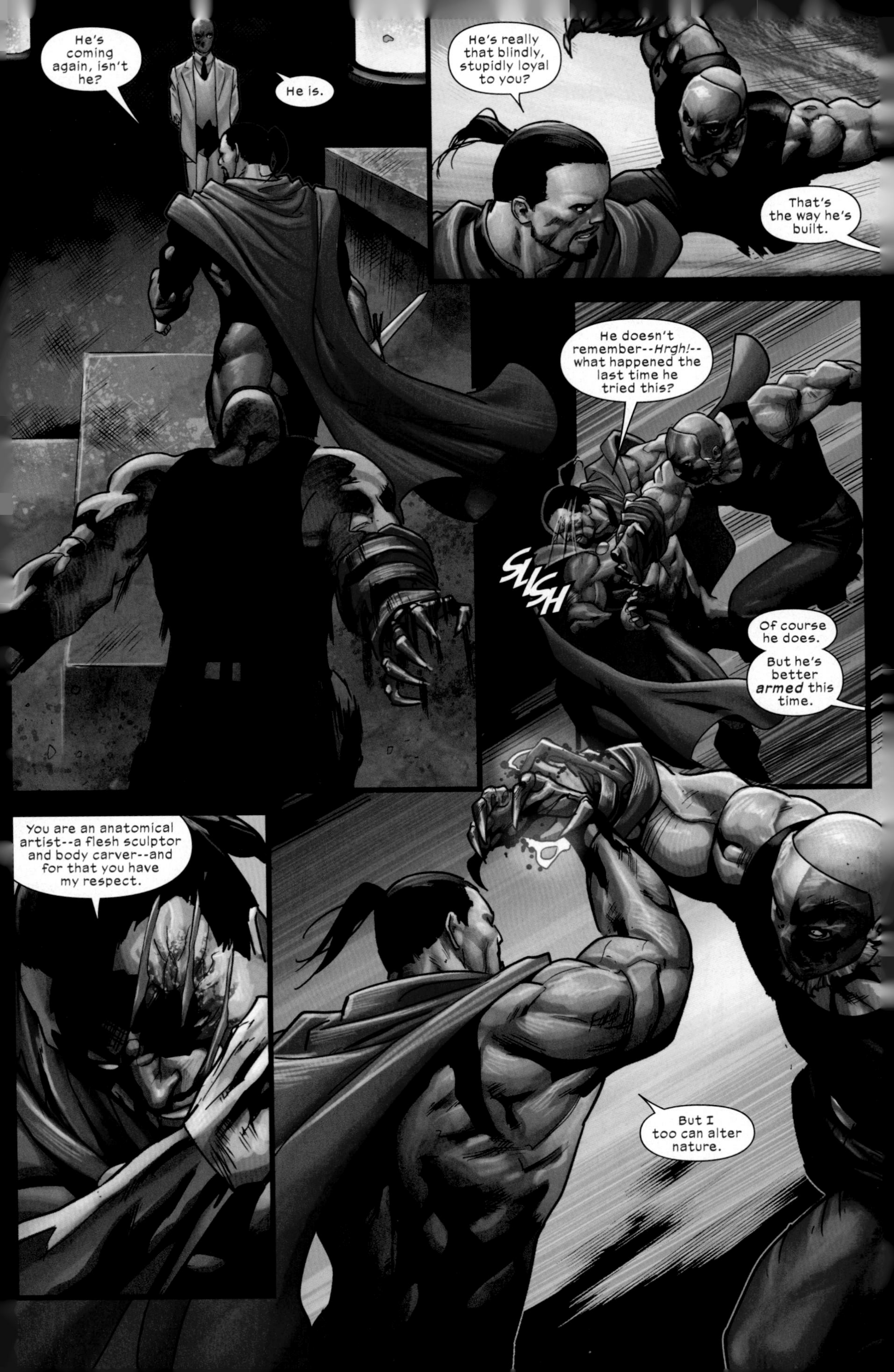
He's coming again, isn't he?
He is.
He's really that blindly, stupidly loyal to you?
That's the way he's built.
He doesn't remember--*Hrgh!*--what happened the last time he tried this?
SLISH
Of course he does.
But he's better *armed* this time.
You are an anatomical artist--a flesh sculptor and body carver--and for that you have my respect.
But I too can alter nature.

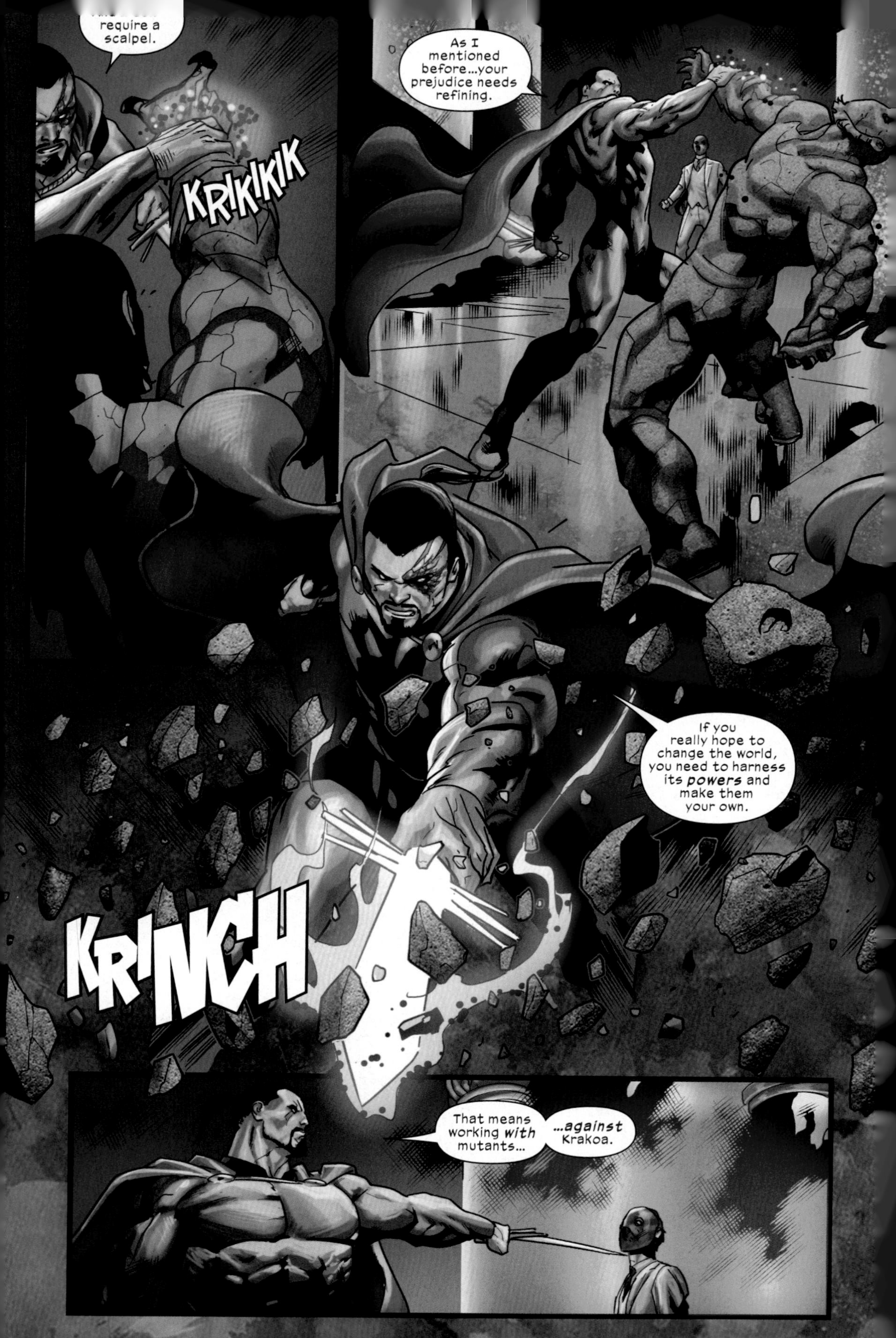
require a scalpel.
KRIKIKIK
As I mentioned before...your prejudice needs refining.
If you really hope to change the world, you need to harness its *powers* and make them your own.
KRINCH
That means working *with* mutants...
...*against* Krakoa.

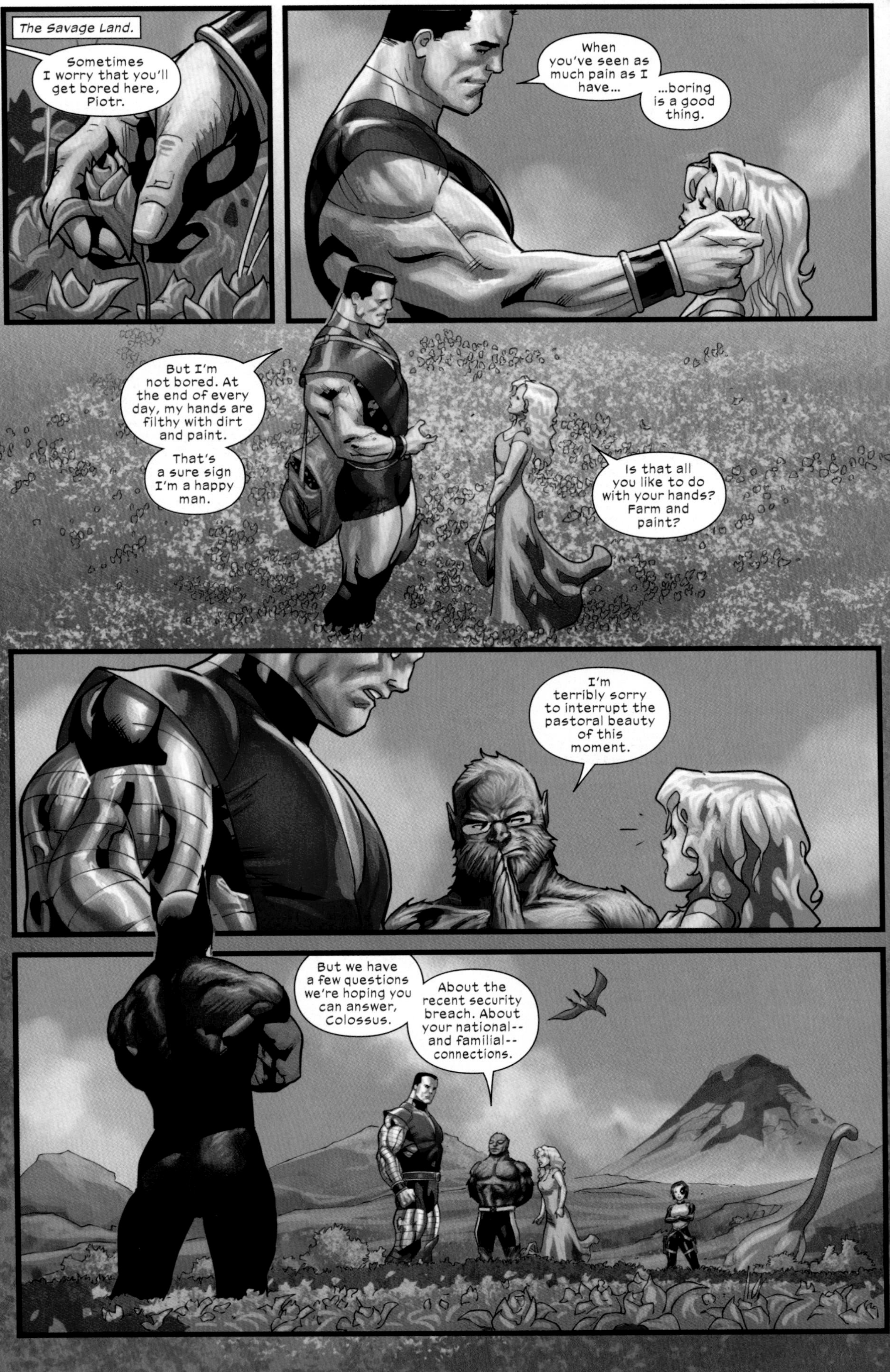

The Savage Land.
Sometimes I worry that you'll get bored here, Piotr.
When you've seen as much pain as I have...
...boring is a good thing.
But I'm not bored. At the end of every day, my hands are filthy with dirt and paint.
That's a sure sign I'm a happy man.
Is that all you like to do with your hands? Farm and paint?
I'm terribly sorry to interrupt the pastoral beauty of this moment.
But we have a few questions we're hoping you can answer, Colossus.
About the recent security breach. About your national-- and familial-- connections.

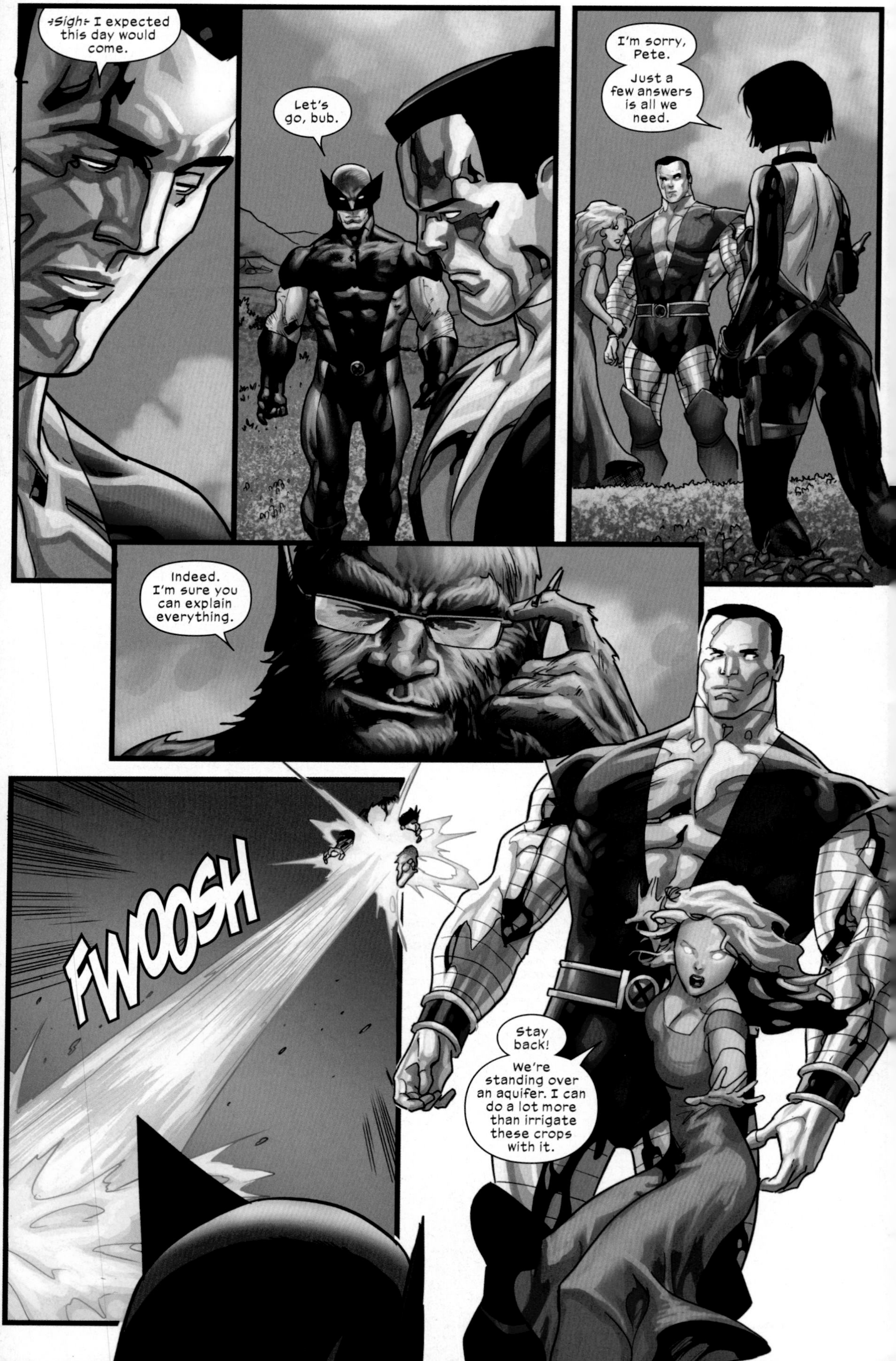

-Sigh- I expected this day would come.
Let's go, bub.
I'm sorry, Pete.
Just a few answers is all we need.
Indeed. I'm sure you can explain everything.
FWOOSH
Stay back!
We're standing over an aquifer. I can do a lot more than irrigate these crops with it.

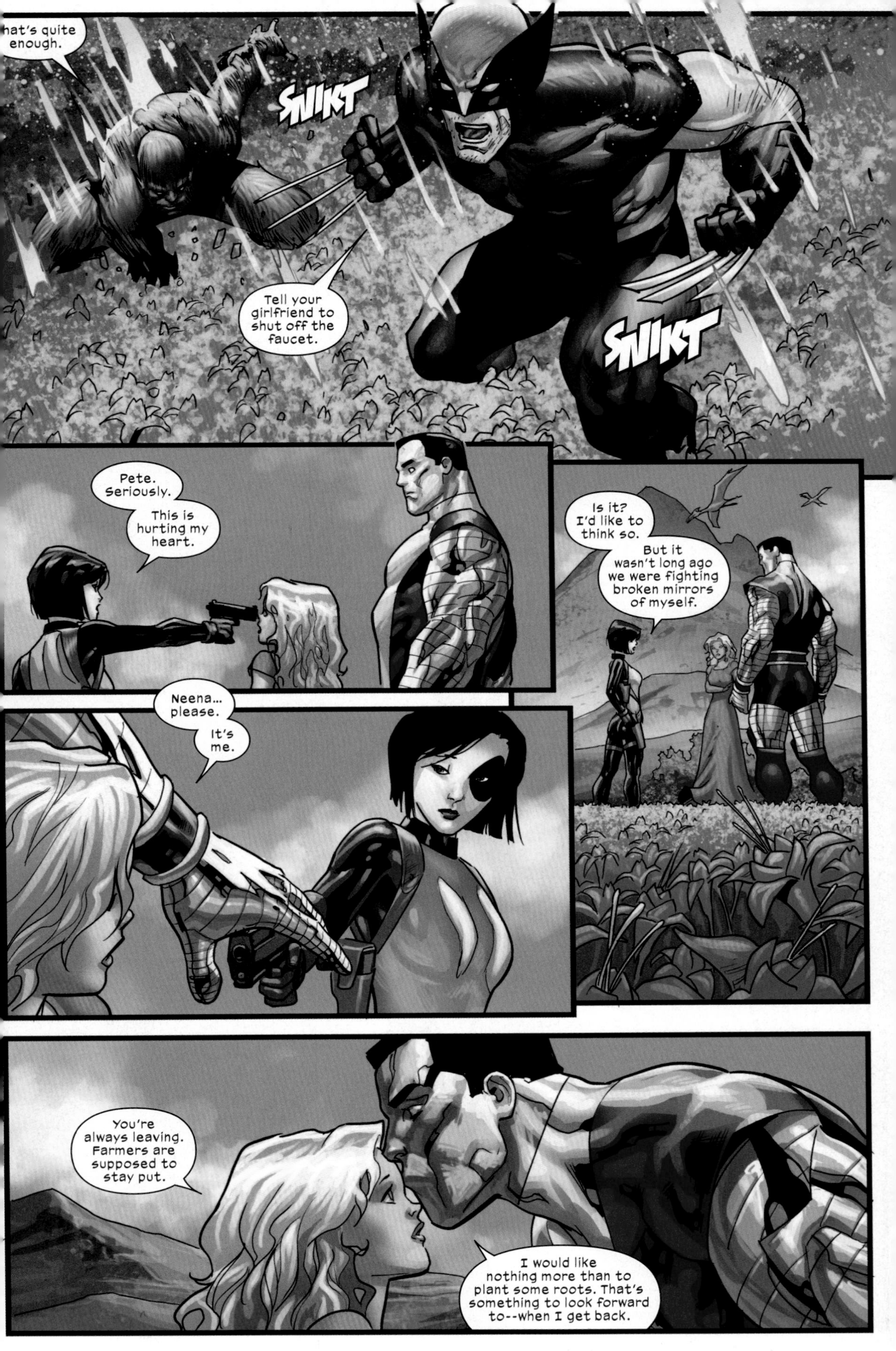
hat's quite enough.
SNIKT
Tell your girlfriend to shut off the faucet.
SNIKT
Pete. Seriously.
This is hurting my heart.
Is it? I'd like to think so.
But it wasn't long ago we were fighting broken mirrors of myself.
Neena... please.
It's me.
You're always leaving. Farmers are supposed to stay put.
I would like nothing more than to plant some roots. That's something to look forward to--when I get back.

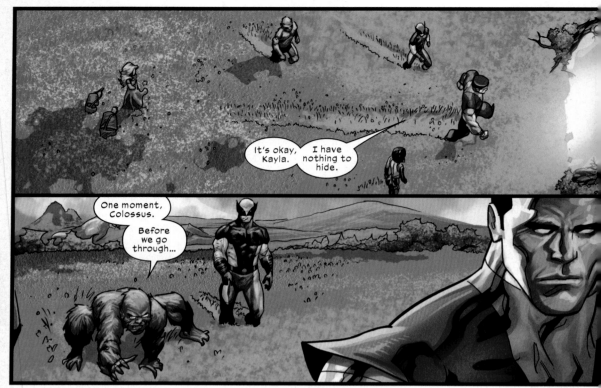

It's okay, Kayla. I have nothing to hide.

One moment, Colossus.

Before we go through...

I was wondering if you might humor me by putting these on?

I realize you can rip through them with not much effort.

But it's a new policy.

I'm sure you understand.

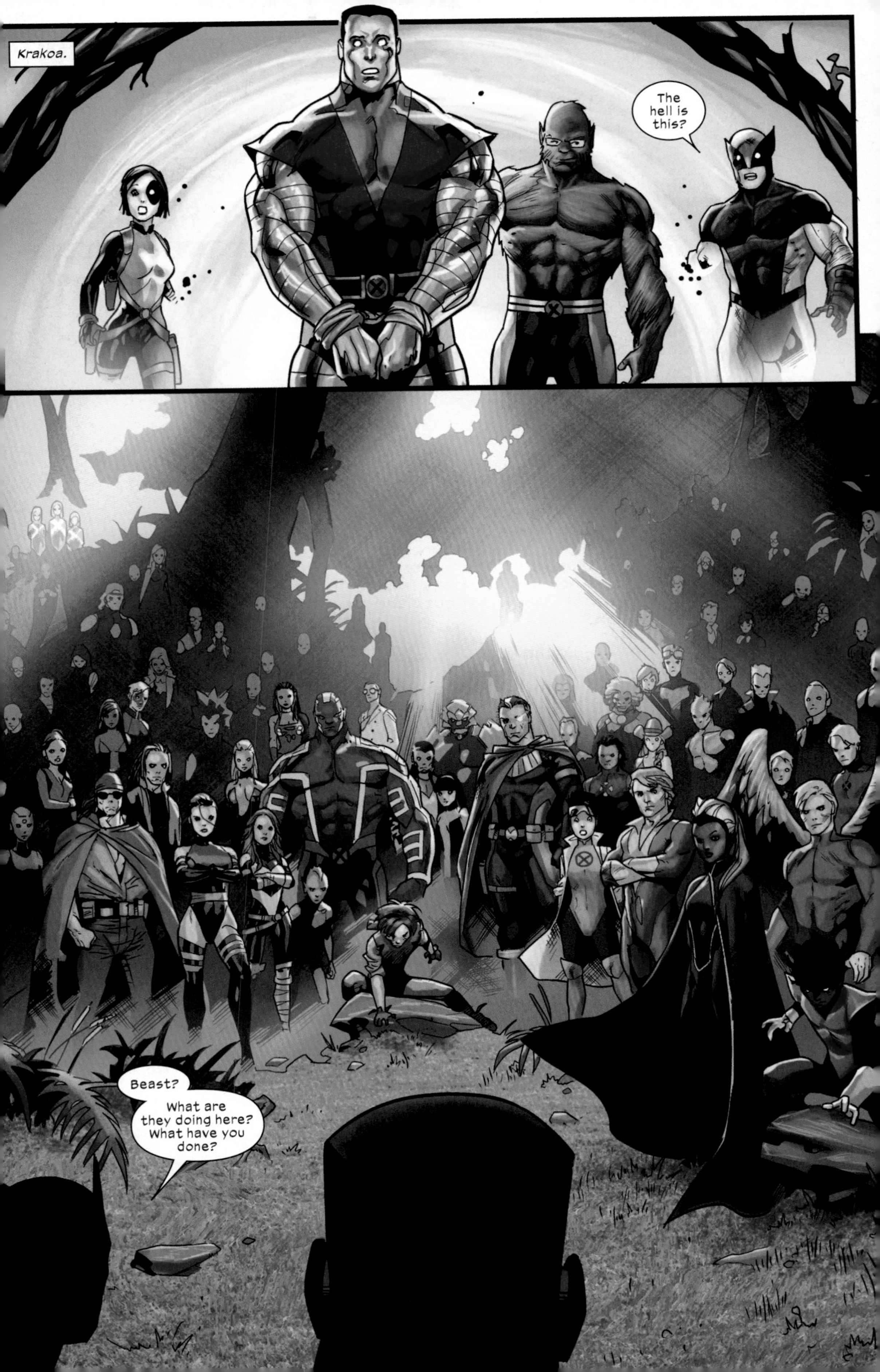
Krakoa.
The hell is this?
Beast?
What are they doing here? What have you done?

BEAST'S LOGBOOK: THE TRAITOR'S PARADE

Our efforts to celebrate mutantkind -- to forgive the sins of our individual histories and build a fresh future as a sovereign society -- is of course commendable.

But I can't help but think it might also be blindly optimistic?

By focusing on the hopeful collective, Xavier's dream ignores the selfish impulses of the individual.

Here are very relevant fears: pollution, incursion, traitorousness.

We are so focused on guarding our gates...that we've neglected to realize what we might have locked ourselves in with.

I have brought this concern up with Xavier several times, but he rebuffs or dismisses or sometimes attempts to placate me by saying things like, "Oh, Beast. Always anxious," and "This is why you're so good at your job."

When I last pressed the issue, this was his response:

"Because I have everyone here," he said and tapped at Cerebro, "I also trust everyone here," at which time he held a hand over his heart.

But we all know this is not a fail-safe. Mind-wipes and mesmerism and telepathic blocks (and, and, and, and -- I'm sure there are many other tricks I haven't even considered) could bypass Cerebro.

Jeremy Bentham's Panopticon was not merely a brilliant design for a prison -- it was a brilliant insight into the philosophy of control. The central guard tower makes the inmates unsure whether they are being observed, and so they behave accordingly. In much the same way, America's crime rates are significantly down due to doorbell cameras, traffic cameras, cell phone cameras. The want to do wrong will always be in us. But the fear of being seen overrides it.

I have a plan, and though it may be controversial and condemned by some, I know it is right. We will detain all mutants with Russian ties. And we will make their detention a spectacle. I don't want to keep this quiet. I want to it to be a parade. I recognize this is unfortunate, but it is also the best possible thing we could do for Krakoa.

A little fear and paranoia keep people safe. It's possible our citizens may come forward with valuable information about their neighbors. It's certain our citizens will know that being watched is the same as being watched over.

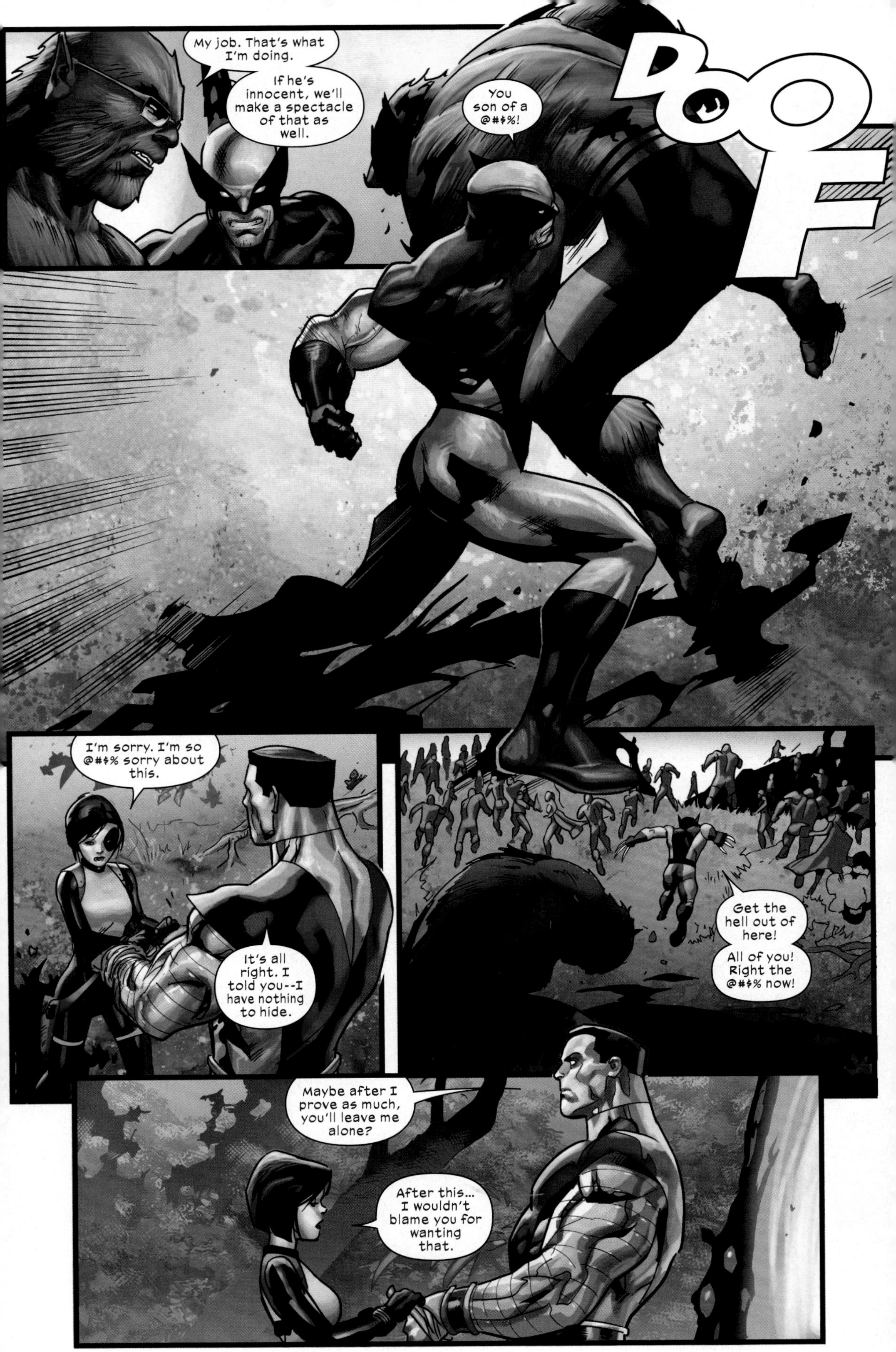
My job. That's what I'm doing.
If he's innocent, we'll make a spectacle of that as well.
You son of a @#$%!
DOOF
I'm sorry. I'm so @#$% sorry about this.
It's all right. I told you--I have nothing to hide.
Get the hell out of here!
All of you! Right the @#$% now!
Maybe after I prove as much, you'll leave me alone?
After this... I wouldn't blame you for wanting that.

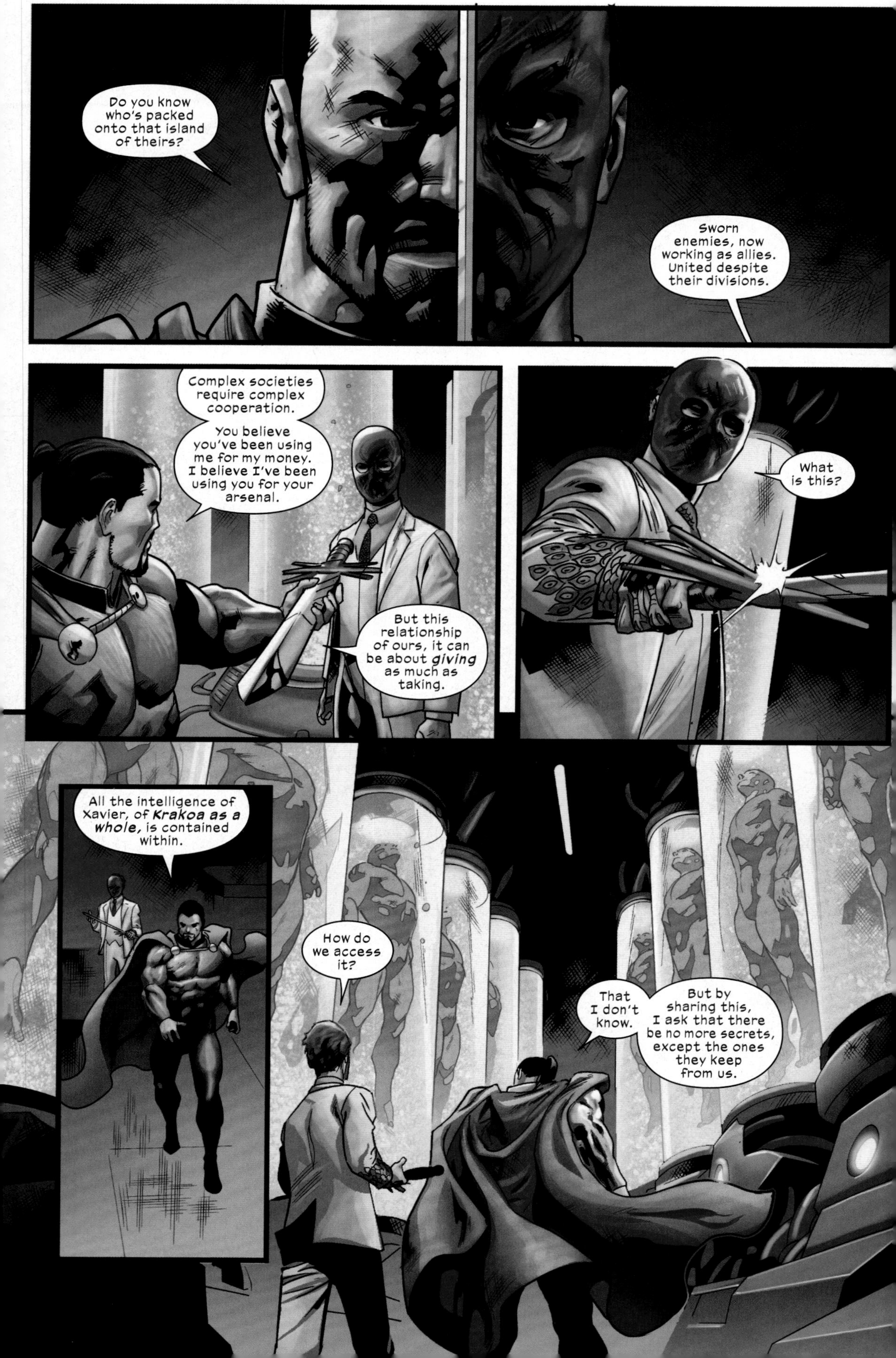
Do you know who's packed onto that island of theirs?
Sworn enemies, now working as allies. United despite their divisions.
Complex societies require complex cooperation.
You believe you've been using me for my money. I believe I've been using you for your arsenal.
But this relationship of ours, it can be about *giving* as much as taking.
What is this?
All the intelligence of Xavier, of ***Krakoa as a whole,*** is contained within.
How do we access it?
That I don't know.
But by sharing this, I ask that there be no more secrets, except the ones they keep from us.

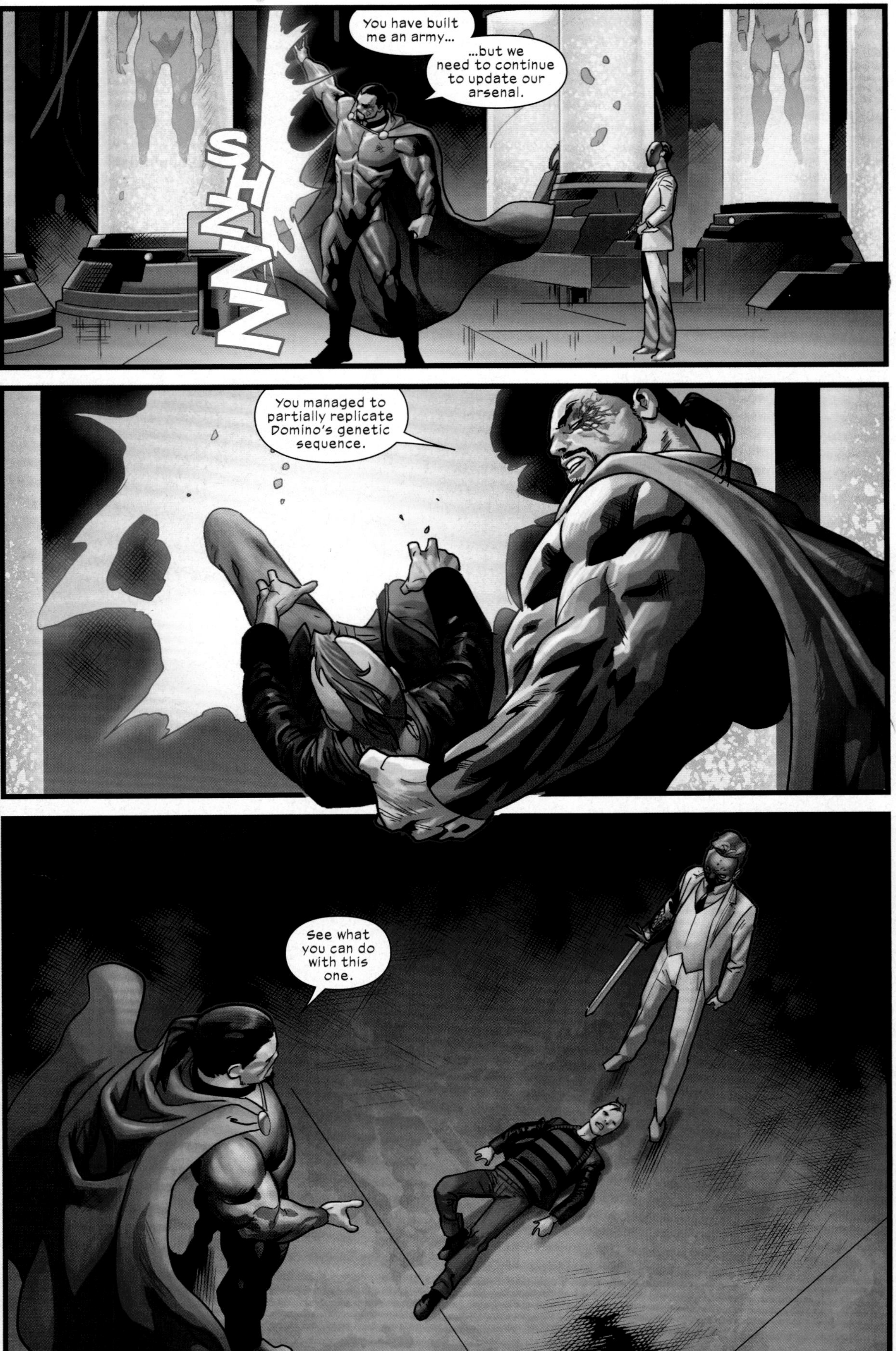
You have built me an army...
...but we need to continue to update our arsenal.
SHNNN
You managed to partially replicate Domino's genetic sequence.
See what you can do with this one.

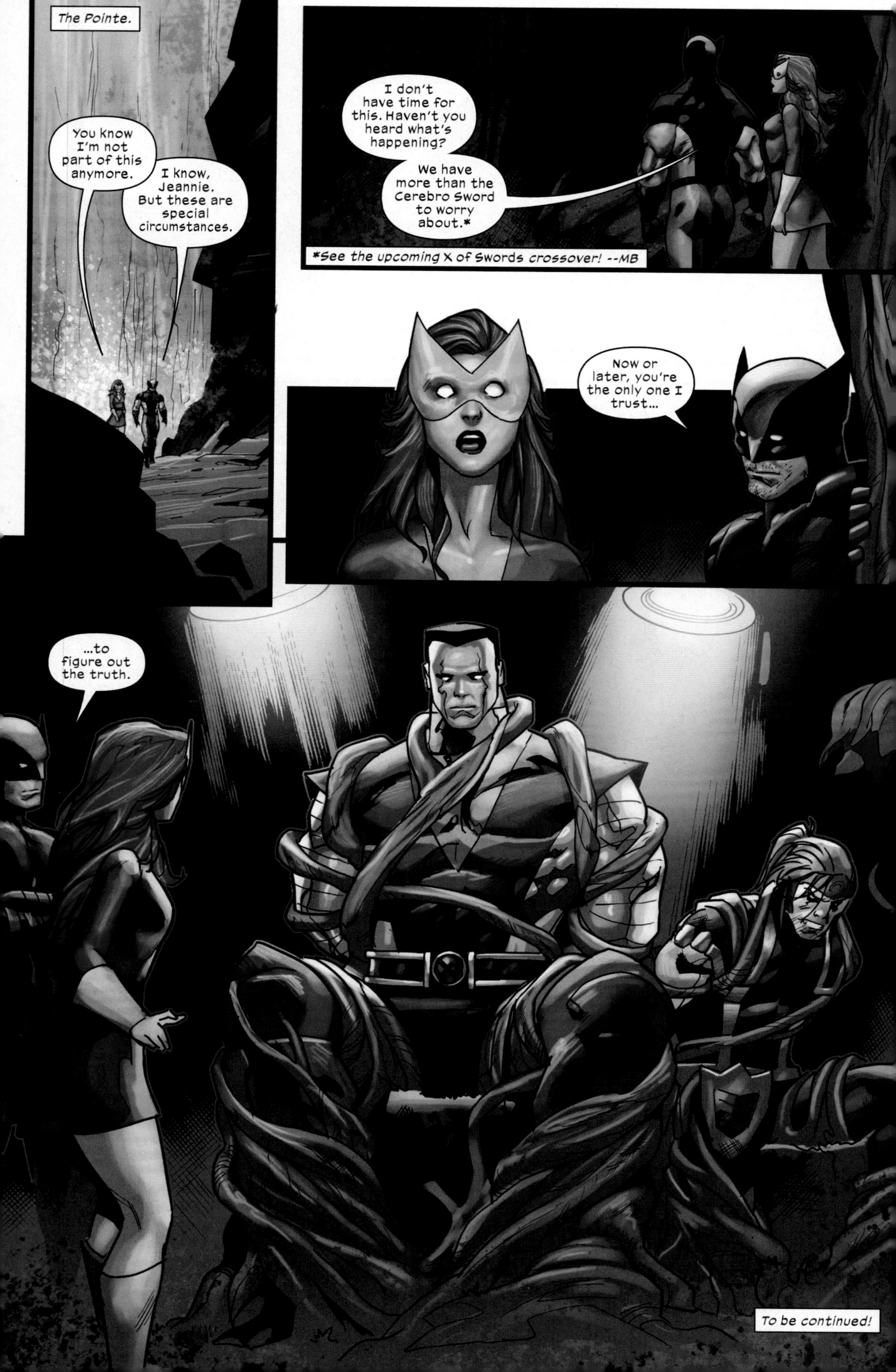
The Pointe.
You know I'm not part of this anymore.
I know, Jeannie. But these are special circumstances.
I don't have time for this. Haven't you heard what's happening?
We have more than the Cerebro Sword to worry about.*
*See the upcoming X of Swords crossover! --MB
Now or later, you're the only one I trust...
...to figure out the truth.
To be continued!

The sun shone in the Savage Land and fields of flowers bloomed brightly. The air was thick with their perfume, and though there was work to do, Piotr could not help but pause in his harvest. Because the pink petals of one breeze-shaken flower had caught his eye, reminding him of a woman swirling her dress as she kicked up her heels in a dance.

Sometimes his hands felt too big and clumsy. If he filled up a glass of water, it sometimes cracked in his grip. If he turned the page of a book, he sometimes tore the spine. But he concentrated now—really concentrated—on pinching off the stem so that he might tuck it gently behind Kayla's ear.

She smiled at him, even her eyes showed her concern. "I'm worried you'll be bored here," she said, and he tried to explain to her how much this place meant to him. As a sanctuary. He liked to put his hands in the dirt in the morning. He liked to dirty his knuckles with paint in the afternoons. He liked to run his fingers through her hair in the evenings. It was easy to forget about pain—the pain of what had come before—when he had so much simple pleasure to focus his attention on.

And then a voice called out to him, saying, "I'm terribly sorry to interrupt the pastoral beauty of this moment."

It was Beast. He smiled with condescension. He held out an arm in invitation. He wanted Piotr to come with him. He wanted to ask questions. He wanted to dredge up everything Piotr had tried to forget, to dig his claws into his still-bruised mind. He wanted to take away this sunlit day, this flower-filled field, this quiet moment with Kayla.

~~Piotr's skin changed—in a flash over silver—as he armored himself. He became something else then. A Colossus. The sun's reflection streamed across his skin when he charged forward. Beast was big, but he was bigger. He seized his old friend and swept him up and slammed him to the ground—once, twice, three times—rag-dolling his body. Beast cried out for him to stop but Colossus' fist met his face with enough force to silence him.~~

~~Blood soaked the ground and the flowers would soon suck the moisture greedily up, reddening their petals.~~

летописец

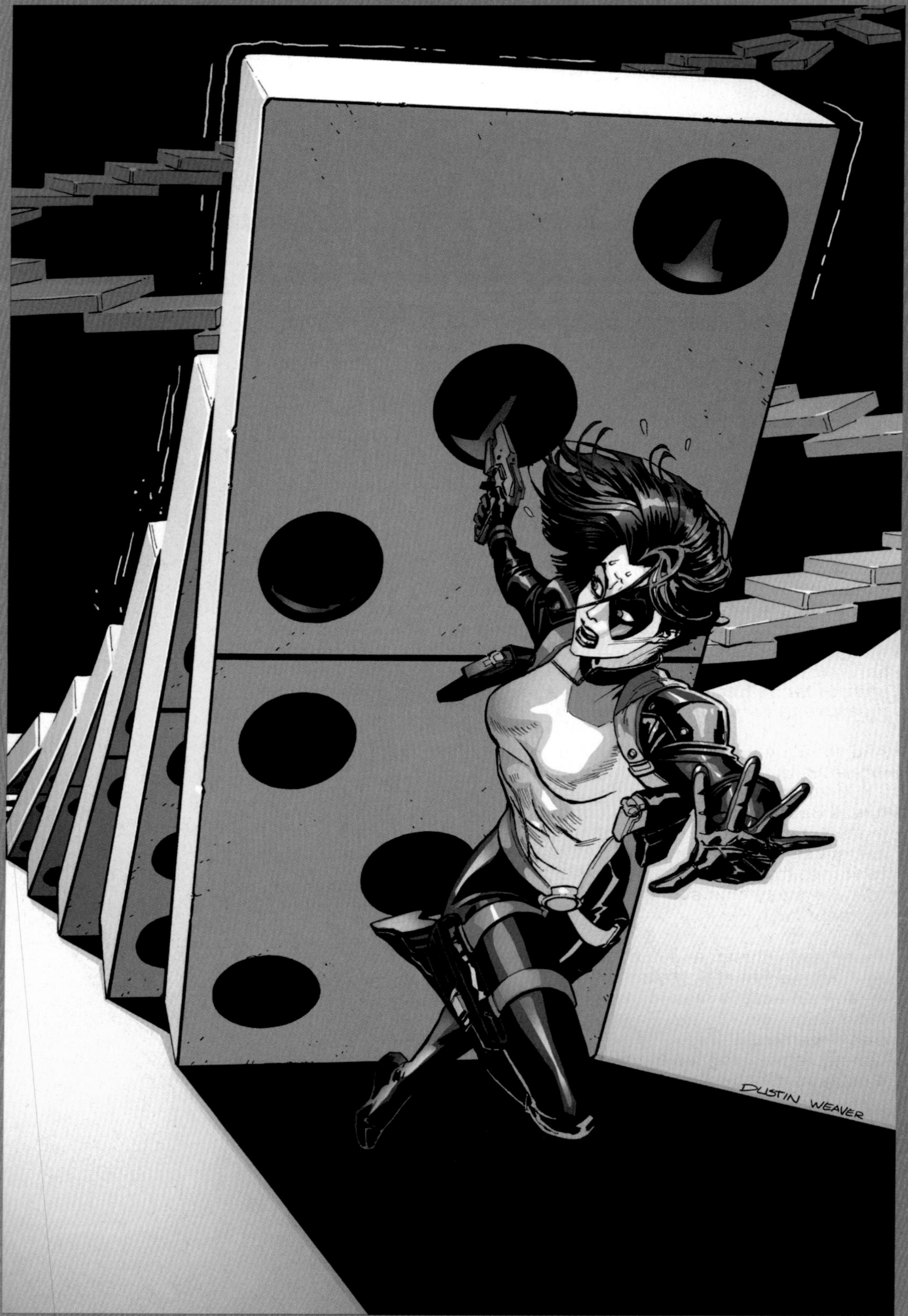
DUSTIN WEAVER

X-Force #7 by Dustin Weaver & Edgar Delgado

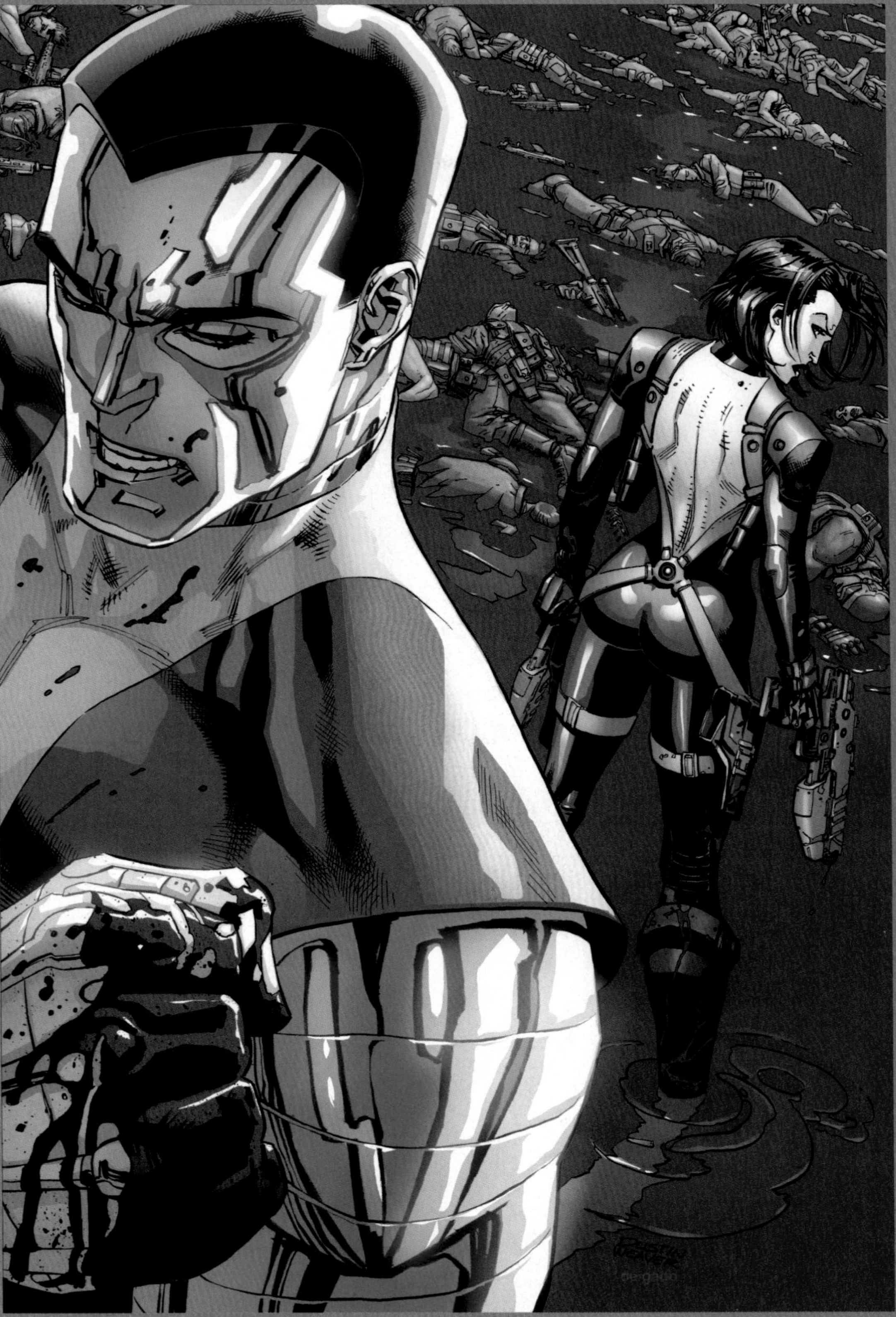

X-Force #8 by Dustin Weaver & Edgar Delgado

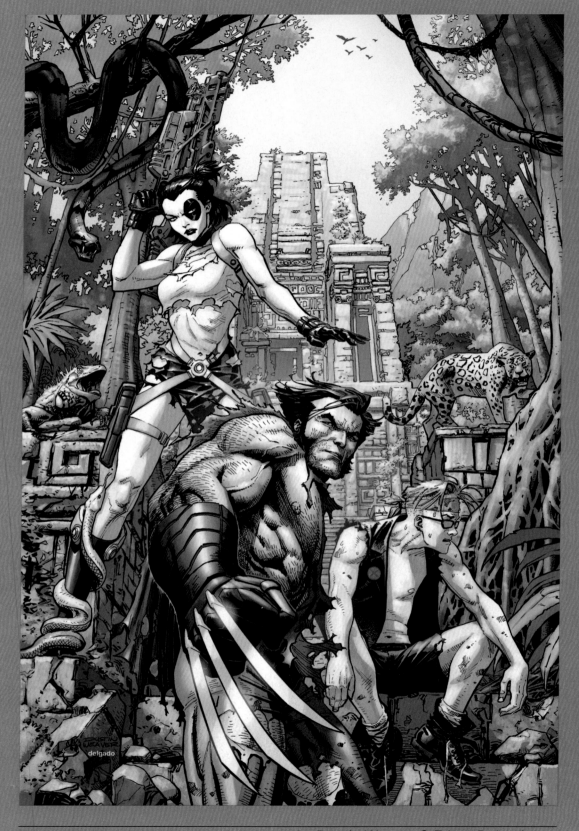

X-Force #9

by Dustin Weaver & Edgar Delgado

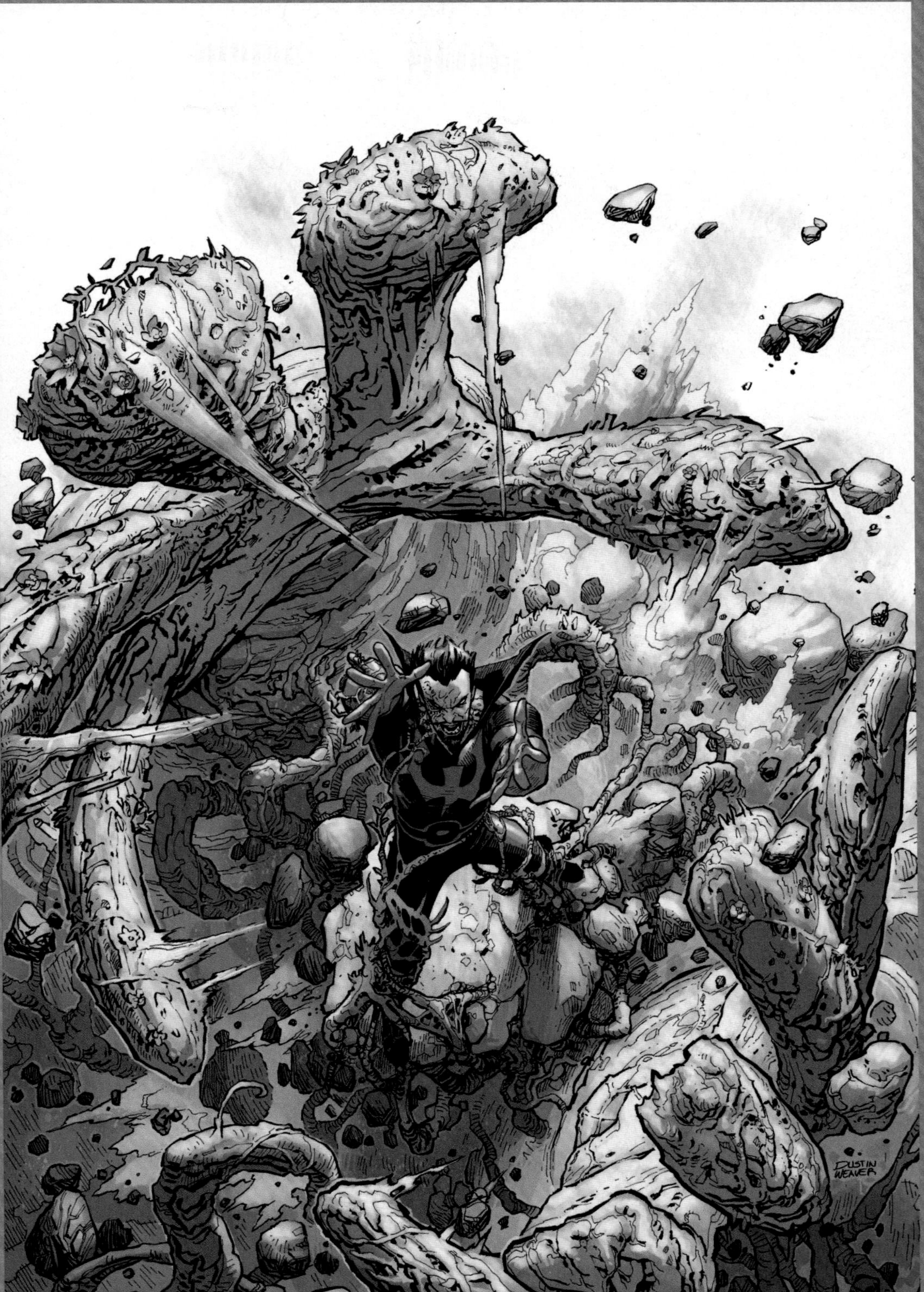
DUSTIN
WEAVER

X-Force #10 by Dustin Weaver & Edgar Delgado

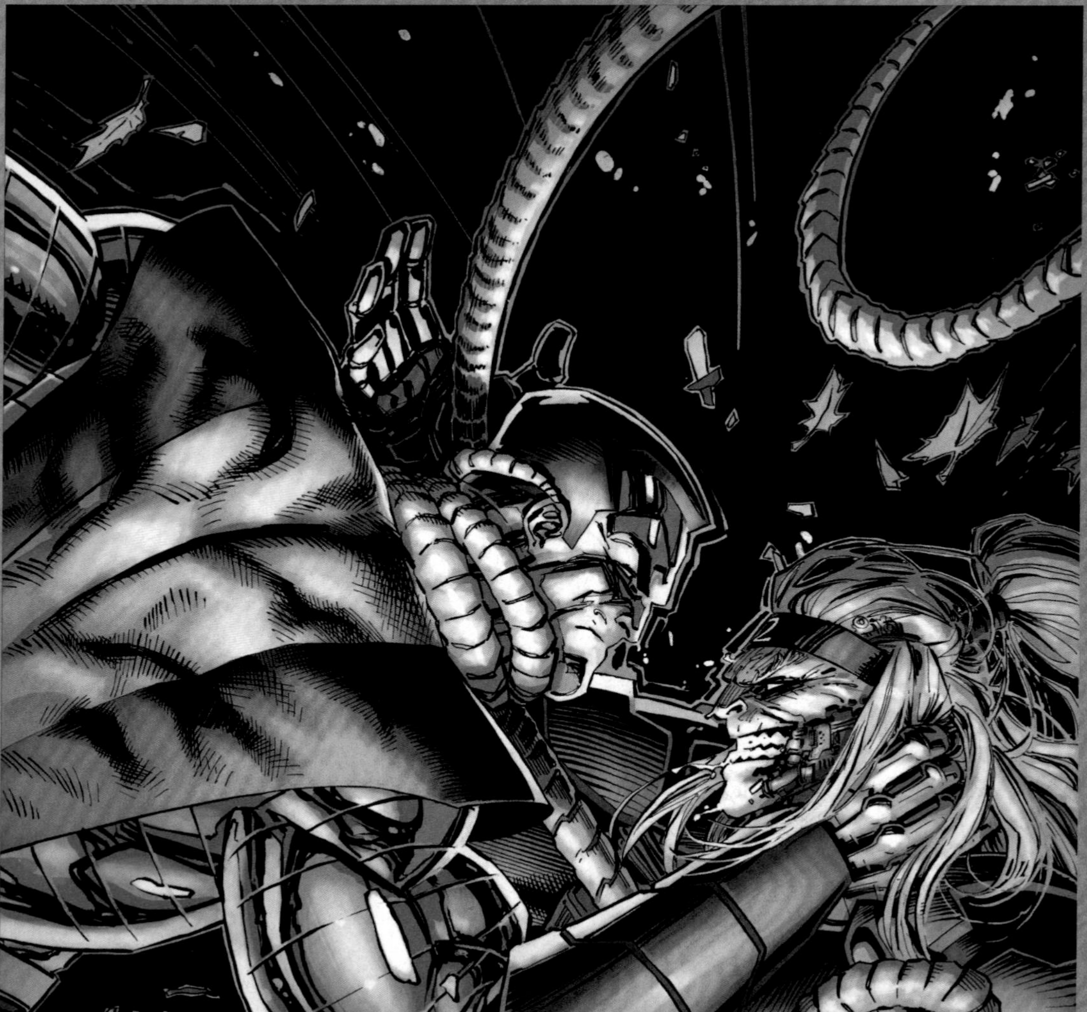
DUSTIN WEAVER

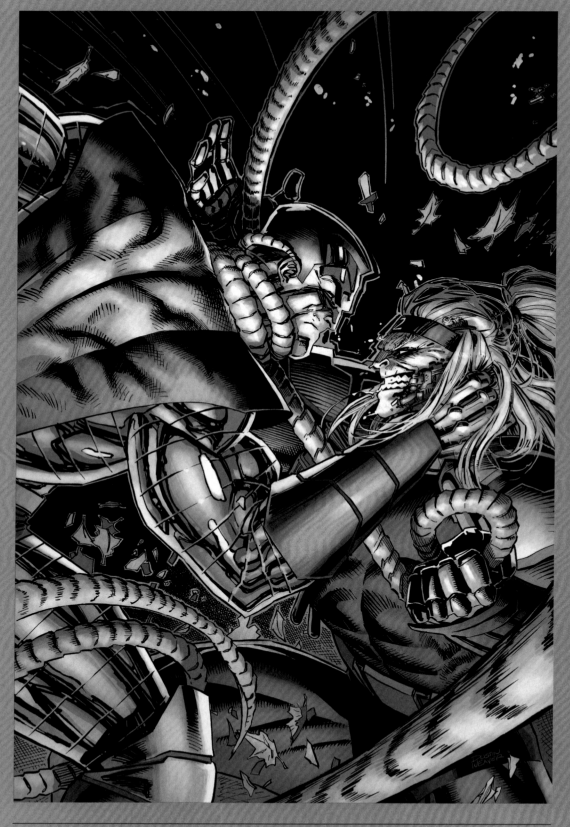

X-Force #11 by Dustin Weaver & Edgar Delgado

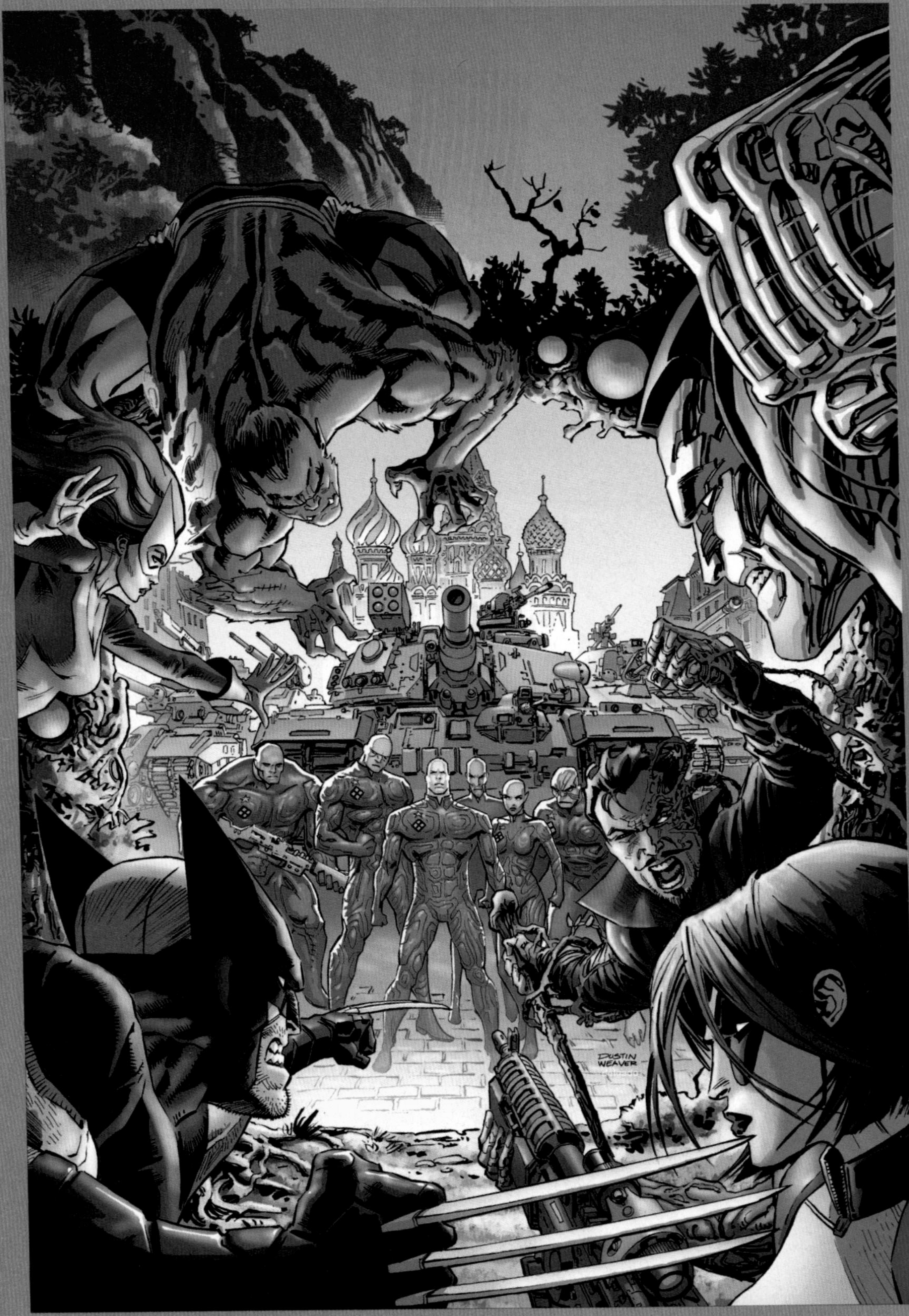
DUSTIN
WEAVER

X-Force #12 by Dustin Weaver & Edgar Delgado

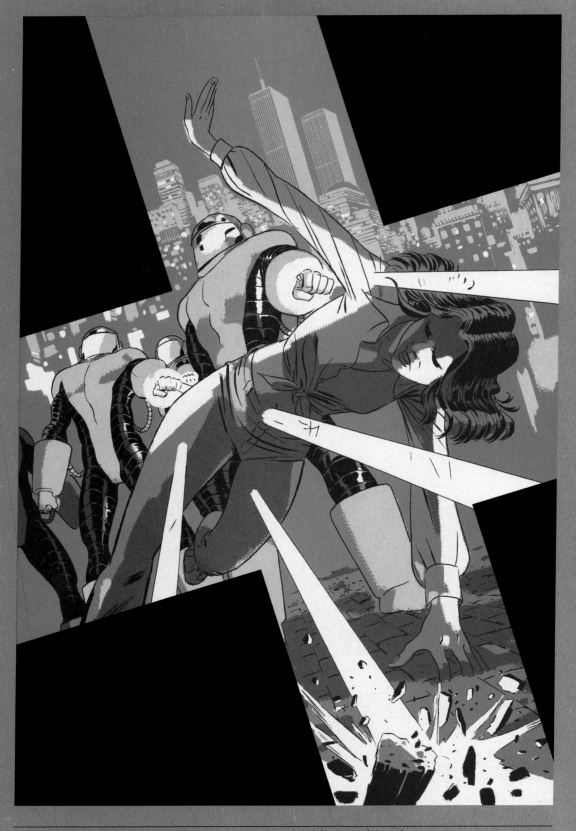

X-Force #9 God Loves, Man Kills Variant   by Marcos Martin

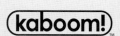

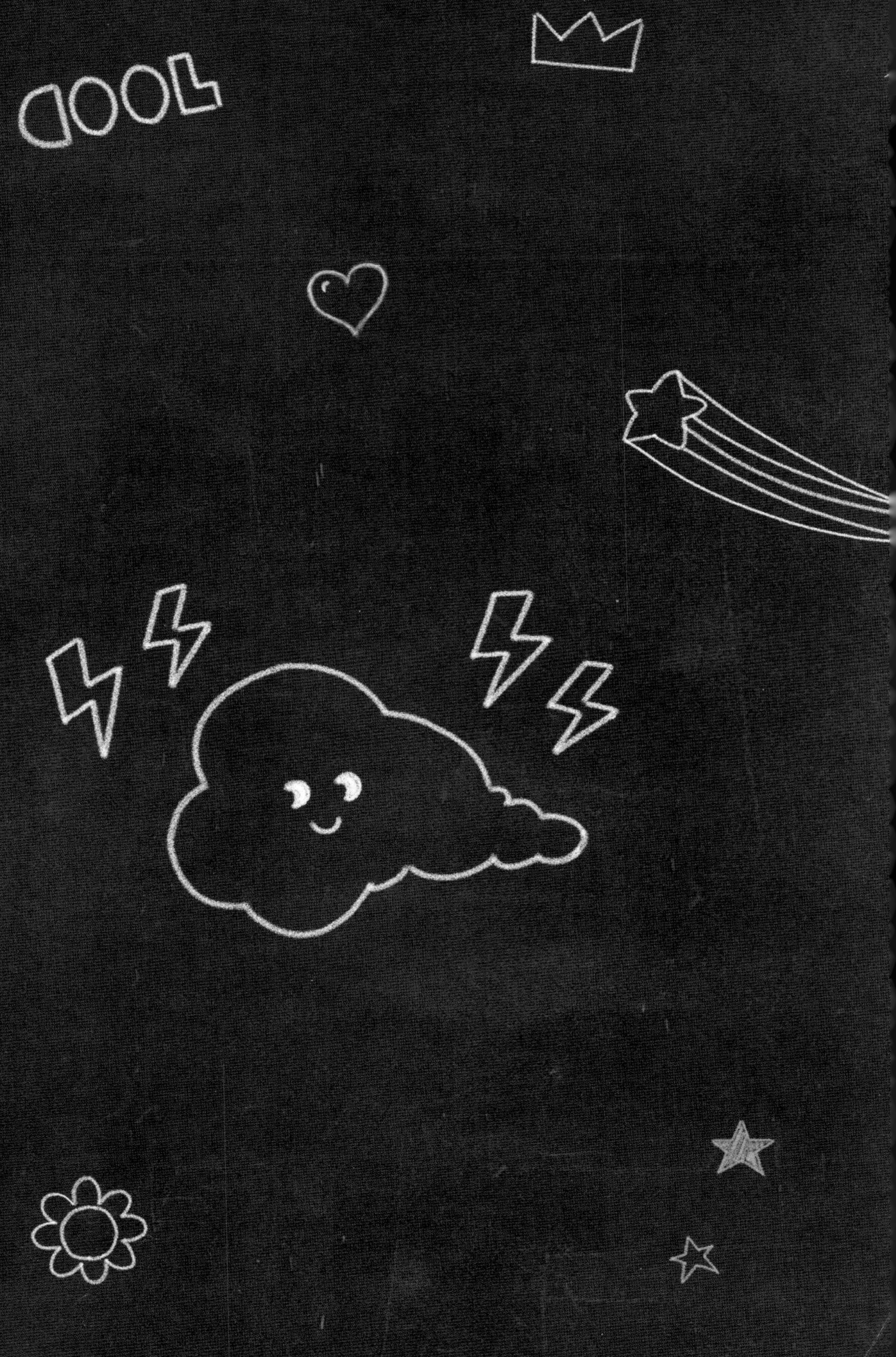